THE AMERICAN PUBLIC SERVICE
POLITICAL BUREAUCRACY

LEWIS C. MAINZER
University of Massachusetts, Amherst

with an introduction by
SENATOR EDWARD W. BROOKE

SCOTT, FORESMAN AMERICAN GOVERNMENT SERIES
Joseph C. Palamountain, Jr., Editor

SCOTT, FORESMAN AND COMPANY
GLENVIEW, ILLINOIS   LONDON

For

my Mother, whose spirit never failed
and my Father, exemplar of honor

(C

Library of Congress Catalog Card No. 73-188616
ISBN: 0-673-05913-8

Copyright © 1973 by Scott, Foresman and Company,
Glenview, Illinois 60025.
Philippines Copyright 1973 by Scott, Foresman and Company.
All Rights Reserved. Printed in the United States of America.

Regional offices of Scott, Foresman and Company are located
in Dallas, Oakland, N.J., Palo Alto, and Tucker, Ga.

FOREWORD

The American system of government strikes a balance between unity and diversity. There is a unity to our system, but it is a unity which tolerates—indeed, requires for its vigor and viability—a broad diversity of institutions, processes, and participants. By organizing the analysis of the sprawling complexity of the American system into smaller, coherent, but interlocking units, the Scott, Foresman American Government Series attempts to reflect this pluralistic balance.

This approach, we believe, has several important advantages over the usual one-volume presentation of analytical and descriptive material. By giving the reader more manageable units, and by introducing him to the underlying and unifying strands of those units, it puts him in a better position to comprehend both the whole and its components. Moreover, it permits us to tap the expertise and experience of distinguished scholars in the fields of their special competence.

At a time when the plain fact is that most books about administration and bureaucracy are dull, and also at a time when the recurrent cry for participation in the administration of governmental policies by those affected by them reflects popular unease about the seeming inflexibility of administration, Lewis C. Mainzer's book is most welcome. While recognizing the special characteristics of a bureaucracy, he puts first things first by stressing that it is political. While showing the need for rational order and expertise in a bureaucracy, he gives equal stress to political control and to responsiveness. It is a timely and interesting study.

Joseph C. Palamountain, Jr., *Editor*

PREFACE

Is it fitting that a book on bureaucracy should emerge from Amherst—a town which nourishes poets? Perhaps an author's experience with Washington and Boston bureaucracies, Weber and Kafka, the sociology of organization and political science, excuses so bucolic a setting for writing on public administration. Perhaps a somewhat detached atmosphere helps keep first things first. For me, for this book, the first thing about governmental bureaucracy is that it is a political institution. This book considers sympathetically the concern with efficient administration and the concern with the well-being of bureaucrats, but it denies primacy to those two perspectives. Governmental bureaucracy is a central institution in our governing, and that is the prominent perspective in this introduction to the American public service and the problems of public administration.

I accept the necessity of authority in the service of good purposes, and have no great hopes of a world without bureaucracy but with the good things of modernity. But I do not look with ease upon government by bureaucracy. This book concerns itself with the means of controlling government bureaucracy without crippling it or degrading the people in it. The rule of law in public administration is carefully examined, in terms that any diligent reader can make sense of. And the methods of political control of the American public service are explored. Can the virtues of government under law and under democratic control be had, along with effective conduct of the public services?

The book seeks to convey a sense of change, problems, proposals, and potentialities. Ought we have an ombudsman, an administrative court, or neighborhood information centers? —Commissions or corporations or departments?—Congressional or presidential control, party or interest group influence, or professional self-direction? Should we choose centralized bureaucracy or community action programs or neighborhood government?—A career corps of neutral officials or advocate administrators responsive to the poor or politically accountable executives? Should we and can we have a representative bureaucracy reflecting the whole society, a bureaucracy which is equalitarian rather than hierarchical? The problems dealt with are inherently interesting and full of political significance. I trust that the readers' own observations and reflections may enrich this book's efforts to point toward a future less grim than administrative tyranny, if less cheering than the best dreams of all who envision pure freedom.

I am especially indebted to William Rouleau, at the beginning stages, and to Arlyn Blake, at the completion of the book, for intelligently and cheerfully performing burdensome chores. Caden, Edward, and Daniel Mainzer sustained me throughout; together we conspired to justify life and art.

Lewis C. Mainzer

INTRODUCTION

The great American playwright, Arthur Miller, once wrote: "The birth of each man is the rebirth of a claim to justice." Each of us is born into a society we did not make, whose form and content we may affect only marginally in our lifetime. Each of us will be required to contribute something to society, and each of us has a right to expect certain things from society. Not least among our expectations is "equal justice under law."

Yet it is in the nature of human beings that we do not think about the dispensers of justice until we ourselves come face to face with them. Then we ask: Who are they? What do they know? What is the law? Will they be fair?

"Justice," under our system of government, is dispensed by a multitude of men and women. There are the judges and clerks of our courts—from the traffic court in proverbial East Oshkosh to the U.S. Supreme Court itself. There are the men and women of the regulatory agencies who decide the keen economic issues of radio and television licenses, railroad rates, and tariff levels. There are the thousands of civilian employees, from the Federal through the regional and local levels, who decide on matters of social security and welfare payments, immigration visas, veterans' claims, and agricultural supports. There are the local officials who decide the price of a dog tag or the number on a license plate, who issue hunting and fishing permits, and set property taxes.

All told, the dispensers of justice in America total two and a half million civilian Federal employees, and an estimated ten million state and local officials. One sixth of our labor force, one third of all the professional and technical workers in this country, are engaged in the exercise of judicial and administrative authority over their fellow citizens.

It is in such facts and figures that a book of this nature finds its primary relevance. For if we would understand our society and our system of government, we must necessarily understand the bureaucracy which is its most numerous and frequently its most influential component.

Yet the men and women who comprise the bureaucracy—that vast collection of Federal, state, and local government employees —are among the least understood of all American workers. How often have we used the term "bureaucrat" in a disparaging way? How often have we criticized the decisions, or lack of decisions, of our public employees? How much do we know about the sources, and the limits, of their authority? And how frequently is our criticism justified?

I remember reading one day an editorial in a large American newspaper. The editor was obviously expressing a long and deeply held frustration when he referred to the "three-party system" in America—the Republicans, the Democrats, and the Bureaucrats —and said, "Of the three, the Federal bureaucracy is the strongest and most powerful."

Interspersed throughout the editorial were a multitude of pejorative adjectives: "arrogant," "dictatorial," "collectivists," "bullies and blackmailers." Unfortunately these terms may apply to some employees on the public payroll. But such broadside attacks fail to take into account two very important factors: first, that the bureaucrats, the civil service employees, seldom make policy and more likely carry out the policies either commanded or condoned by elected officials and the public alike; and second, that public service—at least up to this point—has attracted far more honest and conscientious employees than scoundrels.

We cannot be assured that this will always be so. Speaking before a Public Service Awards luncheon in 1971, Health, Education and Welfare Secretary Elliot Richardson expressed deep concern that the "credibility gap" which has afflicted American foreign policy for so long is finding increasing reflection in public attitudes toward all of government. The Secretary warned, "What first was meant to apply only to the Federal government and a specific issue—appears in some respects to have widened into . . . a void which threatens to separate the people and their government at all levels and on all issues."

We cannot permit the continued existence of widespread public doubt regarding the effectiveness and the credibility of government. These doubts will do more than widen the gap between the government and the governed. They will also help to insure the realization of the very fears they project, by discouraging participation and employment in government by those best qualified to assume the public trust.

All students of government—indeed, all American citizens— should know as fully as possible how government operates. It is important to know more than the structure and organization, for these cannot be fully perceived and understood without knowing something of the framework within which the people operate, as they fill the various slots. How does an employee of the Veterans Administration relate to his superiors or to his clients (the veterans)? To what extent are his actions controlled by decisions of the President and Congress? Psychologically, how does he feel about the tasks he performs; do they give him a sense of personal satisfaction or of frustration?

All of these questions and more are essential to an understanding of our system of government. And all of these questions, and more, are addressed in this book, *Political Bureaucracy.*

Edward W. Brooke
Senator from Massachusetts

Op 1-14.

TABLE OF CONTENTS

CHAPTER ONE

Three Faces of Governmental Bureaucracy

Bureaucracy is the distinctively contemporary arm of American government. Its size, responsibilities, and power have grown markedly in the last generation. Seeking to cope with an intensive concentration of people and substantial common obligations, an intricate economy and complex technology, and a major role in world politics, we demand much of administrative agencies. But if governmental bureaucracy is essential, it nevertheless wins little enough praise. It seems less the beautiful flower of modern civilization than a dull-fierce creature—incompetent at its task, degrading to both its members and the spirit of society, and politically irresponsible if not oppressive.

THE EVALUATION OF BUREAUCRACY

Critics of governmental bureaucracy speak from three major perspectives, each with an implicit criterion for the evaluation of public administration. One set of critics charges that governmental bureaucracy is incompetent. They view it as a kind of social machine, a means to achieve goals established by those external to the bureaucracy, but they berate it as inefficient, a blunt and rusty tool, an engine full of friction and inertia. Though some critics regard all bureaucracy, public and private, as bungling, many persons attribute special inefficiency to governmental administration. For example, the economist Ludwig Von Mises argued (rather simplistically) that private business is not bureaucratic but that government is. Private management produces what consumers want, guided by the standard of profit and loss. Responsibility is delegated, men are judged by their competence, and freedom is preserved, because profit provides an objective standard by which to evaluate men, products, methods, and companies. Bureaucratic management (that is, government, by his definition), in contrast, is concerned only to comply with rules and regulations. Lack of the profit standard of success kills initiative and the incentive to do a really good job. Guided by rules rather than by profit, public administration is necessarily inefficient, Von Mises concluded. Those who condemn governmental bureaucracy as sluggish and of low quality speak not only from the political right. Harold Laski, the British socialist intellectual, despaired that governmental bureaucracy could ever break out of its rule-bound, precedent-oriented, paper-shuffling, self-protecting, experiment-resisting, conformity-rewarding, responsibility-avoiding, and delay-filled ways, to effectuate new public policies and bring about necessary social change. Many a ruling political leader, in democratic, communist, and fascist nations alike, has expressed similar frustration in the face of challenging new tasks. More than one scholar of American foreign policy has argued that if the understanding of Vietnam had been better in our governmental bureaucracies (State Department, Defense Department, CIA), where ignorance of Vietnamese language, politics, culture, and military potentialities was distressing, we might never have become so involved in that nation's destiny. What is alleged is a technical defect, incompetence.

A second condemnation views bureaucracy—both governmental and private—in terms of its degradation of the bureaucrats themselves, its corruption of the human spirit. Existentialist philosophers, for example, decry the bureaucratization of life and the loss by individuals of the ability to see others as persons. Gabriel Marcel, a religious existentialist, has explicitly warned that the modern bureaucratic man is identified with his functions. His life is a timetable, and the individual "tends to appear both to himself and to others as an agglomeration of functions."[1] The noble Karl Jaspers has seen bureaucracy as a characteristic of the contemporary West, where selfhood is so easily lost. "The whole apparatus," he wrote, "is guided by a bureaucracy, which is itself likewise an apparatus—human beings reduced to apparatus . . . ."[2] To the philosophers are joined poets, who sing for the free person whom officialism destroys, and academicians, who mistrust large organizations as a human environment. From the New Left and from nonideological but disaffected young people comes a passionate rejection of the bureaucratization of life, a rejection tied to rebellion against the whole social and political system. In the coldness and hierarchy which presumably make bureaucracy efficient, they see something which threatens the human being's worth. The corruption from bureaucratization of relations pervades and degrades the whole society. This criticism alleges a spiritual defect, the destruction of human selfhood and mutual affection.

A third criticism charges governmental bureaucracy with political oppression. James Burnham argued in a provocative book that our age is in the midst of a social revolution, a rapid change in political and economic institutions, dominant beliefs, and the group of men in top positions. We are moving from a bourgeois, capitalist society to a managerial society. The communists and fascists had, he thought, moved farther than we along this road, but all are on the same route. Not capitalists, not politicians or Congress, but managers in government and business will control society. As government increases its control of the economy, the line between the two loses significance; politics and economics become fused. It is the experts (administrators, production engineers, or bureau chiefs in government) who will increasingly have real power and who even now actually manage the technical processes of production. These confident young managers, he thought, are already the real possessors of power, and the systems of rule are more alike than different in the various great nations. Burnham's 1941 book is dated in its details, but his warning is continually echoed. The condemnation of bureaucratic power takes varied forms: the businessman charges that governmental bureaucrats oppress private enterprise, the poor man and his advocates charge that police and welfare officials abuse the least powerful citizens. Nor is it only in democracies that criticism arises. From dissenters in communist nations come eloquent voices, nurtured often enough by a spell in prison, charging political oppression by ruthless, self-seeking bureaucrats who have perverted revolutionary ideals of liberty. Whatever the specific form, the criticism alleges a political defect, oppression of the citizen.

In summary, therefore, in an era characterized by the importance of administrative agencies, we must ask whether governmental bureaucracies are competent, humane, and politically responsible. Let us look further at each of these criteria.

COMPETENCE

What is the nature of large organizations and by what methods can they achieve efficient operation? One can usefully view a bureaucracy as a piece of machinery, a marvelous, intricate machine to be sure. A substantial literature asks how governmental agencies operate and whether they are competent. It assumes that public administration is like business administration, and suggests means of achieving efficiency, without regard to the goals or the public authority of the organization. Some authorities on administration even aspire to emulate natural scientists in renouncing ethical judgments about the value of the goals being served (though perhaps they import a hidden premise that efficiency matters most). One can, thus, study bureaucracy and ponder the techniques of efficient bureaucracy, without yet sharply distinguishing public from private administration.

The possibility of analyzing a wide variety of bureaucracies objectively was established by Max Weber, a social scientist with a remarkable range of knowledge and ability at systematization. He observed the world becoming increasingly "rational," less and less governed by sacred and traditional ways or by the force of personality of a dominant leader. Weber discerned elements of bureaucracy in varied cultures throughout history, but he saw the twentieth century as a period of increasingly bureaucratized life. "The decisive reason for the advance of bureaucratic organization has always been," he wrote, "its purely technical superiority over any other form of organization."[3] Bureaucratic organization might be used to administer civilian governmental functions, armies, businesses, or churches, without fundamentally changing the nature of the organization form.

Who is the bureaucrat? According to Weber, he is one who occupies an office (position) in an impersonal system bound by rules. Each office has a clearly defined sphere of authority. A set of functions is marked off to be performed by the incumbent of each position in the administrative organization, and the official is provided the necessary authority and means of compulsion through clearly defined regulations. The organization of offices follows the principle of hierarchy, with the pattern of subordination to a superior officer carrying through all the ranks. Though the bureaucrat is subject to discipline in the conduct of his office, he is personally free. His private life is distinguished from his official obligations, and is not controlled by the organization. He owes obedience to the higher authority not as a superior individual, but as occupant of a specific office in an impersonal hierarchy. If the boss resigns, or transfers, that individual no longer has authority over him, or he can dissolve the superior's authority by leaving.

Bureaucratic officials often have had specialized training and are selected on the basis of technical qualifications. They are appointed, not elected. (Election threatens such values as hierarchical discipline, continuity, and professional competence.) The job is a man's full-time, primary occupation, part of a career, in which promotion is by seniority or achievement. The administrative staff does not own the means of administration (as the factory worker does not own his machine) and the work offices are separated from the home. Nor does the bureaucrat own the position, which can be neither sold nor inherited. The official may not retain fees which he collects in his work, but is paid a salary, graded primarily by rank rather than by the amount or quality of work done. He is protected against dismissal, he has the right to a pension, and he is free to resign.

Why is bureaucracy efficient? The technical or professional competence of bureaucrats and their continuity in office are obviously valuable. The administrative process is marked by a large role for technical knowledge (including special knowledge derived from the experience within the bureaucracy itself) and systematically organized files of information. The administrative process carried out by bureaucracy consists, according to Weber, of applying to specific cases rules which have been set down in general terms. (Citizens over 65 years of age are entitled to X benefits, Mr. Y is a citizen over 65, and he is therefore to be supplied with X benefits.) Decisions and rules are carefully formulated and are recorded in written form. Results are highly calculable, for they accord with rules and are quite impersonal (all persons are treated alike, without discrimination). Bureaucratic administration is highly rational, that is: calculated, systematic, technically informed, efficient in use of means to attain given ends, and matter-of-fact rather than imbued with sacred mysteries or personal emotions. Weber compared the superior efficiency of this system to the superiority of machine production over nonmechanical production. He was deeply impressed with the remarkable ability of bureaucracies to perform large tasks well. Outside of his academic writings, however, he expressed a deep uneasiness about the bureaucratic way of life.

Weber's formulation of bureaucracy, like a good many fruitful social science concepts, is subject to serious criticism. (1) Confusion arises from treating bureaucracy as an "ideal type," which is an abstraction to which no actual organization fully conforms. Weber realized that actual organizations are only in some degree bureaucratic, but the reader of Weber easily begins to think that all large-scale administration must be such as Weber described. (2) Weber failed to explore the relation of hierarchical authority (which treats men as subordinates) to professionalism (which emphasizes self-control or group action by equals). He emphasized the careful training and technical competence of bureaucrats, and modern critics have observed that such experts are not easily controlled by hierarchical superiors who can hardly match them in specialized competence. Can the general manager actually direct his subordinate technical experts and certified professionals? (3) Weber's analysis does not take account of human relations within organizations. Informal organization of subordinates is a strong fact of life, sometimes running counter to the commands of formal organization. (4) Actual decision making within bureaucratic organizations is not so simple as the application of general rules to specific cases in an impersonal, efficient manner. What about the serious inefficiencies apparent in large-scale organizations? What impact have the goals of the bureaucrats themselves on their official actions? (5) Weber leaves much uncertainty respecting the political influence of and political control over governmental bureaucracy. Sometimes he implied that bureaucrats will do what they are told; at other times he emphasized the vast influence of the career officials and the impotence of amateur political chieftains of the bureaucracy. (6) Though he was deeply concerned about preserving vitality and individualism in a bureaucratic age, in his academic writings Weber failed to analyze systematically the effects of bureaucracy upon the character of individual members. That question seemed to him outside the realm of a value-free sociology, but its absence leaves a gap in his analysis of bureaucracy.

Bureaucracy is, then, only a rough model, not a precise description of contemporary organizations. The qualities which Weber emphasized reflect his special concern with the development of the modern state out of the feudal system, where authority was more personal and administration less professional. Nonetheless, Weber's analysis provides a useful introduction to key aspects of twentieth-century large-scale organizations, including American governmental administrative agencies. Even where we criticize Weber's work as ambiguous or misleading, he stimulates us to explore further the nature of modern organizations and a heavily bureaucratized society.

Not all joint human activity is essentially bureaucratic, of course. Nonbureaucratic forms of human organization include communes, slavery, family-operated enterprises, cell organization of subversive political action, clan organization, feudal power inherited by nonprofessional noble officials, mob action, congregational control of local churches, community work bees, prophet-disciple-community relationships, volunteer committees, and so forth. For contemporary American nonbureaucratic government officials, think of the justice of the peace who is a part-time amateur and retains the fees which he collects (perhaps to the sorrow of the unwary motorist) or the spoils appointee who holds his job through personal connections and only until his patron loses an election. The inheritance or purchase of administrative office, venerable practices in the world's history, probably occurs only informally in the United States today. American public administration is, with some exceptions and qualifications, "bureaucratic," though it probably still is less bureaucratic than European public administration.

The applicability of categories such as Weber's to diverse organizations suggests the possibility of treating governmental bureaucracy as fundamentally akin to that of business, military, church, and similar institutions. Thus Chester Barnard, in a book about the executive function, noted that "clergymen, military men, government officials, university officials, and men of widely diversified businesses, when not conscious of an attempt to discuss organization as such, have seemed to show an understanding—or better, a sense—that is quite similar."[4] Of all sorts of large, formal hierarchies one may ask how they operate, which easily leads to asking how they must operate to perform well and survive. Thus, the attempt to ascertain the essence of bureaucracy leads directly to the question of efficient bureaucracy, for the nature of a thing is close to its health, its perfection.

The concern with efficiency and the assumption that one bureaucracy is essentially like another is seen in some of the reports of the (Hoover) Commission on the Organization of the Executive Branch of the Government in the late 1940's and its successor in the 1950's. The law establishing the first Hoover Commission required it to offer recommendations for "eliminating duplication and overlapping" and "abolishing services, activities, and functions not necessary to the efficient conduct of Government." To accomplish this, task forces of experts (including business accounting firms) studied problems such as water resources projects and "business enterprises" of the government. In some reports, government agencies were treated basically as business agencies, to be tested by efficiency: if inefficient, private business should assume the function. It seems natural to Americans to close down government navy yards, as Defense Secretary McNamara did, on the grounds that private shipyards are more efficient. There is some sophisticated academic literature, too, which assumes that the goals for an agency can be set sufficiently precisely that administration is essentially the devising of means to reach those goals with the least expenditure of money and effort.

A somewhat broader view of efficiency requires of bureaucracy not merely minimization of the costs of doing prescribed tasks but also the imaginative response to needs. Far more than economy is required in this vision of the bureaucratic contribution to the task of governing. *Efficiency* suggests simple ability to perform without waste in the approved technical manner; *competence* suggests vigor and positive contribution. Efficiency and competence are closely related, however, and both test whether bureaucracy can do its assigned job well.

Competence, therefore, is a significant focus, one of the criteria for judging American governmental bureaucracy. If school teachers are deadened by routine or children lack books because of administrative confusion, if public works officials are political appointees who use old-fashioned methods and a touch of corruption, if branch offices do not communicate regularly with headquarters, if police officials maintain inaccurate records, if aviation authorities do not respond to the introduction of jet aircraft, we assume these agencies will not fulfill in full measure the tasks assigned to them. Most citizens who deem government and its tasks legitimate would judge such incompetence to be a bad thing. If government's bureaucracy fails, so may equal employment, education, public health, and our other common strivings. It is reasonable to ask both how our bureaucracies operate and whether American public administration is competent.

Though Weber described bureaucracy as remarkably efficient, we have common sense reservations. Is not sheer size often a barrier to prompt, effective action? Does not information get lost or distorted as it wanders up and down and across bureaucratic channels? Do not bureaucrats typically pass responsibility for decisions on to other bureaucrats? Is not government often bogged down in red tape—valuing adherence to rules at the expense of accomplishing objectives? Having safe jobs in government and no profit motive, do not administrators prefer caution and precedent to initiative and imagination? Does not political interference, especially from legislators and interest group spokesmen, block efforts to choose the best men and to act honestly on the evidence? We cannot, in the face of such questions, simply assume that the American public service is competent. It accomplishes large tasks, but it may do so despite serious mistakes, at high cost, and with significant failures. Is it sufficiently competent?

SELFHOOD

The second aspect of bureaucracy is humble and human: every institution has to be tested not only by how well it performs functions for the whole community, but also by what it does to its members, those most intimately involved in it. What shall we say, for example, of the factory which produces a fine product but destroys the health and self-respect of its workers? In terms of numbers of employees, government is a highly significant employer in America. The public service includes over two and one half million federal civilian employees and over ten million state and local government workers. Government employs over one sixth of our labor force and more than one third of all professional and technical workers. Because government is so full of symbolic significance, its practices take on added meaning in realms such as collective bargaining and loyalty-security clearance. In truth, though, we slip beyond politics to ask whether modern men are faring well in their bureaucratic environs. The bureaucrat may appear less an oppressor than a brother in bondage, himself burdened by a system of rules, by a hierarchy which towers above him. We must ask whether his personal freedom and worth may not be much impaired by a lifetime in such a system, so far removed from the yeoman's sturdy independence. We ask whether the government bureaucracy provides a humane, dignifying environment for government employees.

Bureaucracy evidently embodies qualities inconsistent with man's fullest dignity, for it seems to require anonymity of each participant, joint participation in every action, compliance with precedent and rules, and hierarchy in relations among members. A position exists in bureaucracy prior to and independent of the personality who fills it at the moment. If the individual officeholder leaves, another takes his place and the work goes on. In this way bureaucracy achieves a sort of immortality but the individual member loses significance. Thus, a dying official can rest assured that he is only opening up the possibility of promotion to a subordinate. Could not one wish for lowered flags, for speeches of praise, for the closing down of offices for a day, or even so humble a recognition as the bellowing of unmilked cows when their master comes no more? But to be so replaceable, not to matter—what fate is that for a man!

Bureaucratic action typically moves up and down and across channels, requiring participation by many persons, thus seeming to deprive any one person of responsibility, of the power and satisfaction of accomplishment. Regulations replace judgment in bureaucracy, thereby permitting equal treatment of citizens and lessening the talent or experience required for reaching a judgment. Reliance on precedent and rules seems to deprive the bureaucrat of creative possibilities, of personal judgment. Because of the hierarchy, bureaucrats become accustomed to thinking in terms of the approval of their superior officer, whose ill will threatens not only promotion but even peace and self-respect. If bureaucratic action is anonymous, joint, rule-bound, and subordinate within hierarchy, how can the bureaucrat achieve his potentialities as a person? It was Max Weber, he who praised bureaucracy's efficiency, who told a political party group in 1909 that the passion for bureaucracy is such that we seem to be turning into men who are "little cogs," who sacrifice everything to achieve order; he asked what we can do "to keep a portion of mankind free from this parcelling-out of the soul, from this supreme mastery of the bureaucratic way of life."[5] No wonder the existentialist cry to be fully a person resounds through a bureaucracy-laden civilization.

Dangers surely lurk in any attempt to describe a way of life lived by millions as if it had the same content or meaning for all. One might wonder whether the bureaucratic experience is really anything more than the experience of living in a modern, industrialized society. And many will object that however rigorous bureaucracy may appear in formal descriptions, in fact it is full of humanity, full of personal relations and informal group organization. More than that, the apparent impersonality is matched by an only apparent authority, for the subordinate really has means of tempering or thwarting the power of his official superior. The administrative superior ordinarily needs the willing cooperation of his subordinates if the unit is to compile a respectable record and the superior is to be judged an effective leader by his own superiors.

These objections to the very significance of the question of personal degradation in the bureaucratic life merit careful consideration. There is danger, too, of applauding a selfish careerism which turns bureaucracy from serving public purposes to mere individual and corporate self-service. Most simply, in an era when men have used great force against their fellows, when stultifying poverty is widespread, when irrational racial antagonisms disrupt community, who dares weep for the little woes of the middle-class American bureaucrat? The man with a comfortable and remunerative job, safe tenure, an opportunity to use his talents, is not a man to appeal to us for sympathy.

To all these arguments, however, we must at least respond that bureaucratic organization does impose its own kind of chains, that there is a freedom outside the organization not fully known within it, and the sacrifice of freedom always concerns us. Nor is the bureaucrat unworthy of our concern, however fortunate in many respects he is, compared with most of the world's men. The ancient Greeks were not wrong to find fascination in the greatest men and states, and we would not be wrong to ask about the life lived in the most powerful and wealthy societies. It is increasingly the typical human life, and, above all, for many contemporary Americans it is their own life.

In the 1950's William H. Whyte, Jr., wrote a popular and influential book in which he argued that "the dominant members of our society" are the middle-class organization men.[6] These young white-collar workers have rejected the Protestant ethic of hard work, thrift, and competitive struggle, of rugged individualism, and "between themselves and organization they believe they see an ultimate harmony." They believe that it is morally right to want to do things with and for others; they trust cooperation, they distrust the self. What they will be must be determined mainly by the system, which is essentially benevolent. After brilliantly describing the ideology and way of life of the modern American bureaucrat, Whyte urged him to fight the organization; the book ends with an appendix titled, "How to Cheat on Personality Tests." The Machiavellian touch suggests the importance of bureaucracy as a formative milieu within which men must live, and it testifies to the difficulty of surviving the bureaucratic life unscarred. Perhaps bureaucracy finally crushed the organization man's spirit. A spunky 1970 book by Robert Townsend, *Up the Organization,* finds the employees at every level in the average company to be docile, bored, and dull. "Trapped in the pigeonholes of organization charts, they've been made slaves to the rules of private and public hierarchies that run mindlessly on because nobody can change them."[7] (Townsend's highest goals, however, seem to be the joy of work and the pleasure of profits.)

If the young generation of the 1950's were compliant organization men, by the 1970's a significant proportion of those under age thirty seemed quite the opposite. Bureaucracy and all it stands for—its impact on its members, its clients, and the entire culture—were denounced in the name of personalism, love, community, spontaneity, freedom, and equality. Charles Reich's vigorous, if somewhat crude, condemnation of the culture of "the corporate state" based on hierarchical administration and his eloquent statement of a new life style (a new "consciousness") based on personal responsibility and equality seems to have crystallized what a good many young people were trying to articulate.

Is bureaucratic life uniformly and unalterably oppressive? Do those qualities which distinguish public from private administration in any way redeem the bureaucratic life within the government service?

POLITICAL RESPONSIBILITY

Though much that is true of governmental bureaucracy is true of private large-scale organizations too, only a limited understanding of the American public service could come from the study of large organizations in general. The politics and the authoritative policy choices of government go beyond simple efficiency. The third aspect of governmental bureaucracy is the perspective of politics, an examination of the contribution of governmental bureaucracy to the whole political system. Government's bureaucracy is not simply a machine. We must ask what purposes are being served. Are we creating death camps or cathedrals, is the agency serving the rich or the poor, party organizations or corporations, freedom or oppression? The basic value in terms of which we test government bureaucracy is constitutional democracy—a system of government based on political equality among persons, with wide popular participation and influence, including regular meaningful elections, a government limited by law and respectful of wide freedom of expression and political action. A democratic system reflects and is presumed to reinforce respect for each person's dignity and political competence. Therefore, in judging the public service, we must ask whether or not it contributes to the health of constitutional democracy. Patronage provides an example. If patronage proved necessary to the survival of political parties and if parties proved essential to our democratic functioning, any recommendation that patronage be abolished in order to increase administrative efficiency would obviously be subject to the gravest criticism. Or if patronage were shown to be a key technique of achieving equality for those ethnic groups which have least wealth and prestige in our society, it could not be rejected without serious consideration. A showing that it leads to bureaucratic inefficiency is not conclusive in its evaluation.

The political aspect of government bureaucracy turns our attention to the problem of power. It is no simple matter to determine to what extent the government bureaucracy possesses power, to what extent it is in fact the ruler of the community. Milovan Djilas, the brave, disenchanted Yugoslav Communist, has argued that communist bureaucrats constitute a brutal new exploiting class; James Burnham argued that bureaucrats are the new ruling class in all the great nations. A scholarly English student of European democratic public services calmly observes that "it is the higher civil service which represents the state, round which legislatures, ministers, the public and the judiciary revolve."[8] Scholars are surely not agreed that America is ruled by bureaucracy, nor is there agreement concerning the degree to which the public service ought to be a major policy-forming force. There is wide agreement, however, that the government bureaucracy has important, sometimes decisive, influence over the shape of public programs and over decisions of great importance to individual citizens. Administrative agencies determine, for example, who receives a television channel or an air route franchise of great financial value or, at the state level, the right to practice as a doctor, lawyer, or barber—decisions of great personal importance. They may destroy a farmer's sick cows, refuse a man admission to the country, deny a man a pension, or inquire of his neighbors whether he is a bad character. Administrative officials often play a chief part in preparing and even winning approval of legislation which guides public policy toward agriculture, taxation, urban renewal, and similar basic areas, for they have a detailed knowledge and continuing concern which congressmen cannot match. And it is bureaucrats who will actually carry out these statutes, fundamentally affecting program success.

If we give bureaucracy the name of the state and its means of compulsion, how then can we control its purposes? Some see internal self-control as the only feasible technique for limiting bureaucratic power, and are not overly suspicious of the intentions of the bureaucrats. Others insist on control by legislature or courts, and harbor deep doubts whether the bureaucracy, whatever the personal decency of its members, is a proper ruler for a democratic state. The French civil service, for example, has been characterized by professional competence and integrity of a high order, with a long tradition of self-control, but has not been subject to effective political direction; thus France is said to be administered (by a centralized, autonomous bureaucracy) but not governed (by democratically responsible politicians). If political parties and elected officials are essentials of democracy, can they control the career-oriented, tenured bureaucrats? Can they do so without a critical loss of competence—that is, are political control and administrative efficiency compatible? Can the courts, our special guardians of legal regularity, assure the rule of law in public administration without preventing effective public service?

The principal means to secure responsible governmental bureaucracy include:

(1) Cut down on the size and functions of governmental bureaucracy; that is, have less government;

(2) Subject public administration to the rule of law, under precise substantive and procedural rules, with court supervision, and with ombudsman-type officials to assist citizens with complaints; thus, the discretion of the person with legitimate authority is subject to a constitutional rule whose standing is higher than his own official authority or the dominant political will of the moment;

(3) Tighten political control, through (a) control by the legislature, the elected representatives of society, (b) control by the chief executive through the hierarchy and with the aid of politically appointed executives, (c) control by the party through patronage, (d) interest group influence through ties with bureaus, (e) citizen

influence through committees representing particular economic interests, (f) local citizen organization through community action programs, and (g) neighborhood autonomy through decentralization of government;

(4) Encourage self-control through professionalism and expertise, relying on (a) objective guidance through management science used by bureaucratic executives, (b) objective guidance through policy-area expertise of professionals in bureaucracy, (c) representative bureaucracy, a microcosm of the population served, (d) advocacy administration by bureaucrats actively committed to advancing the public interest, especially the needs of the least privileged.

Some of these methods assume, in turn, other phenomena, such as free elections and a free press. No doubt there are other possibilities, but these suggest both the range of methods of invoking responsibility and also the need for a variety of methods concurrently at work to hold public administration accountable to the public for whom it exists.

To understand this political aspect of the government service, one turns less to sociologists (who have contributed much to the understanding of bureaucracy as a modern institution) or to students of business administration (who have examined the factory as a social institution, from which we learn something of large-scale formal organization in general). It is the political scientists who teach us most concerning the politics of public administration, and that is the core of this study. As we are unlikely to have less government, the remaining chapters of this book are focused on contemporary problems in achieving political responsibility through the other approaches above. Even our first criterion of efficiency finally finds its practical justification as a means toward democratic political ends which we approve. The third face of public bureaucracy reveals, under its servant disguise, a growling political beast to be tamed.

PUBLIC VERSUS PRIVATE ADMINISTRATION

To say that public administration is governmental or political is not simply a truism. Some see the presence or absence of the profit motive and measure as the chief distinction between private administration and government, treating business as the primary form of the former. Conservatives typically cite this as the cause of the superior efficiency which they attribute to business; liberals are inclined to cite the concern with profit as one which corrupts the morals of business, preventing a commitment to the public good. But profit may not be the key factor differentiating business from public administration. In the modern corporation profit, in any rigorous sense, seems to be a significant motive for relatively few employees (even top managers may seek goals other than maximization of profit for the business), and the profit measure of performance is applicable in only a crude way to many functions and units. On the other hand, not only business corporations, but government agencies, armies, churches, museums, and the like face the need to maximize results, or achieve some level of effectiveness, with limited resources. Qualities such as prestige, salary, ethical standards, or size similarly seem not to be the basic differentiating qualities.

Public administration in a constitutional democracy seems to be distinguished from private administration by the greater presence of these qualities: authority, legalism, politics, and value complexity. By authority is meant the unique scope and weight of government's legitimate power in our society—power to tax, take property, imprison, conscript, license, charter, adjudicate, and so forth. This is a mark not only of its administration but of government as a whole, compared to all the other institutions of society. The question is not simple; for example, the government may permit a person a divorce but the refusal of his church may seem final to him; or a corporation or university may dismiss a member without government intervention. But government's authority does cover a wider range of concerns, and government has a greater arsenal of compulsion, more and tougher sanctions and modes of enforcement than others. In a special way government is the comprehensive institution, the possessor of awesome power. Public administration embodies the authority that society presumably grants to government alone.

Second, legalism means simply that public administration takes place within a constraining web of statutes and rules; it is full of red tape, courts, and controls. Thus lawyers have had a major role in American public administration, for they are experts in what is permitted and in how to do what should be done while remaining within the borders of legality. The General Accounting Office, which checks government expenditures to assure that they have been made in accordance with legal requirements, has been a pervasive and annoying force for federal administrators. Personnel experts guide public administrators through the labyrinth of rules for hiring and firing people. Democratic societies want a rule of law, so they demand that their public administrators operate within the laws and regulations. Private administration, it is true, is hemmed in by government rules, such as tax and antitrust laws and labor and fair employment regulations; also businesses create their own internal rules for the sake of efficiency and accountability.

When all is said, however, government administration is peculiarly enmeshed in limitations, in questions of what is permitted. Private administration is freer to act as the administrators wish. If a businessman wants to hire his son and dismiss someone else to make room, give a gift to or receive one from a business acquaintance, make partisan election pronouncements, enjoy deluxe air flights, give his employees a Christmas bonus, engage a consultant at whatever fee he deems reasonable, or the like, he can do these things; public administrators may be forbidden all these actions. Skillful public administrators learn to work within the rules so well that one is scarcely aware of the art they bring to the task, but businessmen new to public administration sometimes blunder from not understanding the legalism which·is one of the glories and burdens of public administration in a constitutional democracy.

Third, public administration is also more political than private administration. Apart from any quite abstract meaning one may impute to this statement, it says that government administration is closely tied to elections, parties, interest groups, public opinion, the press, the legislature, the chief executive—to all the institutions and occasions which we recognize as highly political. A governmental bureaucrat, agency, or decision may be more or less political, depending on politicizing factors such as these: (1) an official may be appointed by an elected official or be appointed for political reasons, (2) his tenure—promotion, transfer, demotion, discharge—may be affected by changes in elective posts, (3) other politically sensitive officials or agencies may be involved in the same or a competing activity, (4) organized interest groups may be concerned, (5) wide discretion may be permitted the agency, and technical criteria alone may not determine the course of action, (6) there may be no consistent precedents for the decision, (7) passions concerning ideals or the protection of interests may be highly inflamed, (8) the issue, person, or agency may have been dramatized by political campaigns, professional politicians, or the mass media.[9]

Some agencies or programs seem quite unpolitical, very like agencies in private administration. Quiet social security administration may seem closer to a private insurance company than to the Defense Department. The National Institutes of Health, conducting scientific research, may call to mind a university medical school rather more than the sometimes turbulent Federal Communications Commission, which has to decide who will win a valuable television license. A municipal electric power plant may appear much like a private power plant, and little like a public liquor-sale-licensing agency. In its least political, most routine or expert places and moments, public administration may greatly resemble business administration, but politics slumbers within all public administration. Some agencies live always in the lion's den of politics (pulling thorns to save their dear lives), others tend genteel gardens till the dragons of Congress, vultures of an angry press, or sly foxes of ambitious politicians looking for an issue, catch them up; none is really safe from politics. Public life involves the whole range of values of a society, the most complex weighing of largely intangible costs and gains against one another, the frequent conflict of group against group with confusing blends of public interest and private goals, the most inflammatory mixtures of "ideological" with "practical" issues. This is not to suggest that most public administration is conducted in a partisan way, serving Democratic or Republican purposes, but simply that it is always subject to influence or control from the more continuously and overtly political forces in our system.

Finally, then, public administration in a constitutional democracy is distinguished from private administration by greater value complexity. Though a governmental bureau focuses primarily on achieving its particular purposes, it is susceptible to praise or condemnation for its impact on a whole range of values. There is a weight of responsibility upon it from politics, from being answerable to the whole nation, from government's special obligation to the public interest. The difference from private administration is only a matter of degree, but in government there is a special tendency to question the means used in administration, to ask about the total impact of a program. Are the incidental effects of a program desirable? For example, the federal General Services Administration is an unglamorous "housekeeping" agency. Yet in selecting sites for federal buildings it now takes into account the contribution made to underprivileged minority groups by locating buildings in their areas of cities. In running the government's automobile fleet it has begun to try alternatives to gasoline as a fuel, to seek means of lessening air pollution. In purchasing supplies it will pay a premium for goods produced by firms owned by minority group members, under a preferential procurement program. Thus, efficiency is not the sole test of an agency's performance in its own eyes or those of others. Although business, universities, churches, and other organizations are increasingly called to responsibility for the effect of their actions on race relations, pollution, and similar issues, and though government and business corporations are closely linked in such ventures as aerospace and military equipment, government is especially sensitive to the total impact of its operations, the whole range of values affected.

In summary, despite ambiguities and marginal cases, public administration in a democratic society differs from private administration primarily because it is: (a) possessed of such wide authority and strong sanctions, (b) so limited by rules, (c) so bound up with politics, and (d) conducted and judged according to so complex a set of values. Senator Robert Taft, the able and politically experienced Republican Senate leader who was a hero to conservative businessmen, commented skeptically on President Eisenhower's appointment of business executives to high government posts: "Anyone who thinks he can just transfer business methods to government is going to have to learn that it isn't so."[10]

THE UNITED STATES GOVERNMENT BUREAUCRACY

Understanding something of bureaucracy in general and the special characteristics of public administration, can we suggest specifically what sort of agencies and officials constitute government bureaucracy in the United States? We do not include legislators or an elected chief executive, such as the President or a governor, among those who are bureaucrats; election to office, partisan identification, lack of career tenure, and other qualities distinguish the clearly political figures from the bureaucratic ones. We also exclude judges, though in some countries judges are career professionals.

Top political appointees, such as cabinet members and aides whom they may bring along, are not bureaucrats of the Federal Government. Equally clearly, however, they are leaders of the bureaucracy. One must distinguish such short-term, politically appointed chieftains of the bureaucracy from regular career bureaucrats, yet recognize their importance in the bureaucracy. What of lower-level employees, if they owe their appointment to politics, yet secure tenure in the office? Most Federal civil servants today secure their appointment through a merit system; in some state and local governments, a good many of the officials are patronage appointees. As with the chiefs, we must recognize their difference from their bureaucratic bedfellows, but if we find them snuggled in the bureaucratic bed, we shall have to take them into account. So much for those who are not bureaucrats.

For many purposes government agencies ought to be classified in terms of the area of policy with which they deal, for example, foreign affairs, environmental quality, or the banking system. Involved in each function one may discover subunits of various departments (often called bureaus), scattered bureau subunits (typically called divisions), and even smaller subdivisions. A description of the federal bureaucracy in these terms is nothing less than a summary of all the functions performed by the government. We can, alternatively, categorize government agencies in terms of forms of organization such as the six below. Form is not always the critical factor, but it does matter for it affects the policies to be pursued and the effectiveness of the effort. One must consider both organization form and policy commitments when seeking to understand administration.

(1) Cabinet departments, headed by secretaries, are part of a great and continuing administrative tradition in the United States Government. State, Treasury, and War (now Defense), and the office of Attorney General (who heads Justice) date from 1789, the Postmaster General from 1792, and Navy (now in Defense) from 1798. The most recent of the twelve departments are Health, Education, and Welfare, created by the Eisenhower administration, and Housing and Urban Development, and Transportation, both established under Johnson. Defense is the giant, with over one and one quarter million civilian employees, the Post Office has nearly three quarters of a million, but the other departments are mostly under 100,000. In his State of the Union Message of January 1971, President Nixon proposed maintaining the Department of State, Treasury, Defense, and Justice, but reorganizing the others into four new Departments: Natural Resources, Human Resources, Economic Development, and Community Development. Later, in response to political protests, he agreed to preserve Agriculture as a department. The Post Office was already scheduled to lose its departmental status; it became a public corporation in 1971.

The cabinet departments contain many bureaus of long tradition and great political strength, so that some departments have seemed little more than a collection of loosely associated, barely coordinated bureaus. In formal terms, however, there is a nice line of authority from the President to his cabinet secretaries to their bureau chiefs and down another few layers, whereby everyone is accountable eventually to the President. Actual control is not so easy, but the organizational clarity (often absent in state and local government) has been of genuine value. When the President or a department head really intends to enforce a policy, at least the structure supports his authority.

(2) For lack of a better term, "executive agency" may be used to describe organizations which are essentially like departments, but are not titled "department" and are not headed by an official called "secretary." The Veterans Administration, a large organization (over 170,000 employees), is an example, as is the National Aeronautics and Space Administration (over 30,000); a more modest example is the Smithsonian Institution (under 2500). In

1939 a law was enacted permitting the President to reorganize the executive branch, subject to Congressional nullification, over a two-year period. However, the law prohibited the President from creating new departments. President Roosevelt, undaunted, created the Federal Security Agency, the Federal Works Agency, and the Federal Loan Agency under this legislation, and asked the administrators of these agencies to sit with the cabinet. Such agencies differ hardly at all from regular departments in form, but may lack the political and administrative dignity and the endurance of departments.

(3) Certain units are typically called auxiliary or overhead agencies. Three substantial Federal agencies fall in this category: the Office of Management and Budget (until 1970, the Bureau of the Budget), the Civil Service Commission, and the General Services Administration. The Budget Office works on the preparation of the budget and the supervision of orderly spending under it, as well as on legislative proposals from government agencies and problems of administrative efficiency. It is a unit within the Executive Office of the President, a location emphasizing that control of the budget is a key method of presidential control of the administration. (The Bureau was created in 1921 within Treasury, but moved in 1939 to the President's office.) The Civil Service Commission, a three-member bipartisan body created to fight the post-Civil War spoilsmen, is responsible for the government's personnel system. In cooperation with the departments and executive agencies, it assists in providing personnel and systems for recruiting, testing, granting veterans' preference, rating efficiency of employees, and the like. The General Services Administration, which is a post-World War II agency, deals especially with real estate, supplies for government agencies, transportation needs, and records management. Its more than 30,000 employees contrasts with the Civil Service Commission's approximately 5300 and the Budget Office's staff of about 550. These three are identified as auxiliary agencies because they seem to be assisting and controlling the "line" agencies, which appear more directly to be carrying out the actual public programs of government. One hires people, provides funds, and secures a building in order to conduct foreign affairs, assist farmers, or the like.

The entire federal budget or personnel function is not performed within the Office of Management and Budget or the Civil Service Commission. Budget, personnel, and similar auxiliary units operate within, as members of, the various departments and subunits, to aid them in their work and to provide a link with the auxiliary agencies of government-wide scope.

(4) Staff units are those concerned with planning, research,

drafting reports, inquiring into agency actions and checking out complaints, offering alternatives to policies urged or adopted by agency subunits, or performing other activities for which a line official is formally responsible but can use help. Though staff officials may be attached to an executive at a high level, they do not have formal authority over the executive's subordinates. (Because they are close to the seat of power, however, staff officials may actually wield power; who wants to cross the king's secretary?) Some staff aides (including "bright young men") serve in an "Office of" the chief of any unit or as "Assistant to" an official, some are in units responsible for "planning," "program analysis," "special studies," or the like. Even at modest hierarchical levels, an official may be blessed with at least one staff aide, if not a staff unit. The definition of staff emphasizes the absence of responsibility for administering a program and the obligation to serve an official with such authority. Real cases are not always so clear. Where the classification of an actual agency, function, or individual position as "staff" versus "auxiliary" seems unduly difficult, or where there is no need to distinguish precisely, one may join the two categories, content to distinguish them from "line" agencies.

The essence of the staff idea was enunciated by the President's Committee on Administrative Management in 1937, when it sought for the President a small number of aides with "a passion for anonymity." These aides "would have no power to make decisions or issue instructions in their own right. They would not be interposed between the President and the heads of his departments. They would not be assistant presidents in any sense. Their function would be, when any matter was presented to the President for action affecting any part of the administrative work of the Government, to assist him in obtaining quickly and without delay all pertinent information possessed by any of the executive departments so as to guide him in making his responsible decisions; and then when decisions have been made, to assist him in seeing to it that every administrative department and agency affected is promptly informed. . . . They would remain in the background, issue no orders, make no decisions, emit no public statements. . . . "[11] Significant growth in the staffs of the President and cabinet secretaries since 1939 has enabled the effective functioning of the government as something more than a collection of essentially autonomous bureaus.

(5) Government corporations are so elusive a category that it is difficult to agree on either number or definition, and the qualities which distinguish them have faded over the years. These agencies are typically headed by a board, engaged in a business-type function, and incorporated. They used to be distinguished as

enjoying more discretion than regular government agencies, though there was always great variety among government corporations; now more uniform but less distinctive than earlier, they still enjoy some autonomy denied to regular agencies. The Tennessee Valley Authority, engaged in navigation and flood control, electric power production, and fertilizer production, is a government corporation, as is the Federal Deposit Insurance Corporation, familiar as a guarantor to bank depositors. One must add that there are some regular cabinet departments which perform functions not less businesslike than those of government corporations. Establishment of government corporations often reflects a distrust of public administration, as in the conversion of the Post Office—derided as grossly inefficient—from a regular executive department into a corporation.

(6) Independent regulatory commissions are agencies headed by a board, whose members are appointed for fixed terms with judicial protection against removal without cause, typically with a requirement that the board be bipartisan; they regulate a particular industry or a particular function or aspect of business. The oldest federal regulatory commission is the Interstate Commerce Commission, established in 1887 to regulate the railroads; others include the Federal Communications Commission, the Securities and Exchange Commission, and the National Labor Relations Board—a total of nine or ten by common count. (There are state commissions, too, regulating banks, insurance companies, and the like.) To some extent they are the policemen of business, but they also act at times as the promoter and protector of the businesses with which they deal. They are especially identified with administrative hearings of a trial-like nature, with hearing examiners, but cabinet departments, such as Agriculture, engage in these activities in similar fashion. Commissions are praised and blamed for exercising a combination of legislative, executive, and judicial powers. They have been challenged as a threat to presidential control, effective regulation, and the rule of law, but legislators and the regulated interests often have a kind word for them.

There is much imprecision in this terminology of organization types—cabinet department, executive agency, auxiliary agency, staff unit, government corporation, and independent regulatory commission—but at least the terms provide a useful language for administrative analysis. In subsequent chapters the specific contributions and problems of various of these organizational forms will be considered in more detail.

The variety in function, as distinct from form, among government agencies is as great as the complexity of modern life and government. In size they range from Defense and Post Office down to modest servants such as the Subversive Activities Control Board, which counted thirteen employees on January 1, 1969. They all share certain traits, however, beyond those qualities common to all bureaucracies or to all American bureaucracies. They share a role in American political life; if none can claim to be sovereign, each is touched with the dust of that mystical power. Despite differences in form, function, size, and tradition, they are brethren, parts of a single government. Their governmental nature distinguishes them from their nearest counterparts in the world of private organizations.

Is it possible to characterize more specifically the entire American public administrative system, to find an essence that unifies such diverse and changing services? Leonard D. White, distinguished historian of American public administration, set forth stable characteristics "deeply embedded in the preferences and attitudes of the American people and in the history of over a century and a half," which he thought were likely to persist.[12] These are: (1) American public administration is based on the rule of law, with an important role for the courts in controlling administrators and an important role for lawyers. (2) It depends on representative, elected legislatures for its policy and powers; it is subordinated to democratic control, responsive to public opinion. (3) It is democratic in spirit. The bureaucrats are not a special class, public service is freely open to all groups, and the ranks within the service are not rigidly separate. (4) It depends heavily upon the consent of the governed, who are ready to resist or ignore what seems unreasonable. (5) Since about 1900 there has been a strong tendency toward professionalism, a career, merit system, full of expertise. (A dissenter might note, however, that party patronage and amateurism have had and to some extent retain a significant place in our public services.) (6) It is civil, rather than military, in personnel and spirit. (Is this still so much the case?) (7) It is flexible, adaptive, experimental, with a strong sense of improvement. (8) It is federal, with autonomous but cooperating federal, state, and local administration. (9) It is deeply rooted in local communities, with a preference for local people as officials. (10) It works on a huge scale, involving great areas, vast projects, many people. White's analysis suggests specifically that public administration differs significantly from nation to nation and differs also from private administration, precisely because it is governmental.

However, White's analysis may be too gentle, missing the tough power of government officials. Much policy originates in the bureaucracy, for legislators cannot hope to know the detailed problems and possible solutions over the whole range of matters for which they are responsible. Of necessity, they turn to the bureaucrats for advice upon courses of action, even while they may be making occasional dramatic interventions or speeches condemning bureaucrats. Legislation often entrusts major decisions to the administering officials. For example, an agency of government is told to grant licenses in accord with "the public interest"; the legislators leave it to the commissioners and career officials to give the term real meaning. Public welfare officials determine which particular individuals are eligible for specific grants and services. Public road officials decide where the roads shall cut through homes and fields. The gap between a statute and an operating program is vast, and in this discretionary territory anonymous administrators govern. A good many political scientists have questioned whether legislators, executives, or judges can effectively control bureaucrats, apart from occasional random intervention and attention to flagrant abuses. One can say this without suggesting that our public officials are individually corrupt or collectively conspiratorial. Our public servants are surely not a group of evil schemers, but neither are they democratically elected leaders. The question is one of who has power and who ought to. Are we moving into the administrative state, into a time of bureaucratic rule?

COMPETENCE, SELFHOOD, AND RESPONSIBILITY: THE COMPATIBILITY OF GOALS

Let us now return to the three criteria for evaluating governmental bureaucracy and ask what insights they give us into the American public service. (1) Is the American government bureaucracy competent, relatively efficient? Can it provide effective public service? (2) Does the American government bureacracy provide a beneficial environment within which bureaucrats may be their best selves, and does it radiate an influence conducive to the realization of selfhood in the society? An answer to this question no doubt depends a good deal on the nature of bureaucracy in general, but may require specific consideration of the governmental bureaucracy in the United States, since large organizations differ significantly from one another. (3) What is the political significance of the American government bureaucracy? Is it subject to control by politically responsible agencies? Does the public service contribute to the political health of constitutional democracy (the whole community), and what particular groups and what goals find support or discouragement in our public administration?

Are these goals mutually compatible? Can one have efficiency, self-realization, and political responsibility, or is one forced to choose among them? The Prussian bureaucracy had a good name for efficiency, but its members were treated as servants without rights and the citizenry were treated as objects to be controlled by a well-intentioned bureaucracy. There is reason to believe that the bureaucrats of, for example, New York City have gained a measure of collective self-control which, while affording protection for their own rights and dignity, impedes effectiveness by preventing experimentalism and blocks responsiveness to clientele needs and control by elective politicians directly responsible to the public. America tried political control through large-scale patronage, but paid a price in loss of administrative competence. Is it possible that the greatest routine efficiency comes through giving the career chiefs or the professionals within bureaucracy unlimited control, while the greatest responsibility to the public comes through emphasizing control by politicians, and the greatest dignity for the bureaucrat comes through minimizing all controls not imposed by the individual on himself? Efficiency, individual dignity, and control are goals for government bureaucracy which apparently conflict at many points.

Though responsibility is the specifically political goal, all three have deep political relevance. Efficiency, in its fullest sense, involves the ability of the bureaucracy to make a contribution to the art of government. A competent government bureaucracy helps create and shape new and difficult programs, and reinvigorate older programs no longer responsive to basic needs. The army that loves horses or armor too much may, by its technological torpor, threaten the national independence of the state. An agriculture department that is insensitive to scientific advances or to socioeconomic changes may do old tasks well but miss its major contribution. Apart from any concern with penny pinching, one must hope for competence from the bureaucracy. In areas such as the fight against poverty and racial discrimination, the administrative contribution may be as important as purely political actions. We need imaginative, able, determined, experienced administrators—not simply obedient servants—if these programs are to achieve any measure of success.

The internal effects of bureaucracy have political significance, as debates over the right to strike of public employees or the loyalty-security program of the public service testify. If teachers strike, out of despair at bureaucratic controls or resistance to community control or resentment over inadequate pay, the action is treated by the entire community as intensely political, full of meaning about the ultimate sources and purposes of power. The very personal hiding places of human dignity are not so exposed and dramatic, but attempts to form institutions (such as unions) or to act collectively (such as to strike), in ways reflecting personal needs of bureaucrats, finally become political issues. And the

rejection by young adherents of the counterculture of a bureaucratic life which has touched them in actions and in fantasy has
political implications for the whole society.

If technical competence emphasizes organizational autonomy,
and if personal dignity leads toward personal autonomy, the issue
of constitutional responsibility leads to problems of control. If the
solution were simply "the more controls the merrier," one could
proceed to invent means of control. But controls may conflict with
technical competence and with personal dignity. Too much control
or the wrong kind can ruin the public service, which requires
talent, initiative, professional judgment, and imaginative innova-
tion. Too little control can transfer power from those directly
responsible to the public to career employees, who may give
primacy to their own needs or to their own definition of the public
good. Our goal is to devise controls which work, yet which leave the
public service rich in competence and in dignity for its members.

CHAPTER TWO

Public Administration Under Law

Subjection of rulers to the law distinguishes constitutional authority from tyranny. We would be ill at ease with a governmental bureaucracy guided solely by its own views or by the current attitudes of a ruling elite or even a majority, heedless of limitations found in community traditions and constitutional provisions. The essence of constitutionalism is that it so binds those currently in power that they consent to use that power in limited ways. But lawfulness in administration seems not to touch equally all activities of government; thus it focuses less on foreign affairs than on the power of government to impose punishments on, and to grant or withhold benefits from, its own citizens. Nor does lawfulness guarantee wise or popular or effective public policy, for law may inhibit the democratic majority or impede a discretion necessary for effective government. The United States has experienced tension between the rule of law and democratic responsiveness of the bureaucracy in such areas as economic regulation, especially during the 1930's, and loyalty-security clearances in the 1950's. At this time there is tension in American politics between those who, in the name of the majority's right to physical safety and order, seek more authority for government in criminal law enforcement, and those who emphasize the constitutional rights of the accused.

Similar tensions arise in the administration of public welfare, between demands for more vigorous action to prevent or punish abuses of the system by welfare recipients and efforts to protect the rights and dignities of the recipients. Can the public service be effective and politically responsive, while respecting limitations imposed by the rule of law?

THE RULE OF LAW

At the turn of the century, A. V. Dicey, an English constitutional scholar, analyzed the rule of law brilliantly, if not entirely correctly. England had been marked, he suggested, not by the leniency of the laws, but by legality itself. Continental powers may not have been oppressive, but there the citizen was not secure from arbitrary power. In three principles, Dicey held, is the rule of law: no one may be punished except by conviction under the ordinary law through the ordinary courts; public officials hold limited power, subject to the same ordinary law and ordinary courts as private citizens; constitutional principles grow from well-established ordinary remedies for protection of private rights, the principles being inductions from judicial decisions in specific cases.

Dicey's analysis has been influential in England and America, as an assertion both of the actual tradition and of the ideal in terms of which to evaluate government. Yet his analysis leaves one uneasy. Are the ordinary courts, applying ordinary law to government officials, satisfactory controllers of government? A private suit against a public official in a regular civil court is not always a feasible way for a citizen to prevent abuse of power. Controls within the administrative branch or specialized administrative courts sometimes prove more effective. The French created a system of special administrative law and administrative courts on the assumption that the ordinary judges were the enemies of administrators and of social reform. Dicey deplored such administrative law, but the modern verdict is more favorable. He argued that the common law—the traditional law, drawn from judge-made precedents rather than from legislative statutes—is the basic protector of individual rights. But is the ancient common law always better than statute law made contemporaneously by the legislature, and can the regular courts deal with abuse of administrative power? Jennings, a later student of the English constitution, argues that basic freedoms are protected less by judicial review than by democratic political devices such as ministerial responsibility to the current majority in Parliament or free, regular presidential elections with competing parties. Dicey may trust too much in the courts to control administration.

Is administrative discretion always an evil? If not, what is the proper extent of official discretion? To Aristotle's "vexed question whether the best law or the best man should rule," Dicey, not trusting men with power, gave all right to law. He equated administrative discretion with arbitrariness and oppression. Yet almost all governmental tasks require discretion in interpreting the law, in shaping policies and rules, in judging claims and ascertaining the facts. If we forbid all this to administrators or involve the courts each time, public administration will bog down. Dicey's political position was conservative (what Englishmen would call Whiggish or Liberal). He believed strongly in individual freedom and was unsympathetic to governmental control of the economy or provision of extensive social welfare services. He was especially concerned with police interference with individual liberties, and tended to see governmental actions as a threat, not a service. The need for lawfulness has not declined since Dicey wrote, but the need for effective government—even then racing ahead of his analysis—has grown greatly. Harmless government is not good enough. We seek to combine administrative virtues (expertise and ability to cope with large numbers) with judicial virtues (impartiality and careful procedure in reaching a decision). We seek effective public administration under law.

ADMINISTRATIVE REGULATION

That administrative adjudication is not entirely modern is suggested by such examples from English history as commissioners with power to enforce excise taxes, sewer commissioners with power to fine and imprison, and administrative licensing of wine and liquor dealers. However, most nineteenth century American regulation of railroad and public utilities rates, for example, was conducted by the legislature with enforcement through suit by an aggrieved party in the courts. Why have we departed from regulation through the courts, which emphasizes law and judges in the spirit of Dicey, to adopt administrative regulation, which significantly empowers bureaucrats and opens wide the problem of administrative power?

RETREAT FROM THE COURTS

The first difficulty with using the judiciary as regulator is that courts have policy defects. Ideological conservatism in the late nineteenth and early twentieth centuries led courts to nullify legislative efforts at regulation of the economy. Thus courts interpreted the Sherman Act so as to defeat its antimonopoly purposes and, in defense of the property rights of employers, undermined statutes to protect workers. Legislatures then turned to administrative agencies to effectuate policy more faithfully to legislative purpose than had the courts, whose dominant concern, rooted in the old common law, was private property. Courts emphasized the rights of the parties before them, "with only an accidental regard for the interests of the public at large, and with a disregard for the exigencies of social policy."[1] Courts focus on the particular case and on adjudication as an end in itself, not on its implications for public policy; however, agencies could use adjudication as one technique toward policy goals which are relatively explicit and responsive to political and statutory control. Public policy is often implicit in particular judicial decisions, but it is a more remote consideration for courts than for agencies, unless—as has happened often with the independent regulatory commissions discussed below—the agency has lost its sense of policy responsibility and tries to act like a court.

Second, courts suffer from lack of expertise. Courts cultivate procedure and nourish great principles, while handling a considerable variety of issues. We occasionally create a specialized court, such as the Court of Customs and Patent Appeals, and Europeans use administrative courts, but our tradition is of general purpose courts. These courts lack not only specialization, but also an expert bureaucratic staff and the ability to gather facts other than those which parties choose to put on the record. The question of a reasonable rate for a common carrier, which courts used to decide, involves a considerable amount of financial, economic, and technological sophistication. An administrative agency can include varied experts, who together provide impressive knowledge of a specialized area.

Third, courts have procedural defects. They cannot deal expeditiously with large numbers of cases, though presumably one might multiply indefinitely the number of judges. In 1789 there was created an agency to determine which claimants were entitled to veterans' pensions, rather than leaving the decisions to judges. Its descendant, the Veterans Administration, adjudicates through the formal procedures of the Board of Veterans Appeals almost half the number of cases adjudicated by the entire federal court system; it adjudicates informally more than thirty times the number of cases adjudicated by the federal court system. Even if one haggles about definitions of case and adjudicate, the point is clear: courts can hardly inquire into all decisions about social security, drivers' licenses, admission to public universities, and so forth. If courts went through the entire decision process for even the contested decisions, they would bog down. Also, the costliness of judicial procedure punishes the weak and helps the rich. Workmen's compensation used to depend on a court trial, rather than administrative determination. The injured workman often was forced to settle on company terms, rather than wait for and pay for justice. The courts are also too much attuned to formal battle, unsuited to informal action, though they now accomplish a good deal in settling cases without trial. An administrative agency is well suited to resolving controversies through means less formidable, costly, and slow than trials.

Fourth, courts lack preventive and supervisory mechanisms. They can issue injunctions and some similarly flexible writs, but they excel at leisurely allocation of rights and wrongs after the fact, not at preventive action. To prevent explosions in coal mines or the sale of impure drugs or the floating of wobbly ships or shoddy securities, agencies are better suited. Courts receive cases, they do not initiate action; an official or a private citizen must come to the courts and ask them to prevent harm. Regulation which relies on aggrieved citizens or busy district attorneys and which must go through the courts before any control is effected is not likely to be vigorous, consistent, effective, or preventive of injury. The Supreme Court itself has held that the federal courts cannot be empowered to fix rates or prices, though they may review and reject rates. Nor can the courts be empowered to issue broadcasting licenses or perform similar discretionary functions. "This insistence of the courts upon confining themselves to judicial, as distinguished from executive or legislative, functions," wrote the Attorney General's Committee on Administrative Procedure in 1941, "has made inevitable the conferring of a wide range of power, if the powers were to be conferred at all, upon some one of the executive departments or upon an independent agency."[2] To these tasks the agencies can bring research, inspection, testing, licensing, rule making, warnings, or formal charges—a panoply of preventive and supervisory techniques not used by the courts.

Like the courts, the legislature cannot adequately perform the regulatory function. State legislatures once fixed rates by statute and Congress formerly handled all money claims against the United States. Legislatures have the authority but lack the time and expertise to make and continually adapt the rules required for effective regulation, although occasionally they try to set policy for an industry or problem area, often failing even at that. In sum, administrative regulatory agencies were established in the hope of flexibly combining legislative (general rule making), executive (rule enforcement), and judicial (adjudication of charges, laying penal-

ties on rule violators) powers, all aimed at vigorous expert enforcement of policy consciously formulated in the public interest,
willing to limit the property rights of the economically powerful.
These observations on limitations of courts and legislatures are
put somewhat sharply and should not be taken to mean that
agencies work perfectly or always better than courts. (Recently
environmentalists unimpressed with the record of governmental
agencies in fighting pollution have been working for citizen initia-
tion of suits against private parties or public agencies, to obtain
court orders prohibiting activity that adversely affects the environment—an interesting old-fashioned supplement to administrative
regulation.) They simply suggest why, despite reverence for the
rule of law, Americans have increasingly turned to administrative
agencies to regulate behavior. This seems so natural today that one
may wonder why it is worth telling. But Dicey, very many nine-
teenth- and pre-New Deal twentieth-century Englishmen and
Americans, and a substantial number of people today, would think
that the governmental bureaucracy has grown large and powerful
beyond all wisdom.

From the 1930's to the 1950's it was especially businessmen
who complained bitterly of excessive governmental regulation and
power-mad bureaucrats; today the poor and the Blacks complain
of arbitrary, lawless power in welfare, police, and other public
agencies. Scholars look with renewed interest at protections against
administrative authority; students, among others, seek regulations
to assure fairness in their dealings with large organizations. Our
goal is to use the giant governmental administrative system, created
largely since 1933, without losing the rule of law.

RESISTANCE TO ADMINISTRATIVE REGULATION

Our system of administrative regulation has been shaped by
the tension between our tradition of the rule of law and vigorous
resistance to the growth of effective administrative regulation, on
the one hand, and the recognized needs of a modern society and its
complex economy, on the other. Resistance to administrative
regulation has been led by lawyers steeped in court tradition and
the spirit of Dicey and by businessmen trying to impede governmental regulation. (Some businesses, such as radio broadcasting in
its time of chaos, wanted regulation, and many became accustomed
to it after a while or even dependent on it to prevent more vigorous
competition.) The American Bar Association has a splendidly
consistent record of opposing administrative regulation, ever since
it appointed a special committee on administrative law in 1933.
The first attack on administrative regulation asserted its un-

constitutionality and sought to reject it entirely. In the 1930's the combination of legislative, executive, and judicial powers within administrative agencies was challenged as violative of the separation of powers, and the delegation of legislative power to administrative agencies was called unconstitutional. The federal courts now accept the mixture of powers in administrative agencies, but state courts do not always. The second attack sought to control administrative regulation through extensive judicial review. The third, dominant since the late 1930's, sought to impose procedural requirements, to make the administrative process like the court process. The ABA has led the fight to formalize the process of administrative regulation, on the court model, and to extend judicial review of agency action. In 1940 President Roosevelt gave a blistering veto to the ABA-sponsored Walter-Logan bill, which promised enough judicialization to cripple administrative regulation. Questions of fair procedure and of judicial review are now the stuff of administrative law.

Out of the battles of the 1930's came the report of the distinguished Attorney General's Committee on Administrative Procedure (1941). Because it is balanced and thoughtful and rich in details of the actual working of administrative regulation, it remains a valuable source. The committee accepted the role of administrative regulation, and its studies did not uncover shocking procedure, grave abuse of rights, corruption, or gross power seeking. Though it tended to use the judicial process as a standard, it saw the practical problems of administration and sought to balance the protection of private rights against the achievement of public purposes.

The reform movement was interrupted by the war but came to fruition, much tamed, in the Administrative Procedure Act of 1946. This was a compromise between those who opposed any effort to require uniformity and judicialization in the administrative process, on the one hand, and the ABA and allied proponents of procedural reform or curtailment of administrative powers, on the other. The major change was somewhat greater independence for hearing examiners, who conduct formal administrative hearings. Musolf concluded of the rights guaranteed by the statute: "They caused no great upheaval in agencies for most agencies already had incorporated most of them into their procedural rules and, with the numerous exceptions which accompany these rights in the statute, existing variety in agency practices was to a considerable extent preserved."[3] Most scholars now agree with such a restrained appraisal.

Have we reached consensus? Evidently not. In 1952 strong pressure was observed in the states for "further and more drastic legislative action that would over-judicialize the procedures of state regulatory agencies."[4] A task force of the second Hoover Commission in 1955 spoke of administrative procedures much in the old, harsh Walter-Logan spirit of the need for extensive judicialization of regulatory procedure and expanded court control. The Hoover Commission itself almost visibly choked as it barely swallowed the recommendations, and the Eisenhower administration's Attorney General thought the proposals "would substantially 'judicialize' the administrative process, with disastrous results to efficient and effective government."[5] The American Bar Association is not reconciled and "in 1963, as in 1933, the ABA and some groups in the legal profession seem to be pushing for complete formalization of the administrative process in terms of internal agency procedure, and in some instances legal opinion favors administrative courts which presumably would solve procedural problems by entirely removing the function of adjudication from the hands of administrative agencies."[6] The ABA continues, at this writing, to press, with sympathetic legislators, for legislative action which would push much further than the Administrative Procedure Act of 1946 in the direction of court-like procedural requirements. Those who measure the performance of regulatory agencies in terms of the court model (for example, lawyers and judges, detailed rules of evidence and formal testimony, lengthy opinions and elaborate appeals procedures) may well find the agencies lacking, but one must remember that the agencies carry on programs of a sort the courts could scarcely undertake. The opposition to administrative regulatory procedures has come from a mixture of devotion to traditional legal procedures and search for a means to block programs of economic regulation which had political legitimacy but were seen as a threat to corporate interests.

ADMINISTRATIVE POWER TO PUNISH

Concern with administrative regulatory procedure is based partly on recognition of the power administrative officials have over citizens. Including sanctions imposed by agencies directly and with the assistance of the courts, what can officials do to a person? It is obvious that the police may arrest a person and that the prosecuting attorney may initiate action to have a person fined or imprisoned, but these actions must go through the courts finally. Normally administrative officials must turn to the courts to secure enforcement of whatever laws are entrusted to them, if they seek formally to punish an individual. The individual may refuse to obey, then await prosecution by the government. Ordinarily, then, until he has secured judicial warrant for such action, the administrator cannot use force on the person or property of one who violates a law or a rule made under the law. Thus the courts are a safeguard.

Exceptions are the "summary powers" which come from the common law or from statutes. Under summary procedure, compulsion may be applied against person or property without a judicial warrant. The person is required, if he protests, to seek redress afterwards. Ernst Freund in 1928 cited such examples as: a New York State law authorized the Superintendent to take possession of a bank for various reasons, the banker being required to seek judicial aid in reclaiming his business; the Post Office was authorized to refuse to carry obscene matter, lottery tickets, and fraudulent schemes; statutes permitted summary power over the movement of ships, refusing entry or clearance papers for departure; aliens seeking entry were subject to exclusion by summary administrative procedure; summary procedures were commonly authorized in collecting taxes, normally by sale of the delinquent's property to satisfy the taxes and charges; or unpaid customs duties might be obtained by sale of the merchandise. The most numerous grants of summary power in legislation are probably in connection with safety, health, and public order, concerning which officials may "abate a nuisance." Freund cited New York City's sanitary code, which authorized condemnation and destruction of food or drink unfit for human use, and New York State law, which authorized the destruction of unlicensed dogs or false weights and measures. Sometimes the law requires summary action to be taken only after failure of the party to obey an order; sometimes no such order need be given. Sometimes an individual can ask a court to enjoin the summary action before it occurs, but that may be forbidden or may simply be impossible from lack of time. Summary powers, most typically at the local level, are a most dramatic instance of administrative power.

The Supreme Court has upheld varied "civil sanctions" assessed by administrative agencies, referring to their character as remedies and distinguishing them from sanctions with a punitive, criminal element. Thus in a 1944 case the Court upheld an Office of Price Administration suspension order prohibiting a fuel oil company from receiving fuel oil for resale for almost one year.[7] (OPA had determined that the company had violated the fuel ration order.) The Court said that the suspension order was not a means of punishment, but a method of assuring equitable oil distribution. Though commitment by administrative authorities is exceptional, one can find instances of it, even outside quarantine and immigration cases. In 1957 the Supreme Court sustained a jailing by a fire marshal of persons who refused to testify before him (because he would not permit their counsel to be present).[8] The punishments imposed by administrators may, by common standards, be severe indeed.

Administrative officials may also withhold the good or necessary things government has to bestow, imposing burdens instead. They may refuse a grant—social security, welfare aid, pension, and the like—or may delay a decision for a long while. They may refuse a license needed to engage in any of a vast variety of businesses or occupations, or may suspend or revoke the license once granted. Sometimes they levy fines and may cut off service until a fine is paid, or an agency may blacklist a firm, refusing to purchase from it. In performing such actions, they may investigate a person intensively or repeatedly and may publicly announce their doubts or adverse decision, thereby harming personal or corporate reputation. In the field of securities registration, for example, the very announcement of a challenge by the SEC is generally regarded as eroding the market for the securities, regardless of the eventual decision. Administrative denial in such cases may be subject to court challenge, but this exacts a price in money, energy, and time, and of course the individual may lose.

Agencies may instigate prosecution, which is burdensome regardless of ultimate acquittal, or, as the price of not prosecuting for an alleged violation, they may require future compliance with their demands. The licensing power, with its potential threat of nonrenewal, may similarly be used to control actions—it has been argued that the FCC does this to broadcasting stations. A good many agencies can assess penalties but mitigate or remit in particular instances, normally with no real standards to limit their discretion in each case and with few procedural safeguards. By assessing a penalty and then offering to compromise on the amount (probably coming down a good deal), an agency may induce a defendant to settle his case in order to avoid the burden of court proceedings and the risk of the full penalty, even if he believes himself innocent. Or an agency may be empowered to suspend the operation of statutes or administrative regulations, exempting whole groups by a general rule or dispensing with requirements in a particular instance, without precise standards to guide the decision.

Legislatures grant broad powers to agencies. A statute may authorize a board to fix penalties, even imprisonment, within definite limits. Sometimes a statute fixes the penalty and authorizes the agency to issue the rules and regulations whose violation will subject one to the penalty, as in public health and motor vehicle regulation. The agency may also be authorized to determine if the individual has committed a violation and is therefore liable to the penalty. Thus the Federal Power Commission has the authority to fix forfeitures not exceeding one thousand dollars in cases of willful failure of licensees to comply with FPC orders. The Department of Agriculture and the Interstate Commerce Commission have power to make reparations orders, in effect deciding controversies between two private parties. A state board has been authorized to establish a minimum fair wage for women and minors in an industry. The National Labor Relations Board can order an employer to reinstate an improperly discharged employee and make payment of lost wages. The NLRB or the Federal Trade Commission can issue a cease and desist order, subjecting a party to contempt action in court for repetition of an unlawful act. Agencies may set rates, deny permission to undertake or drop a service, order reorganization or dissolution of a company, take or limit the use made of one's property, require detailed record keeping and reporting, or issue subpoenas requiring production of information or personal testimony. A public welfare official may, with the potential sanction of cutting off aid, control details of family life.

In sum, administrative agencies have substantial powers to punish, sometimes through the courts, sometimes directly. To abide by the spirit of the rule of law, the authority must be exercised fairly. Those who say that it is impossible to eliminate discretion should be the most vigorous opponents of what is simply arbitrary. No stripping of all authority from the administration is called for, this world being no garden of gentle folk. Rather, fair administrative procedure is needed, under the laws and administrative rules and subject to scrutiny by the courts.

ADMINISTRATIVE DUE PROCEDURE

The effort to keep regulatory powers out of administrative hands has failed. As a practical matter, so has the attempt to define fair administrative procedure as identical with fair judicial procedure. H. W. R. Wade, a law professor at Oxford, suggests that the British and American governmental administrative systems share a unifying concept of administrative justice and that, using the experience of the *courts,* we need "to point out which of the numerous rules of legal procedure are sufficiently universal to apply equally to *administrative* acts."[9] Very few of our fundamental rules of court procedure are sufficiently universal to be copied uncritically by administrative agencies, he suggests. In contemporary American administrative law, despite the Administrative Procedure Act and mountains of court opinions, the standards of administrative due process are extraordinarily indefinite. Of state law, one must especially note that its variety is carefully nurtured by our federalism. Difficult though it is to say what "administrative due procedure" is, let us tease a little meaning out of chaos.

RULE MAKING AND ADJUDICATION

The distinction between a rule and an order is basic, though various terms may be used and though borderline cases blur the distinction. A *rule* is analogous to a legislative statute, with a quality of general and future applicability. It controls the action of anyone who subsequently comes within its terms. An *order* is like a court decision in a case. It absolves or imposes a penalty or grants an award to a particular party in connection with a particular dispute or application. It is specific in the parties to whom it is directed and relates to action already taken, although it may serve as a precedent influencing future actions. Administrative agencies make both rules and orders. In general we demand more careful procedures, fuller protection of a specific party's rights, in making orders.

The opportunity to be heard seems a basic element of fair procedure, but a uniform requirement will not cover all administrative situations. Kenneth Davis suggests a distinction between two kinds of facts, which seems to parallel that between rules and orders: legislative and adjudicative facts. *Adjudicative facts* concern specific parties and their actions, answer who did what and why, and are the kinds of facts typically before juries. Adjudicative facts ordinarily ought not to be determined without giving the parties a chance to know and question the evidence. *Legislative facts* do not concern specific parties, but are general, helping a tribunal decide questions of policy. Concerning legislative facts, trial procedure is frequently not appropriate. For example, Davis suggests that a selective service registrant should be able to meet evidence against him concerning his behavior (adjudicative facts) but not to testify concerning the army's eyesight requirements (legislative facts). The terminology seems to be Davis', not the Supreme Court's, but he discerns some recognition of the distinction in its cases. He does not argue that a formal trial-like hearing is always called for where adjudicative facts are being determined, because inspection, examination, or testing is preferable in some circumstances. For example, gradings of grain, inspections of locomotives, and testing of candidates for the bar are rarely or never challenged in the courts, though they are settled on the basis of expert judgment, without an administrative hearing. The basic principle which Davis urges, however, is that "a party who has a sufficient interest or right at stake in a determination of governmental action is ordinarily entitled to opportunity for a trial type of hearing on issues of adjudicative facts."[10]

Because of the legislative character of rule making, it has not been subject to the stricter procedural requirements established for administrative adjudication. Examples, cited by Kenneth Davis, of rules which may be made without any participation by the affected parties are that trucks must have two headlights and bus drivers must speak English, that aircraft about to collide should turn to the right, and that lawyers are not exempt from the draft. Some states require hearings for rule making. The federal Administrative Procedure Act of 1946 does not, and unless a statute specifies a hearing for the particular agency or function, none is required. Some federal agencies, notably the Interstate Commerce Commission, have used elaborate trial-like procedures for framing rules, but a less formal hearing seems preferable, and informal written or oral consultation with affected parties is an important feature of federal agency rule making. Publication in the *Federal Register* (an official daily publication) of notice of proposed rule making is required by the 1946 statute, along with the opportunity for interested persons to submit at least written views, though generous exemption from these requirements at agency discretion is permitted. The relatively convenient publication of federal regulations since the mid-1930's is valuable; many states do not make readily available regulations that have the force of law. Agencies no doubt make vast numbers of rules day by day with nothing but internal procedures. Some of these rules govern the bureaucrats' work procedures, but others affect outsiders as well or primarily. Think of all the rules made by a state university governing admissions applications, dormitories, libraries, motor vehicles, and what not. Some rules should be made in simple bureaucratic style, others only after full, formal consultation.

Critics of expanded government distrust administrative rule making, and emphasize that the only power agencies should have to issue rules binding on outsiders is that clearly granted by the legislature. However, for agencies to carry the major load in regulation requires the delegation of substantial rule-making powers to administrators. If the legislature grants powers sparingly the price may be ineffective regulation. And, as critics of administration correctly note, if a rule has been formally issued, at least one knows the basis on which the agency commits itself to act. More serious today than the critics who object to too much administrative power are those who protest that the agencies are insufficiently willing to engage in rule making or to state general standards, and instead may proceed case by case under no apparent general principles.

Judge Henry J. Friendly has attacked as a basic irrationality in administrative regulation, "the failure to develop standards sufficiently definite to permit decisions to be fairly predictable and the reasons for them to be understood."[11] Congress often gives a regulatory agency no precise standard to guide its decisions, either because of the belief that current knowledge of the problem does not permit more precision, or that flexibility is necessary in a technically complex area, or because political conflict dictates a compromise which leaves open the question of what should be done. The Supreme Court states that Congress cannot delegate its legislative power except under a prescribed standard, but the Court has accepted such vague standards as: "just and reasonable," "public interest," "public convenience, interest, or necessity," "unfair methods of competition," and "excessive profits." State courts too are likely to insist on standards but to accept very vague ones. Even if Congress or the agency cannot initially state clear standards for dealing with a problem, over the years the agency might develop and articulate more specific standards. Adjudication can contribute to rule making if, from time to time, the general principles which have emerged from a series of administrative cases are set forth in rule form. The goal is clear standards to guide agencies and those subject to regulation.

The Federal Communications Commission and the Civil Aeronautics Board may enjoy the dubious distinction of being most frequently cited as agencies which fail to provide standards. FCC was given no policy guidelines by Congress for licensing stations, beyond the criterion of the "public convenience, interest, or necessity," which leaves vast discretion in determining which competing applicant wins a valuable license. Nor has FCC ever made clear with consistency which factors count most—local control, past performance, diversity of ownership of mass media, or others. For principles to emerge from cases, as they do in the courts, requires at least substantial consistency. When Pennock reported in 1941 that the Federal Trade Commission case decision method since 1914 had not yet clarified the legislative standard prohibiting combinations "in restraint of trade," he properly regarded this as a failing. (FTC opinions gave little detail and failed to serve as precedents; SEC, in contrast, published many rules and, in adjudication, careful opinions, sometimes including even dissents.) In his 1959 memorandum to the President, on the occasion of his resignation from the Civil Aeronautics Board, Louis Hector explained why he felt that independent regulatory commissions were not competent to regulate vital national industries. In part his objection was to a lack of standards in CAB proceedings and to the inconsistency of decisions. "Actually the Board has almost no general policies whatever. . . . In almost all fields of economic regulation, the Board proceeds on a pure case-by-case basis with policies changing suddenly, without notice, and often with no explanation or any indication that the Board knows it has changed policy."[12] The case for standards seems to be the case for an administrative rule of law, rather than pure discretion.

Detailed specification of standards by the legislature may, however, interfere with a beneficial flexibility and use of expertise and experience by the agency. In fact, independent regulatory commissions, such as the Interstate Commerce Commission, have been accused of too willingly accepting the invitation to fall into routine administration of detailed rules, failing to bring imagination and initiative or responsible discretion to its task. An agency ought to learn from experience and adapt to change. Those who have reservations about rule making as the basic regulatory technique justify the case-by-case method. The great tradition of the English common law, created by the consistent decisions of judges in actual cases, serves as a model. Davis suggests that the strength of this method may be its "thorough consideration of one problem at a time," for the human intellect is weaker in dealing with abstraction and generality than in "thorough consideration of narrow, concrete, and particular problems."[13] Thus he emphasizes adjudication with proper procedural safeguards, rather than rule making and general standards.

We can accept the goal of consistency, which affords equality of treatment and lends predictability to agency action. One function may be more susceptible than another to formulation of a comprehensive, clear set of standards to guide agency and citizen, so that disputes concern only the facts of citizen behavior. Even where standards are harder to formulate, however, we may ask that an agency's adjudicative judgments show consistency, that one may be able to understand inductively the reason which guides the agency. This may be assisted if formal opinions are issued or at least an occasional opinion in a key case is published or if rules are issued from time to time summarizing a principle which has emerged from a series of cases or which has been formulated in response to a thorny case. Lawyers can make sense out of our law because in general precedents are respected. Lawyers who practice before administrative agencies such as the Federal Communications Commission or the Civil Aeronautics Board feel deeply that the whole procedure is absurd, a Kafka-like trial with no substantive rules. That is flexibility gone rancid. The demand for standards serves to remind us that though every case is unique, unless one sees some similarities, some principles of law relevant to a whole series, there is no rule of law. Most administrative agencies probably succeed in considerable measure in being lawful, if for no other reason than their own internal needs. Uniformity, routine, consistency, rules—of such poor straw is bureaucratic competence contructed. The goal of a reasoned interplay between general principle and unique cases is close to the heart of the mystery of the rule of law.

A FAIR HEARING

In adjudicative hearings the rights of a particular person or corporation are being determined, perhaps a privilege granted or a sanction imposed. But the courts do not require procedure in administrative adjudication to follow the rules which guide jury trials, rules which have been elaborately developed over a long period. Nonetheless, it is reasonable to expect hearings to be in accord with statutes and agency rules and to be fair. Fairness is the responsibility of each agency, whether it be a local liquor licensing board or a great national agency. Demands for a highly detailed, restrictive statutory code of standards of administrative procedure have been pressed for decades. It may well be that the enormous variation among agencies, and the value of prompt, inexpensive action, argues against pressing further in this direction. The Administrative Procedure Act of 1946 did impose certain uniform requirements, rejecting the argument that only procedural diversity made sense where the functions are so diverse, "but for the most part little was added to the requirements of notice and hearing developed by the courts under the aegis of the due process clause."[14] The generality of the provisions of the 1946 act, and usually of state administrative procedure acts, leaves to the agencies and the courts the setting of standards of fairness.

Requisite to a fair hearing is adequate and timely notice, but there is no uniform, detailed rule of notice for administrative proceedings. By how long a time must the notice precede the hearing—a day, a week, a month? To whom must notice go—to immediate neighbors if the question is a petition for permission to erect a glue factory? By what method may notice go—publication in fine print in a newspaper? How specific must notice be concerning the issues, evidence, or proposed order—is it enough for a person to be accused simply of unethical conduct meriting revocation of a license? Specificity about the subject of the hearing and adequate time for preparation of an answer not only serve justice, but make for briefer hearings which focus on the real issues and get to the facts. Statutes permit the NLRB to give a minimum of five days' notice; NLRB rules increased the minimum interval to ten days, proving more generous than the legislators. But in 1911 the Supreme Court indicated that a few hours' notice to parties that they were to be deprived of certain rights was, at least in that instance, insufficient.[15] The courts accept diverse practices provided their sense of constitutionally required due process is not offended.

Fairness also requires that he who decides should not have an improper bias, such as prior strong feelings toward a party involved, or a personal interest in the outcome of the case. Abuses may be a real problem at the local level, where personal friendships and family ties, grossly partisan political maneuvers, indelicate use of public office for private gain, and crude bribery sometimes survive. Apart from grossly improper bias, it may be difficult to draw the line between permissible attitudes and preferences and those which in effect deny due process. For example, the attitude of a National Labor Relations Board hearing examiner that unions are a valuable protection to otherwise impotent workers might seem bias to a harried employer in the midst of a dispute with a union, but this attitude would not provide a basis for voiding a hearing conducted by such an officer. Because of the nature of its work, the NLRB has been especially susceptible to charges of bias, which are sometimes sustained by the courts. Regulated interests are not above charging bias in order to intimidate agencies. Agency officials are likely to be committed to particular goals and programs, but they should be guided by statutes and regulations and be detached in judging particular individuals, as distinguished from social purpose.

Administrative adjudicatory procedure varies from very formal, court-like to conversational, conference atmosphere. What evidence is admissible in administrative adjudication? Our legal system provides rules for exclusion from jury trials of unreliable kinds of evidence, not suitable to be weighed by lay jurors. Especially is this true of hearsay statements (a report of a statement made by someone who is not in court testifying and so is not subject to cross-examination). The 1946 act requires exclusion of "irrelevant, immaterial, or unduly repetitious evidence," but not hearsay. State statutes, too, generally permit something less than jury trial rules. What of lawyers? The 1946 act provides that one who is compelled to testify before a federal agency has the right to be represented by counsel; the right rests on the statute, not on a constitutional provision, and applies to the federal level only. State courts do not come down uniformly on the question of right to counsel in administrative proceedings, and in 1957 the Supreme Court divided five-four in denying the right to counsel in a state agency's administrative investigation (into the causes of a fire) whose consequences might be very serious for the participants.[16]

Legislators and a good many judges have been willing to accept an administrative procedure which does not employ jury trial rules of evidence and courtroom methods. This makes sense;

otherwise administrative regulation would bog down hopelessly. The danger, of course, is that this may deteriorate, as it did in loyalty-security administrative hearings, into failure to specify charges, use of gossip, denial of opportunity for cross-examination of prosecution witnesses, and similar flaws which the court system long ago rejected. Informality does not preclude a requirement of elemental fairness.

Both federal and state courts typically require that in a formal case an administrative tribunal present a systematic statement of the facts that it finds from the evidence. Courts sometimes require agencies to state reasons (considerations of law and policy) as well as facts of the case. Regulatory agencies such as the FCC, ICC, and NLRB publish opinions which resemble court opinions, and they cite these as judges cite earlier court cases. Agencies which handle vast numbers of adjudications are not likely to publish opinions, but the Social Security Board does select some significant opinions which serve as precedents. In 1967 the Department of Housing and Urban Development ruled that a public housing tenant is entitled to a statement of the reasons for his eviction and a conference with his would-be evictors. (The Supreme Court was then considering a case in which a local housing authority had terminated a lease without hearing or explanation the day after a tenant's election as an official in a tenants' organization.) Giving a reason for an order (a decision directed to a specific individual) is generally good practice, though with varying formality to fit different situations.

During the 1930's and 1940's those concerned with administrative regulation focused on the role of the hearing examiner. There were in 1954 only some two hundred eighty federal hearing examiners, of whom over one hundred were in the ICC and almost fifty in the NLRB. The examiners preside over hearings, prepare the record, and make or recommend to higher officials a decision. (Most cases are actually settled by less formal means.) Critics of administrative regulation attacked the combination of prosecuting and judging functions within the agencies, and sought to force examiners into the mold of judges, independent of the agencies, making decisions in isolation from agency influence. In some agencies examiners were rather separate and judge-like; in others, more like regular members of the agency. The 1946 act rejected proposals for a complete separation of examiners into a single independent central corps. It accepted the view that specialization of examiners and their sense of responsibility to agency programs is valuable, and that one can have both policy commitments and detachment in judging particular cases. The act does, however, lessen agency control over examiners and makes the Civil Service

Commission a guardian of their independence. The Supreme Court has indicated that it will take seriously the 1946 act's intent to enhance the status of the examiner, and that agency reversal of an examiner's decision may weaken the case for the agency's decision.[17]

The battle over the status of hearing examiners seemed of major importance, but it was substantially a battle over symbols. The vast bulk of administrative regulation is settled by some procedure short of formal hearing before an examiner. Correspondence, conference, inspections, and the like settle most cases. Even in the formal stages, many shortcuts are taken. "Contrary to the popular scholarly view, full-fledged legal procedure (notice, hearing with cross-examination, a record with adequate findings to support conclusions, and decisions based upon hearing records with the opportunity for court review) is rarely employed."[18] The FCC in 1961 received about 700,000 applications respecting radio operation; it relied on correspondence, conference, and staff investigation, assigning fewer than 600 cases for a hearing. The Internal Revenue Service in 1960 received more than 94 million tax returns. It uses a simple, inexpensive procedure for the personal income tax payer, and it provides opportunity for a series of conferences aimed at reaching agreement, so that few cases go to court. The NLRB, working where passions run high, settles about 88 percent of unfair labor practice cases informally, with a field examiner's conference playing a key role. Large volume, professional staff, and technical bases for judgment lie at the heart of much resort to informal procedure, along with the value of speed, economy, and simplicity either to the citizen involved or to the public interest, or both.

Regulatory agencies have sometimes sought to model themselves on the courts, taking pride in the formal propriety of their hearings, but losing sight of program effectiveness and the purposes for which the program was established. Some administrative adjudication is so slow and costly that the courts may do better. In a famous case of rate setting for the Kansas City stockyards by the Department of Agriculture, some 13,000 pages of transcript of testimony were compiled plus more than 1000 pages of exhibits. Where full, formal hearings are held, the procedures are likely to be impressively judicial or at least carefully proper. Of all controversies arising from federal administration in all fields, however, only something over 50,000 a year are decided on the basis of formal hearings; about half of these come from the social security agency, yet fewer than 1 percent of its cases are fully contested. Just, effective regulation need not always be grandly formal. In most administrative adjudication the hearing examiner does not exist or never enters, the courts are not approached. Most of the time it probably achieves practical justice, through reliance on uniform rules objectively applied. But obviously there is a residue of error and corruption, given our fallen nature, and control of so vast a judging process must surely be imperfect. Where less formal hearings are held, it is important that the regulatory staff be honest and competent and that appeal to a superior official or board be available. Techniques such as periodic training sessions for the staff and spot checks of their work are often appropriate bureaucratic means of assuring the integrity of a regulatory process which rests mainly on informal procedures.

Poor procedure may be especially likely where agencies are dealing with actions legally defined as privileges rather than rights. A decision that is very important to a particular individual may be made in mean or slovenly fashion, permitting him no occasion for proper defense. Some of the harshness of the government's loyalty-security program (affording the accused no opportunity to know and respond to the evidence and witnesses against him) came from labeling a government job a privilege, then insisting that fair procedure is not required in depriving a man of a privilege. If there are no valid requirements about such matters as specificity of charges, the procedure to be followed, and the evidence that is admissible, there may be nothing to be hoped for from appeal to the courts. Excluded aliens have a history of bad treatment without resort to court, on grounds they have no right to enter the country. State courts have permitted revocation of various occupational licenses without a hearing, on the privilege doctrine. Even concerning what is called a privilege, however, the courts may insist upon certain kinds of fairness—for example, no religious or racial discrimination—or they may even call some action a privilege yet still insist on due process, by whatever logic.

Viewing provision of services, grants, contracts, and jobs (to none of which one may have a legal right) as a major portion of modern governmental activity, Walter Gellhorn warns that "in large areas of government, procedural safeguards are at present virtually absent because of the old-fashioned notion that fair and careful procedures are not necessary when mere 'privileges' are at issue."[19] What can be done is suggested in the requirement of the Massachusetts Administrative Procedure Act of opportunity for a trial-type hearing before an agency may revoke or refuse to renew any license. That seems reasonable, just as it seems reasonable to give a fairly careful hearing before cutting off someone's welfare payments or dismissing someone from the public service as a security risk if he disputes that charge. The next major need in administrative procedure reform may well be an attack on the privilege doctrine. If the legislators will not, then the courts ought to insist on fair administrative procedure.

Administrative agencies are by no means uniformly insensitive to demands for procedural protection. New York City in 1968 instituted a formal procedure for low-income public housing applicants to request reconsideration of a decision to reject an applicant. Further, it agreed that personal conduct such as having illegitimate children will not be considered in determining eligibility and that deferral of a doubtful application will not result in infinite delay which really means rejection. In 1971 the federal Department of Housing and Urban Development, reflecting pressure from tenant organizations, required inclusion of a grievance procedure in all low-rent public housing leases—covering some 2.8 million tenants. As a minimum, each local public housing authority must provide grievance procedures including an opportunity for a hearing before an impartial official or a hearing panel if a tenant disputes the local housing authority's action (including eviction) or failure to act. HUD suggested use of a hearing panel with equal numbers of local housing authority and elected tenant representatives and one impartial member. The tenant has the right to be represented by counsel and to bring in his witnesses and to cross-examine witnesses, but court rules of evidence need not be used. He must be notified in writing of the decision and of the reasons and evidence relied on.

Procedural guarantees of this sort are adopted by agencies in response to court decisions, to client pressures, and to current awareness of the need for fair procedure. They do not instantly assure justice to the poor, but they point the direction for public administration which is both fair and effective.

JUDICIAL CONTROL OF ADMINISTRATION

Until the 1930's those who sought to prevent administrative oppression emphasized judicial control; then, concern to develop fair procedure within the administrative regulatory process itself gained higher priority than judicial review. Most Americans would probably assert intuitively that one should be able to turn to the courts to correct improper administrative action. We may agree that much responsibility should be placed upon the agencies, provided they adopt fair procedures, and that courts must be guardians of the fairness of that procedure. Yet too tight control by the courts stifles administration. Development of techniques and doctrines of judicial review of administrative action that assure the citizen redress yet do not paralyze the administrative process has been extraordinarily difficult.

By what methods have the courts traditionally controlled administrative action? (1) Courts receive actions for damages (money awards) brought by citizens against the government or against public officials for alleged abuse of authority (illegal acts committed in the discharge of their public duties). The government may give its consent to being sued for damages, either in general or in certain types of cases. The courts may hold, concerning certain proprietary (business) functions of local government, that the government is subject to suit. The official himself may be suable where the government is not. However, in some matters, the law, under the doctrine of "sovereign immunity," may be that neither the government nor the official acting for it is subject to suit. (2) Courts receive criminal prosecutions brought by public prosecutors against officials. (3) Most administrative orders cannot be enforced except through the courts if a citizen resists, and the question of legality of the administrative action may be considered by the court before it grants the action sought. (4) Particular statutes may provide for judicial review of administrative determinations under the statute, or the courts may hold that review is constitutionally required even if not specified or even if apparently prohibited. (5) A set of extraordinary writs, of which mandamus, injunction, and habeas corpus are probably best known, may be sought by an aggrieved citizen. These permit the courts to require an official to perform or refrain from an action; violation of a writ subjects one to court punishment by fine or imprisonment. Thus the courts may award damages against an official or against the government, may fine or sentence an official in criminal action, may refuse to enforce an administrative order, may declare an administrative action to be forbidden by statutory or constitutional provision and therefore null, or may specifically order an official to do or not to do some action. That is a considerable battery of powers.

Sometimes the citizen who believes that he has suffered injustice at the hands of public officials finds the courts closed to him. The courts will not simply substitute themselves for administrative agencies, but insist that parties should first have their case considered by the appropriate administrative agency, not entirely skip that step and come to the court for decision. Similarly, courts invoke the doctrine of "exhaustion of administrative remedies," which requires a party to complete the administrative proceeding before coming to court, even if he believes that the agency lacks power over the subject matter or otherwise has erred to his disadvantage in the proceedings thus far held. This doctrine is not precise nor is it uniformly applied; courts sometimes do permit a challenge to the agency's jurisdiction before the administrative procedure is completed. Another doctrine of the federal courts is that they will not give advisory opinions (there is no actual controversy, risk, with rights of the parties to the proceeding at stake), but will deal only with genuine cases (a concrete dispute, as against clarification of an uncertain matter before the law is enforced). This too is less than clear and the results are less than consistent, but it may mean that one cannot challenge the statute or rule as such, but must await its punitive application to a particular party, who then bears the risk of punishment.

The principle of "standing" to sue (which asks who has a legitimate basis for challenging) further limits one's right to go into court to challenge administrative action. (May a radio station sue to block a permit by the FCC for a new station in the area? May a citizen sue to block public welfare payments?) Federal courts have not been so liberal as some state courts in granting standing, but the 1946 Administrative Procedure Act defined it rather broadly. Courts may refuse to consider a complaint because they consider what the individual seeks from government to be a privilege, not a right. Suit for damages against the government or even against the offending official himself may be rejected by the courts under the doctrine of "sovereign immunity" from liability. In 1946 the federal government adopted a statute to permit suits against it rather freely for damage its agents cause, but most states still do not have any such general waivers of sovereign immunity. Questions of who may attack administrative action in court, at what point, and by what technical procedure are far from clearly settled.

The openness of courts to the complaint of a person who has used the administrative process fully and still feels deeply aggrieved ought to be pretty wide, for agencies may skimp on procedure in their concern with program results. Sometimes speed is necessary to administration, but often not, and even if it is, after-the-fact consideration is usually possible if the courts are willing. Courts can afford to be liberal in allowing an aggrieved citizen at least to state his claim of administrative abuse and in looking at the administrative procedure which was used. But that is only half the issue of judicial control. The other half is how deeply the judges look, how far they substitute their own for the administrative judgment. In that problem is more danger of conflict between the striving for fair play and for administrative effectiveness.

THE IMPACT OF JUDICIAL REVIEW

If courts review administrative action, how deeply will they probe? Simple substitution of the court's judgment for that of the agency raises questions that led to substituting administrative for judicial action originally. Limitation serves the courts as well. It has been variously calculated that a fifth to more than a third of Supreme Court decisions these days involve review of administrative action.[20] If the courts try to repeat the entire decision processes through which the agencies go, they may choke to death. The court may choose which issues it will decide along this spectrum: no judicial review whatever; review solely of the question whether the agency had jurisdiction (the legal right to deal with the matter); review of the administrative procedure to check for due process; review of interpretations of law; review of questions of (the meaning of) law and of fact (what events occurred) on the basis of the administrative record; review of all questions of law and fact on the basis of the administrative record plus such additional evidence as the court may admit; trial de novo, in which the court virtually repeats the administrative process, reaching its own determination on the basis of evidence produced in court, disregarding the record of the administrative proceedings. Even within these categories, the court may tend to give great benefit of doubt to the administrative decision or to view it as suspect. The attitude will vary with (a) the period (tough before the late 1930's, gentle for a while, then a reaction in the post-World War II period); (b) the reputation of the particular agency for objectivity, competence, and careful procedure; and (c) the nature of the function (the courts may probe less regarding favors, government business services, or taxes, but may more carefully scrutinize exercises of the police power or regulation of business).

Despite considerable variation, "the dominant tendency in both state courts and federal courts is toward the middle position known as the substantial-evidence rule. . . . the court decides questions of law but it limits itself to the test of reasonableness in reviewing findings of fact."[21] That is, the court looks closely at questions of statutory and constitutional interpretation and matters of administrative jurisdiction, fair procedure, and abuse of discretion, but asks only whether the record as a whole provides substantial evidence to support the agency's findings of fact concerning the unique circumstances to which the law applies in this case, the actions of the parties to the specific case. The substantial-evidence doctrine or practice was developed essentially by the courts, though some statutes have included it. Even some statutes providing for de novo review (in which the court in effect does what the administrative agency did in reaching a decision) are interpreted by the courts to mean review under the substantial-evidence rule. This rule, which appears in the 1946 Administrative Procedure Act, may be viewed as the compromise solution to the debate of the 1930's between opponents of administrative regulation (seeking tight court control) and the partisans of administration (seeking to minimize judicial review). Actually the formula is anything but precise, and leaves considerable discretion to courts in determining the extent of review. Some state courts go further than the federal courts in substituting their own judgment of the facts of the case. Courts do not always choose clearly or consistently between asking if a reasonable man might have reached the agency's decision or asking if the agency reached the right decision (the decision the judge would have reached, naturally). They tend to the former, using the substantial-evidence rule. Courts tend to interpret the law independently but to accept agency findings of fact if they are supported by substantial evidence. Though a court is suited to interpreting law, the administrative agency is the appropriate place for determining what the facts are, if the whole concept of expert determination under adequate procedural safeguards makes any sense.

And yet the line between law and fact is blurred. Is the question whether a man is an "employee" a factual question of determining his relationship to an employer or a legal one of defining the term? Though courts often call a question one of law if they choose to review it and one of fact if they choose not to review, actual judicial behavior is usually guided by practical considerations of which functions can better be handled by the agency and which by the court. Courts may tend to uphold the findings of one agency more readily than those of another because of greater confidence in its competence, procedures, and integrity. A study of the Supreme Court and the administrative agencies published in the late 1960's observed that "the federal courts are today rarely found in opposition to the agencies."[22] There is harmony, Martin Shapiro argued, because the courts and the agencies generally are in consensus on the policies to be followed (unlike during the 1930's) and because courts and agencies accommodate to each other. Where the Supreme Court finds an agency needs correcting (suffering probably from parochialism or too ambitious growth in its power), the Court's opinions can generally indicate the need for change without coming into frontal collision with the agency. Using the substantial-evidence rule with generally good judgment, balancing a literal interpretation of fact and law with a practical sense of the situation, the courts have pretty well come to terms with administrative regulation. They neither emasculate it nor fear to touch it.

Administrative law is not a finished product, however; we continue learning to use and control administrative powers. In 1968 and 1970 cases the Supreme Court held that local Selective Service Boards cannot reclassify and induct young men who are entitled to exemption or deferment but have turned in their draft cards to protest the Vietnam War; the Court rejected induction as a disciplinary or vindictive measure.[23] In 1967 the Supreme Court required health and fire inspectors to obtain warrants (very broad warrants, it is true) before nonemergency inspection of private premises for code violations without the occupants' consent, finding these "administrative searches" to be significant intrusions.[24] In 1970 the Court denied the authority of an Internal Revenue Service liquor agent to break a lock and enter a storeroom without a warrant or permission of the owner, even though it is an offense under law for a liquor licensee to refuse admission to a federal inspector; Congress has provided the penalty for nonadmission of the inspector, and that is the penalty that should be invoked.[25]

The California Supreme Court in 1967 rejected the discharge for insubordination of a county social worker who had refused to participate in early morning mass raids without warrants on recipients' homes to see if there were a man in the house (to determine welfare eligibility), for the raids were unconstitutional.[26] Thus the court vindicated the rights of both the employee and the welfare recipients. The Supreme Court in 1968 rejected Alabama's regulation denying AFDC (Aid to Families with Dependent Children) welfare benefits to a child whose mother cohabits with an able-bodied man.[27] The state regulation was based on the grounds that he is a "substitute father," though state law imposed no obligation on him to provide financial support. In 1970 cases the Court required procedural due process in terminating welfare grants. There must be a pretermination hearing, which need not be judicial in form but which must provide: adequate and timely notice detailing the reasons for termination; an opportunity for the recipient to appear and to confront adverse witnesses and present his own case orally before the decision maker; the right to retain counsel if he wishes; and a statement from the decision maker, who must be impartial, of the reasons and the evidence relied on.[28] The states involved already had certain procedural guarantees in instances of termination, but the Court found them insufficiently protective of the welfare recipients. However, in January 1971 an increasingly conservative Supreme Court, reflecting the impact of President Nixon's appointments, held six to three that New York public welfare officials may insist on admission to the homes of recipients for periodic inspections, and may cut off benefits of those who refuse them entry.[29]

Court decisions such as those summarized are signs of a sensitivity to the power of public officials over average citizens. The cases renew our appreciation of the importance of the judiciary as guardian of good procedure in administrative regulation.

ADMINISTRATIVE COURTS

Administrative courts, whose jurisdiction is limited to cases involving the public service, can also provide effective judicial control of administration. Combining the virtues of the judiciary with a heavy dose of the specialized knowledge of administrators, they do not suffer from hostility to or ignorance of administrative regulation. The French system of administrative courts is evidently the finest; elsewhere they have less prestige and less vigorous independence of the executive.

The French Council of State advises the executive on proposed legislation before its introduction into parliament and on proposed administrative regulations and, as the chief administrative court, hears challenges to governmental action. As adviser to the executive, the Council is at the center of administration. Within the Council there is a distinction between the advisory and judicial functions, but also active communication among members and a sense of unity, close cooperation, and esprit de corps. All members of the judicial section have had experience in advisory sections and some have served in the active administration. The Council is in no way the enemy of the administration; it is advisory to and judge of the administrator. Yet the judicial section is and is known to be impartial, independent of political or executive influence. Other French administrative courts deal especially with such matters as education and social welfare assistance. Local administrative courts were given wide jurisdiction in 1954; since then the Council has become essentially a court of appeal from all these other administrative courts, though it still has original jurisdiction in important cases. The regular civil courts, unlike those in America, do not generally have jurisdiction in cases involving public officials acting in their governmental capacity.

The Council is easier to use and more helpful than an ordinary court. It is liberal in granting standing to bring action. Procedures required of the complainant are simple, and it is not necessary to use a lawyer or to incur substantial costs. The Council will help prepare the case once it accepts a complaint; a citizen initiates action, but the Council sees it through. The procedure used is essentially written, a collection of comments and materials which bear on the contested action. The Council seeks such information as meets the needs of the particular case, and can order even a minister of government to produce the files on which he based his decision. Especially the Council of State's power to annul an administrative act or decision, whether taken by the lowest official or the highest minister or the President, attracts Americans concerned with controlling administrative power. The Council can require any administrator to give a reason for any challenged act he has taken, and will declare the act null if he fails adequately to justify it. The Council can annul either general regulations or decisions directed to specific individuals.

The law applied by the Council is largely case law, Council-made, without legislation. The Council respects its own precedents, but openly departs when that seems desirable, and its law has a flexible, developing quality. The Council will act even against the use of legal powers in proper form (where the external legal formalities have been respected) if power was used for purposes contrary to or beyond the intention of the law. If a reason is attached to an administrative decision, the Council will annul the decision if it finds the reason was mistaken in fact or erroneous in law. The Council will void an action not in accord with the spirit of the French legal system as the Council understands that, though the act does not violate any enactment or formal code. Thus the Council creates or discovers rules of due administrative procedure which it enforces, and it inquires closely into even discretionary decisions.

What defects are observed? British and American observers worry deeply about the divided jurisdiction of the civil and administrative courts and argue that there is great value in a single, unified system of courts. French administrative law is unsatisfactory respecting the police, who are not included within the Council's domain. The English and American reliance on personal action against the offending official has been justified as a useful deterrent, whereas in France the impersonal proceeding against the state may be useful chiefly for repairing the damage done. The delay and formality of any court, even a helpful one, may be enough to discourage many humble citizens. And the French left has viewed the Council as a politically conservative, traditional institution. Americans of varied politics might feel ill at ease with the concentration of authority and talent in an institution outside political control. Our notion of separation of powers is different, our traditions of the judicial career are different, and the French inquisitorial method of court responsibility for developing a case is different from our adversary tradition. The Council's virtues, based on a career elite judiciary, could not easily be transferred to the United States.

Nevertheless, the French Council deserves praise; informed, sympathetic to, and respected by the active administration, it has been able to inquire very deeply into decisions without imposing a hostile and negative control, such as our courts sometimes have. French administrative courts cover a range of contested decisions more widely and go into reasons more fully than do the English and American courts, and they are more inexpensive, simple, and available than our courts.

There are some specialized administrative courts in the United States, for example, the Court of Claims, created in 1855 to hear certain claims by private individuals against the United States, and the U.S. Customs Court, to hear controversies between importers and the government. These are in most respects like other courts, but with special jurisdictions. In the 1930's the American Bar Association's Special Committee on Administrative Law proposed a federal administrative court, but the main ABA emphasis later shifted to judicialization of administrative procedure. The second Hoover Commission's Task Force on Legal Services and Procedure in 1955 proposed an Administrative Court. It preferred the regular courts, but suggested the administrative court as an intermediate step in the transfer of adjudicative responsibility from administrative agencies to the judiciary. In the late 1950's the ABA, following the Hoover report, sponsored legislation for tax, labor, and trade courts, along with internal separation of judicial and executive functions within agencies, an independent corps of hearing examiners, and stricter judicial review of administration.

Proposals for an administrative court in the United States tend to be based on a distaste for the regulatory powers of the administration, a desire to shift power from agencies to courts. They would give the actual regulation of the citizen to the court. But the French administrative court system is a check on abuse of administrative power, exercised by a body experienced in and sympathetic to administration, a part of the executive yet independent in its operation. There is no thought of the court's doing the work of the administration.

The President's Advisory Council on Executive Organization (the Ash Council) in 1971 recommended an Administrative Court to hear appeals from regulatory agencies in transportation, securities, and power, but not in the spirit of substituting court for agency judgment in substantive questions. The Council urged regulatory agencies to focus on policy, to act with decisiveness, to be less beguiled by the model of a court, while a specialized administrative court would protect the regularity of procedures. Possibly there could be successfully established specialized courts or even less formal but quite independent tribunals, to which could be taken easy and cheap appeal of actions in specific areas—public housing, welfare, mental hospitals, selective service, or whatever seems to be pinching. (Housing courts already exist in at least three cities, to deal with landlord-tenant problems, but leave much to be desired respecting, for example, numbers and expertness of judges.) This would not substitute regulation by courts for regulation by administrative agencies.

However much administrators and judges have been cast as opponents in America, those who respect the public service need not apologize for believing also in the courts as necessary·guardians of the rule of law in administration. Courts and administrators alike have learned a great deal since 1933 about achieving effective administration under the supremacy of law. For errors or abuses by the garden variety of lowly official, administrative appeal may generally be the best resort, certainly the preferable first resort. After review within the administrative hierarchy, there may be review by a "quasi-judicial" administrative tribunal, for example, the Board of Immigration Appeals (in the Office of the Attorney General) or the Board of Veterans Appeals (in the Veterans Administration). Then there may be judicial review. The courts should be saved for the tough cases, insoluble within the administrative process, but they should really be open to those cases. Judicial review suffers from costliness and slowness and does not deal comfortably with the realm of discretionary decisions or the realm of minor misconduct (discourtesy, unresponsiveness, and the like). It cannot easily require positive administration, vigor, and competence. To get wise policy, effective administration, and decent bureaucrats, something more than courts is required. But the courts are an essential check, lest bureaucrats get heady with policy goals and the wine of the public interest, and forget the need of careful procedure, private rights, and lawfulness.

THE OMBUDSMAN

The ombudsman, who investigates and reprimands bureaucrats, has attracted much enthusiasm of late as a guardian of individual rights under the rule of law. There is no single model for the office. Historical precedence goes to the Swedish office (1809), but the Danish institution (1955) has been influential. Most other ombudsmen are more recent. The essence of the ombudsman institution is an office whose occupant, normally a jurist appointed by parliament but independent of partisan identification or political pressures, with the aid of a limited staff inquires into complaints concerning illegal or unjust administrative acts, and sometimes acts on his own initiative. His authority extends to discretionary decisions of administrators, which courts typically are reluctant to touch, but both the Swedish and Danish ombudsmen have written of the extreme caution they exercise in such cases, where the question is not the formal legality of the action but the substantive justice of the decision. A common mark of ombudsmen is that their opinions, which are based mainly on examination of documents and letters, are carefully drawn, clearly discussing the relevant facts and law. This facilitates acceptance of their work by citizens and administrators.

The ombudsman's concerns are both to secure the righting of wrongs in individual cases and to secure improvement of the legal-administrative system where it is operating badly. The subject of most complaints is not the actions of particular civil servants or such problems as bad manners, but the substantive content of administrative decisions or bad procedure and delays within an agency. The Swedish ombudsman has been especially concerned with unlawful restraints on personal liberty, which in recent years has fixed his attention on detention of the mentally ill, alcoholics, juvenile delinquents, and the like—those who are restrained through administrative rather than judicial process. When an ombudsman makes a recommendation to administrators concerning a case, they ordinarily accept his advice, sometimes on pain of being prosecuted. In that way the ombudsman may directly help one or two hundred people each year. But when he makes proposals for legislation or for general changes in the administrative system, his advice is often ignored. He operates through power to investigate and recommend and publicize, through reason and discussion and the hint of bad reports. The Swedish and Finnish officers enjoy strong prosecutive powers as well, and the Danish official can order institution of criminal or disciplinary proceedings. But the modern ombudsman emphasizes persuasion, with at most the implied threat of prosecution for failure to repent. He seeks to assure that the governmental bureaucracy operates in accord with the laws of the land and the spirit of justice and courtesy.

The ombudsman idea is enjoying a substantial popularity in the United States at this time. Bills to create the office have been introduced, for example, in New York City and Baltimore and in over a dozen state legislatures. Hawaii in 1967 adopted the first state ombudsman act, giving the official very broad investigative powers. Nassau County in New York State evidently had the first American ombudsman, appointed by the county executive to serve the 1.4 million residents. At the national level, Congressman Reuss has been introducing bills for some years to establish an ombudsman, who would receive complaints channeled through congressmen and report his findings back to the congressman. Senator Long (Missouri) introduced bills for and held hearings concerning the ombudsman, including the ideas of a general ombudsman and of specialized ombudsmen for the District of Columbia, for tax problems, and for agencies which especially generate complaints. Various universities have established ombudsmen for students and perhaps other campus citizens. Though the form varies widely—the proposed tax ombudsmen, for example, would have the name but would exercise administrative authority that hardly fits any normal conception of that office—the idea is in the air.

What distinctive qualities of American government are relevant to the establishment of an ombudsman?

(1) Large population within a federal union. The United States is so populous that one man and a small staff could hardly deal with all the cases that might arise under even a limited conception of the ombudsman's responsibilities. The personal, one-man emphasis, of which so much has been made in Scandinavia, would probably give way to a bureaucratic office. Functional specialization, such as in taxes, social security, and so forth—Sweden and Norway each have a special military ombudsman, after all—might help. But this may pose problems of coordination, completeness of coverage, and dramatization of the official's role. If the office grows large enough or if there are enough specialized offices to do the job, would it become just another bureaucratic agency? Given the size and diversity of the United States, the ombudsman idea may well enjoy its greatest success at the state and local level. There may then be problems of determining whether a particular program is national or state, if both have contributed legislation and money and personnel toward it. Should we have one or more national ombudsmen, in addition to various state and local officers? Simplicity, coverage, coordination, and legal authority may be problems in adapting the institution from a Scandinavian nation of a few million to a vast federal union.

(2) Politicized civil service. The ombudsman has grown and flourished where the public service is highly professionalized. He deals with career civil servants who are much concerned with the good opinion of their colleagues and with technical competence in doing their jobs. At the state and local level in the United States there is a good deal of raw politics, incompetence, and marginal or even gross dishonesty. How would an ombudsman work where he is most sorely needed? Would many a county official snort at an ombudsman's scolding, unless a public report critical of the of-

ficial's conduct threatened political problems for him in the particular circumstances? (Americans do not seem to want to give the ombudsman the prosecuting authority he has in Scandinavia.) Even at the national level, there is not so sharp a line as in Scandinavia or England between bureaucratic and political officials. We use noncareer men in key public service positions. It is not clear that such officials will be fully amenable to the advice of an ombudsman. The vague boundary between politics and administration in this country would tax an ombudsman's judgment.

(3) Legislative-executive separation. The separation of and competition between the two branches deeply color American government. Our government so often seems to lack concentration of authority or discipline that one wonders who would vouch for an ombudsman's detached but vigorous performance. Would the executive, as the normal American appointing power, select the ombudsman, or would the legislature, as in Scandinavia? A Massachusetts proposal became bogged down in just this question. Apart from appointment, there is the question whether he might become the tool of one branch against the other or be ground under trying to resist the pressure to be defender or opponent of the administration.

(4) Legislator-constituent relationship. The single-member election district system ties a member more closely to a group of constituents than does a proportional representation system, such as those of Scandinavia. The American tradition of a legislator living within the district he represents heightens this. The general lack of discipline over legislative members of our parties leaves representatives largely on their own in winning elections. All this leads to an important role for assistance to constituents in their dealings with the governmental bureaucracy. Legislators believe that such aid builds local support important to winning reelection. Concern of legislators over possible loss of political credit to themselves for giving such aid bothered the British, who provided that complaints must be referred to the ombudsman through a Member of Commons and the answer must also go through the Member. Congressman Reuss' proposal contains a similar provision; ombudsman bills in Massachusetts and New York City ran into legislative trouble over concern that members would lose the gratitude and political support of constituents whom they have helped; and the Joint Committee on the Organization of Congress expressed a similar concern in 1966. This obsession clouds the future of any American ombudsman.

(5) Alienation through poverty and race. Those who suffer the most from defective government procedures are often the poor. They have little political or economic power and limited

political or legal sophistication. It may not be easy to convince them to make claims to an ombudsman. The dependent poor feel alienated and are viewed by significant parts of respectable society with contempt, so efforts to secure safeguards for them may encounter grave difficulties. They have not been used to demanding their rights, and some of society views the idea of their demanding rights as a moral outrage. If an ombudsman insists, for example, on the right of welfare-recipient mothers of illegitimate children to have equal access to public housing, the public may reject the ombudsman. The federal program of legal service to the poor has aroused much political controversy, especially where the poor are helped to challenge welfare or other public agencies.

Racism and the suspicion of racism so suffuse America today that they make difficult the objective search for justice. Could any white ombudsman convince Blacks in the slums that the boy was to blame, not the white policeman? Could any ombudsman (not to mention a Negro ombudsman, an obvious choice in a northern city with a large black population) convince the police and the white working classes that the boy was an innocent victim? (Policemen and white majorities in northern cities have tended vigorously to oppose establishment of civilian review boards to hear citizen complaints against police action.) What would be the ombudsman's role in the toughest corners of the South? If we have state ombudsmen, what will the Mississippi or Alabama ombudsman be like in dealing with alleged abuses against Negroes—an uncooperative voting registrar, a too-tough policeman, a contemptuous county clerk? The ombudsman lives by reason, cooperativeness, faith in justice. The race problem in America is threatening those qualities.

A double caution is necessary. The Scandinavian experience is not quite so glowing as it is sometimes painted. The record is respectable, the righting of any wrong is valuable, but the ombudsman's most obvious contribution is in dealing with a very limited number of cases within a highly receptive system. He has a sense of caution about undertaking, and often enough sustains defeat in, efforts to secure changes in policy or general administrative practice. Although he may lecture an administrator on good behavior, he sticks more to questions of legality than is often realized. Secondly, the institution may not work as well here as in Scandinavia. Perhaps something other than the problems indicated above would turn out to be the real difference, but one cannot ignore the difficulties of transplanting institutions. We are likely to have many ombudsmen, not one, dividing the work in geographic and functional terms. We may well bureaucratize the complaint-examining function. Despite likely difficulties and reasonable doubts, the effort is well worth making, provided we keep a sense of proportion and modest expectations. The ombudsman is a valuable official because he is a supporter of the rule of law, yet not an opponent of effective administration.

AMERICAN PUBLIC ADMINISTRATION AND THE RULE OF LAW

To ask point blank whether American public administration embodies the rule of law is now in order. The answer in general terms is: yes, it pretty well docs, but with significant qualifications. Our public administration operates, on the whole, under statutes and rules and specified procedures, and there is widespread, if extraordinarily imprecise, understanding that this is so. In those areas which have so occupied lawyers over the past generation, notably federal regulation of corporate business, procedures have been quite well regularized and judicial review established in satisfactory manner. While battle calls are still shouted, the sort of procedure which the 1946 Administrative Procedure Act required is on the whole accepted by administrators and regulated interests. Judicial review under the substantial-evidence rule, whereby courts generally give the benefit of the doubt to agency findings of fact but look rather closely at interpretations of the law, is at least for the moment an accepted and practicable rule. Our system of procedural safeguards is impressive—"probably by a wide margin the best in the world."[30] And our judges are bolder than those elsewhere in looking into the administrative process. But the variety in formality and carefulness of procedure is very great. Even the presence of the courts as watchdogs guarding the rule of law barely keeps a common thread running through all of American administrative regulation.

Students of the subject find it difficult to say precisely what due process means within administrative regulation. They may refer to opportunity for formal administrative hearing, or to the availability of judicial review. Despite all the cases and the Administrative Procedure Act, what is required of administrators varies, as it probably should, from one function to another. The British speak of natural justice instead of due process, and their courts are more restrained in reviewing administrative actions than ours, but they too find it difficult to pin down a meaning. We sense strongly that administrative procedures which reward or punish particular individuals should be lawful and fair, sufficiently careful to the purpose, genuinely and not just formally correct, and adequately open to hear the demands or responses or complaints of the citizens directly affected. The spirit demanded is uniform, but the procedures in which it is embodied will vary. Before a person is deported or dismissed from a government job as a security risk or deprived of his right to practice medicine, a very careful procedure is essential, to be sure of having the facts and of applying the rules properly. To seize some putrid meat or reject an application to enter graduate studies at a public university, quite different procedures would be correct. No single procedure constitutes due process. Due procedure as an ideal is so basic and yet so difficult a concept that it is tempting to define it as administrative dealing with the regulated individual justly, under the best relevant laws and traditions that we have. Practically speaking, administrative due process is that procedure which will normally be accepted by the courts as reasonable under the circumstances, whether or not the judge thinks the substantive decision was correct.

The wisdom of insisting that the courts must have the final say is not, as some critics of administration have supposed, that the courts can better make all these decisions. It is that they have a nose for shoddy procedure. Courts embody a long tradition of concern with fair procedure, including a bag of technical tricks which often make much sense but sometimes are not transferable. And good judges are generalists, strong on common sense, distrusting power, greed, and all the other mischief-making motives. Although courts are not the only guarantors of fairness, that is their specialty, and they are without the stake in easy, effective administration that the agency has. Of course courts err. But persons sympathetic to the modern role of government and the equalitarian purposes of the welfare state ought not to belittle the concern for due administrative procedure, nor to assume that it is never violated. We have seen too many shortcuts to political heaven—good ends being used to justify dubious means—to disregard lawfulness.

Nonetheless, an arid legalism which, in the name of high standards, prevents the achievement of public purposes, is a real threat.[31] In those areas to which lawyers, businessmen, and courts have given most attention, and in which the national independent regulatory agencies bulk large, procedural formality has proceeded far—at times, surely too far. While procedural requirements were in part imposed by courts or legislatures in order to cripple regulation of business, in part also lawyers and judges and some administrators look to the courts for a pattern when something seems to them judicial in nature. Excessive judicialization of the administrative process leads not only to excessively slow action but to failure to assume responsibilities to formulate or enforce policy, in the preoccupation with formal case hearings. The first of the great national regulatory agencies, the Interstate Commerce Commission, set the pattern as it chose to regard itself as a tribunal and to obtain a reputation for expertise and impartiality, rather than to adopt a vigorous policy-making role. Other national and state agencies have similarly preferred the dignified model of the court to the politically risky role of promoter of the economy. When highly judicialized procedure is applied to the wrong purposes, it interferes with effective administration. Due process does not require that everything that administrators do should be done as the courts do.

Some aspects of administrative regulation, however, suffer from too little judicialization. Years of concern have helped formalize and protect the role of the hearing examiner, yet there is limited knowledge of or control over what happens when a case reaches the level of agency heads. They actually make the decision, but normally the hearing was held outside their presence. It has been suggested, for example, that the Civil Aeronautics Board almost completely ignores the work of the hearing examiner when it considers a case. Further, the elaborate procedures used by such an agency to collect evidence may be rendered almost meaningless by the lack of any standards on which to base a decision. What is jarring is the disproportion in different parts of the process. We need a clearer sense of the procedures appropriate to the purposes, neither excessively judicial nor insufficiently guided by substantive policy and procedural rules.

Enforcement also evades control by law. Controls over the decision to prosecute, whether in administrative or criminal process, are not comparable to those over the actual hearing. The threat of prosecution can be used to coerce action. The power to publicize an alleged violation of the law, as in charges before the SEC or racial discrimination charges before a Fair Employment Practices Commission, is a real sanction and a difficult one to control. Informal negotiation, for a tax settlement, for example, necessarily leaves considerable room for administrative discretion. A police department or an administrative agency with a substantial policing function usually has to expend its limited resources so as to apprehend some people, warn others, ignore some merely technical violations, and fail to discover some real but minor violations. Total enforcement costs too much and involves some harsh or absurd actions, so discretion is used, but it is difficult to protect against abuse of that discretion.

Still another area of inadequacy revolves around governmental sovereignty. Despite progress, governmental liability is not so well developed in Anglo-American law as in continental administrative law. A citizen who suffers because of the fault of a governmental official or agency may not be able to secure compensation. Procedures for governmental taking of property in most of this country have been criticized as harsh, still suited to a rural society with open spaces. As noted before, where something is labeled a privilege and not a right, the individual may be dealt with by rather crude procedure. It is time that terms such as "sovereignty" and "privilege" were stripped of magic. We ought to look clearly into the question whether, in any area, the needs of government are so urgent that it is not possible to provide procedures reasonably in accord with our best traditions of fairness.

Charles Reich argues we should create a new property in government largess (grants, benefits, jobs, franchises, contracts, subsidies, services, licenses, and the like). Social security, veterans' benefits, government jobs, licenses required to pursue an occupation (by doctor, lawyer, pawnbroker, barber, taxi driver, funeral director, psychologist, plumber, cosmetologist, and endless others in one city or state or another), permits to operate a business (bus, taxi, radio station, liquor store), government contracts (notably defense spending, but also old-fashioned buildings and roads and equipment), subsidies and grants (to farmers, scientists, others), services (the postal system, fire protection, agricultural extension)—all of these put even respectable citizens in a position of dependence on government. Reich sees the growing role of government largess as leading to a state whose underlying philosophy is "the doctrine that the wealth that flows from government is held by its recipients conditionally, subject to confiscation in the interest of the paramount state."[32] Property, he suggests, gave a degree of freedom to an individual, but increasingly society has replaced property with government grants. By creating rights in largess, the individual's dependence would be lessened, his freedom protected. Rejection, revocation, or conditioning of grants should follow reasonable procedure.

Abuse of administrative power is probably more prevalent at the local than at the national level.[33] Not the ICC but the local health board or building inspector, what Dickinson called "the sedimentary levels" of officialdom, are most likely to abuse authority, failing to provide proper notice and hearing when they easily could. Where government uses summary powers, it may seem especially oppressive. The health and welfare regulatory powers in state and local governments have a very long tradition in this country. They are not a modern welfare state phenomenon, as are many of the federal regulatory functions. The courts will react against clear abuses, but accept broad powers of local inspection and control. The local businessman may be especially apt to view government officials as powerful, obstructive, and arbitrary. The fire inspector, building inspector, and the like, actually possess very broad discretion in the application of rules. Personal favoritism, political connections, and business alliances may be or seem significant influences, all the while hiding behind the good name of the public interest. Sometimes the businessman is not really being abused and actually wants nonenforcement, but sometimes the complaints are legitimate.

Compared with other times and places, we enjoy impressive administrative compliance with the law, impressive efforts to be fair in procedure and substance. But the variety in America is remarkable too. In general those with wealth, lawyers, and political power are usually assured of fair and sometimes even excessively favorable treatment. For the large businessman, the complaint may be overjudicialization of the great agencies of regulation, perhaps lack of clear standards with which his lawyers may work. For the local businessman or householder, large discretion in small officials may occasionally be a plague. For the poor man dependent on government, harsh or even illegal treatment without any practical means of objecting may be his lot. Dicey's teaching, despite its flaws, still has meaning for us. The courts are important guardians, though they sometimes fall. If government punishes people through nonjudicial procedures, it should never be done in malicious or slovenly style. The procedure should fit the function and circumstances, but administrative convenience is surely not the sole criterion. Government officials must have discretion, for laws cannot rule of themselves, but it must be *discretion under the laws.* There must be effective remedies, not simply grand guarantees.

Useful protections against abusive administrative regulation may include: (1) public servants of character and qualification (who are especially lacking where professionalism has not yet been established in local government) and regular training of and systematic hierarchical supervision over regulatory personnel; (2) explicit rules and clear precedents to guide regulatory personnel and citizens or their advocates who deal with the agency; (3) an independent inspectorate or an ombudsman-type official to serve a local jurisdiction or a specialized area of administration (a city, a university, soldiers or prison inmates, and so forth); (4) opportunity for a person to present his case when an order specifically affecting him is at stake, and provision of an advocate or attorney to assist him; (5) clear statement of the laws and rules under which a decision was taken and the reasons for it and the means of appeal; (6) the right to appeal to a superior official, that is, someone beyond the original decision maker; (7) a special appeals unit within the agency yet with substantial autonomy; (8) judicial review by the regular courts or by specialized administrative courts with jurisdiction probably limited to a single function, such as housing or public welfare. Though such a listing does not cover all the established modes of fair procedure or all the feasible reforms, it suggests some of the key points at which we might perfect existing procedures or establish new institutions.

If there are abuses, the sophisticated citizen may be able to secure redress through appeals to legislators or others with political influence, administrative appeal, or courts. People are less often abused if it is obvious that they would challenge. The poor are more often abused because we all are susceptible to the corruption of unchallenged power. The legal services programs funded by the federal Office of Economic Opportunity since 1965 have served poor people not only in such unheroic matters as divorce cases, but also in such actions as suing a state for medical aid funds or suing to require cities to institute food stamp programs. Such initiatives have aroused the fury of some governors and other politicians, but the poor obviously have a better chance of justice when they have vigorous lawyers on their side.

Our most notable failure to achieve the rule of law in public administration has been the lesser grade of justice we extend to the poor, both because they cannot in fact secure the rights they admittedly have and because we have been reluctant to extend to them rights analogous to those enjoyed by holders of more traditional forms of property. Reginald Smith, in a landmark study in 1919, argued that our court system had failed to adjust to urbanization and immigration, to the rise of a class that could not secure justice. Justice is denied to the poor because of delay, costs and fees, and the expense of counsel. He considered administrative tribunals "the most important experiment in the administration of justice made in the twentieth century."[34] Between 1911 and 1917 some thirty-seven states had adopted workmen's compensation acts establishing industrial accident commissions, in view of the obvious defects of court procedure in this realm, defects regularly exploited by employers and liability insurance companies. Smith warned that though new agencies enjoy special freedom and informality, they tend to move toward formality, precedent, and attorneys. Finally, then, he stressed that the poor need lawyers if they are to get justice.

Did the New Deal or subsequent programs solve the problem of justice for the poor? Evidently not. What the poor receive from government is typically defined in law as a privilege, a gratuity furnished by the state subject to whatever conditions it sees fit to impose. It is not a right, not property they own. Welfare payments, public housing and the like are provided by a reluctant political majority, in the belief that bad character has brought the receivers to the public trough. Given this legal and ideological context, authoritarian practices and harsh or even illegal treatment have been widespread. The most obvious example has been after-midnight raids on homes of those receiving aid to dependent children, to try to discover signs of a man, if not the man himself. These raids have lacked judicial warrant, resting on the assumption that the welfare given is a privilege, in return for which one sacrifices the constitutional right against search without warrant. Cloward and Elman argue that the chief characteristic of public agencies serving the poor is "the exercise of unlawful discretion—the promulgation of administrative rules and procedures which undoubtedly violate either constitutional provisions or the immediate statutes governing departments."[35] Police departments, with the threat of judicial rejection of their actions to speed them, have in recent years increasingly abandoned the procedures under which they have so often trampled the legal rights of the poor. Now the purely administrative services, not so dependent on court action to effect their sanctions, are properly a central concern of reformers. The search for administrative justice for the poor is unfinished business, high on our agenda of public duties.

CHAPTER THREE

Public Administration Under Politics

The rule of law ties public administration to what is basic and relatively stable, to fair procedures. However, to ensure a democratic community as well as a constitutional one, political control must tie public administration to the changing political will of society. We seek means of granting control to a majority, with wide freedom to participate on equal terms. Elected political leaders transmit policies to the bureaucracy, but there are real problems in making legislative and executive control effective. Political parties and interest groups also influence governmental administration, sometimes formally but often informally. If we accept the commitment to political control over administration as fundamental to modern democracy, we encounter problems of determining what channels of political control are most legitimate and whether administration can be effective when political influence is at work. A bureaucracy isolated from politics is not for democratic tastes; a bureaucracy servile to politics offends concepts of objectivity and equality of treatment and is unlikely to do well the necessary work of government. We need just enough political influence and just the right kind—which is little enough wisdom from which to start.

THE POLICY-ADMINISTRATION RELATIONSHIP

The policy-administration relationship, like the question of the obligation of an elected representative to his constituency, is of such profound importance and complexity that it will evidently not go away or be solved. Public administration scholars in twentieth-century America have moved from the view that there is a sharp split between politics and administration to the view that the two elements are tightly interwoven.

Frank J. Goodnow's analysis at the turn of the century crystallized the view of the politics-administration relationship which was dominant then in America and which remained so until World War II. He argued that we must look beyond the formal, written constitutional document to the administrative system to understand a government. The functions of any state are naturally divided into the expression of the will of the state (politics) and the execution of that will (administration). Governmental organs are concerned primarily with one or the other of these functions, though there can in reality be no absolute separation of them. The legislature expresses the will of the state in most instances where the constitution has not spoken, and the chief executive or his subordinates express the will concerning details; the administration executes the will. The distinction among the functions is clear, Goodnow thought, but their division among organs is not precise.

Should politics control administration? In general, Goodnow argued, administration should be subjected to the control of politics, so that the expressed will of the state is executed. But there must be limits. Especially in municipal government it must be recognized that administration should be freed from politics, for much of it involves activities of a largely scientific, judicial, or business nature, which has little significance for the expression of the will of the state. The work of these technical and professional officials should be free of political influence, for it is no more political than the work of judges. Such officials, as well as clerical officials who simply carry out orders, should enjoy tenure in office. To combine popular government and efficient administration, political control over administration should be sufficient to produce harmony between expression and execution, but the control should not go beyond what is necessary to produce harmony, or the impartiality of administration is destroyed. The political party has provided in the United States what was not formally provided for in a system of separation of powers and election of many officials—a means of coordinating execution with expression of the will. The need for party was, in turn, used to justify the spoils system, which sapped administrative efficiency. The national government, where authority is less splintered than in the states, was able to rely more on hierarchical (presidential) control and less on party control over officials, to secure coordination of politics and administration. As we concentrate authority more, with states emulating the federal government model (fewer state-wide elective officials, more authority over administration vested in the governor), the governmental system itself can provide coordination formerly performed by the party. Party control will be required only for the highest officers, who can control their subordinates, thus transmitting the political will to the lowest employees.

In 1900 the spoils system was rampant, and state and local governments lacked responsible leadership, for their many elected officials were each on his own, not subject to control by the governor. Goodnow urged a responsible chief executive and a hierarchy leading up to him; he argued against having many administrators elected or politically appointed and for the merit system of career public service without partisan obligation. He underemphasized the necessary, useful play of political influence in public administration, but he urged sensible political-administrative reform, if effectiveness of administration is a key value.

The politics-administration distinction, along the lines of Goodnow's analysis, was a dominant note in American public administration writings until the mid-1940's. Students of public administration sought to justify adoption of merit systems, professional specialization, and protection against political interference or detailed legislative intervention. Politics should be democratic but the essential test of administration is efficiency, they argued, and we need more of the competence that nondemocratic nations have developed in their administration. In the attempt to spur reform, they overemphasized the line between politics and administration.

Today the basic view is that the two processes are interwoven; some writers deny any essential difference between the two. Contemporary American public administration enjoys far more autonomy from partisan influence and is far more expert than it was in 1900, so writers are less impelled by reformist motives to insist on a sharp separation. The dominant view accepts as accurate description and proper democratic practice "the intermingling of policy and administration" seen by Paul Appleby.[1] The policy that administrators make is not simply narrow or technical, nor is the process essentially different from legislative policy making. If a decision which is normally made by administrators becomes politically significant, it may be called up to a more purely political level, but these different orders of policy making constitute not separate realms but a continuum from routine administration to pure politics. Nor is policy making by administrators a threat to democracy, for it is "hedged in by pressures of many kinds, checked by competing and complementary prerogatives, exposed to publicity and opposition attack, with responsibility fixed in political officers who can be got at." The administrative process is one of our political processes, Appleby wrote, out of which comes a consensus that approximates the public interest. Not highly partisan, it is responsive, politically aware, and has a policy impact.

A focus among political scientists on interest group politics after World War II also helped illuminate the political qualities of public administration. Administrative bureaus, legislative committees, and interest groups in each policy area constitute a political subsystem. The bureau and its chief are key characters in shaping policy. It is not parties as a whole nor Congress as a whole nor the administration as a whole that copes with most problems; it is interest groups, committees, and bureaus. Some of these analyses go rather far in denying any difference between one kind of participant and another. We have come a long way from the politics-administration distinction.

Attempts have been made in recent years to revive the policy-administration categories in a more sophisticated fashion. Herbert Simon, in a book showing remarkable analytic ability, came brilliantly to questionable conclusions.[2] He sought to make the study and practice of public administration more genuinely scientific. He distinguished fact (description) from value (preference) elements in decisions, and argued that a democratic state is committed to popular control of value elements. Arguing that the value-fact distinction is basic in the proper relation between policy making and administration, he sought "procedural devices permitting a more effective separation of the factual and ethical elements in decisions," and "a more effective division of labor between the policy-forming and administrative agencies." Essentially he sought to give the legislature policy decisions and the administration decisions in which the factual issues are more important. Although Simon's analysis is complex and interesting, it justifies treating administrative decisions as less political and more technical, more a choice of efficient means, than seems to be really the case.

There is a continuing tendency for anyone fascinated with techniques for making administration more efficient—through computers, planning, special budgeting techniques, reliance on technical knowledge, development of a science of public administration, or the like—to wish and to claim that politics can largely be taken out of administration. There is plenty of room for rationality in administration, and the difference between the life of the public administrator and that of the politician is significant, but there is a good deal of politics in American public administration. The most direct route for political control of administration is through elected politicians in the legislative and executive branches, who claim to transmit the will of the people (or a reasonable facsimile) to the bureaucrats.

A contemporary view, expressed by "New Public Administration" critics of our government's failure to cope with grave social problems, rejects political control out of concern for equalitarianism, not from concern for technical efficiency. It is impatient with, if not contemptuous of, political control of public administration. Politicians and legislatures are seen as spokesmen of the established groups and the status quo. Failing to respond to the needs of the dispossessed, politicians sacrifice a moral claim to authority over public administration. Nor is it feasible for either legislators or an elected chief executive to create policy and control its actual development—only administrators can do this. Government bureaucracy governs today, and properly so, argue these critics. With faith that new public administrators will (or must if the system is to survive) identify with and serve the needs of the underprivileged, that only they are equipped to make and administer policy, and that a representative bureaucracy is a more valuable form of representation than an elected legislature, advocates of a new public administration tend to dismiss political control of public administration as neither desirable nor feasible. This is a radical break with the traditional theory of the political role of the governmental bureaucracy—in fact, with the theory of American democracy as a process of government in which the people act through elected political representatives.

CONTROL BY ELECTED OFFICIALS

There is ample ambiguity about the meaning of democracy, but one can reasonably insist that rule by the many, popular control, is its essence. That meaning inheres in its history, in its name, and in the philosophical attacks upon and defenses of democracy. A modern democratic problem is to make popular control work in a vast nation, a problem for which the Greek experience is of limited use. Permanence in office is hardly a hallmark of democracy, which implies direct popular rule or at least periodic elections in which leaders may be replaced. We accept the need for a career bureaucracy, but this is to serve certain practical needs of society, not to foster its democratic impulses. Elected officials rightly claim to be, more truly than bureaucrats, in the democratic stream. In formulating a democratic theory of political control of bureaucrats, the first rule must be that any fundamental rejection of political control is antidemocratic. Then if one wants to argue that effective service or the values to which officials are committed are more important than democratic control, one can argue that case.

Within the category of elected officials, however, are both legislators and executives. Often the division between them seems more important than their common legitimation through election. The competition between Congress and President, state legislator and governor, is a continuing quality of American government, despite examples of relative harmony. Much discussion of political control of the governmental bureaucracy focuses on the respective roles of executive and legislature as controller, partisans of one side flaying the other.

What differences between the chief executive and the legislature are important to control of the bureaucracy? The executive is likely to have a greater sense of responsibility for the effectiveness of the administration, for adequate performance. The legislature tends to be more concerned with bureaucratic abuse, with excess of vigor in regulation, with failure to give favorable decisions, rather than with systematically uniform and effective administration. A century ago John Stuart Mill warned that at least a cabinet minister feels himself under some responsibility for the quality of administration, while a legislator does not, "for when did any member of Parliament lose his seat for the vote he gave on any detail of administration?"[3] A minister's reputation rests on how well his department functions. Not so the legislator, who is, wrote Mill, likely to be ignorant of the matter being decided and easily swayed by any in the assembly who have a bias or a special interest. Such warnings have been repeated since, with direct reference to our own Congress. Further, the chief executive has a sense of responsibility to the entire nation, to the public interest—imprecise though that may be—by virtue of his election from the whole and the nature of the executive responsibilities. As head of the military, for example, it is unlikely a President will think of himself as responsible for anything less than the good of the United States as a nation entire; the same is true to some extent in all his functions. The legislator responds often to his own constituency, to local pressures, partly because this seems the way to get reelected, and partly because he feels a moral obligation to speak for the area or groups who sent him to the assembly.

Legislator and executive look to different groups for support: legislators have been described as provincials, of local perspective, the President as a metropolitan, speaking for the national perspective. The executive tends to respond more to an urban, politically liberal constituency that favors government involvement in the economy and the provision of services to the poor, while the legislature is more responsive to groups which distrust governmental interference, expanded governmental costs, or free services to the poor. This difference is complicated in its cause and manifestations and is not always true, but generally speaking the executive branch takes for granted the provision and expansion of services and regulation that arouse opposition among influential legislators. The small cities and towns find more voice in Congress, the big cities, the labor unions, the Blacks look to the executive as their normal spokesman.

Apart from differences of constituencies and goals, there is institutional rivalry between legislative and executive branches in the United States. If the presidency has enjoyed a period of apparent dominance, congressmen begin to feel they are but rubber stamps and assert their prerogatives and power, trying to whittle the President down a peg or two. Men in politics want to count for something, to have power, and our government is set up in a way that tends to pit legislature against executive. Though the truth is probably not quite so simple, it usually appears that as one waxes the other wanes. In sum, seeking to protect their power and to respond to their constituents and to further the goals they value, legislature and executive so often face each other as competitors or opponents that it is easy to accept their opposition as fundamental.

Both Congress and President feel themselves on good constitutional ground in exercising controls over administration. There are occasional pitched battles, as when a committee tries to exercise a veto over administrative action in a manner constitutionally objectionable to the President, but most of the time the issues are political rather than legal. The Constitution, drawn in nonbureaucratic days, does not settle the question but offers encouragement to partisans of each branch. It vests in the President the executive power, makes him commander in chief of the army and navy, and states that he may require the written opinion of the principal officer in each of the executive departments upon any subject relating to their respective duties. It provides that he shall commission all officers and shall nominate and by and with the advice and consent of the Senate appoint officers of the United States whose appointments are not otherwise provided for by the Constitution (though Congress may vest appointment of inferior officers in the President alone, in the courts, or in department heads). The President shall from time to time give Congress information about the state of the Union, recommend for their consideration such measures as he judges necessary and expedient, and take care that the laws be faithfully executed. Given those powers, one can hardly doubt that the President properly claims substantial right to direct the administrative agencies.

Congress has credentials too. The Senate has the right to participate in the appointment process, and Congress has impeachment powers. Congress has the lawmaking powers, which may be used for the purposes specifically enumerated in Section 8 of Article I and "To make all Laws which shall be necessary and proper for carrying into Execution the foregoing Powers, and all other Powers vested by this Constitution in the Government of the United States, or in any Department or Officer thereof." The Constitution provides that no money shall be drawn from the Treasury except following appropriations made by law. This suggests that Congress has a legitimate concern with what the bureaucracy does. But the Constitution does not appear to settle any fine points of legislative versus executive control.

The dispute between advocates of legislative and of executive control rests more on general conceptions of need and competence than on fine points of the Constitution. Defenders of legislative control emphasize the direct relation of the legislator to his constituency, the essentially democratic quality of the representative assembly. Perhaps implicitly they may link the chief executive with the history of monarchical rulers who sought to govern a realm, who viewed officialdom as their personal servants, and whose primary concern was not the rights of citizens. The legislature, in this historical image with a hint of Magna Charta, emerges as the defender of local and personal rights. The partisans of the chief executive emphasize that only he is primarily concerned to provide effective public administration and that only he provides a truly national point of view. Legislators protect local interests but willingly sacrifice the national interest. To some extent the two sides agree that the legislature excels in concern for local interests, in seeing that administration responds to dominant constituency attitudes, and that the executive excels in concern for coordinated, professionally directed administration, more willing to override interest group, local, and personal objections in order to serve what is conceived as national purpose.

One cannot dismiss the question of legislative versus executive control, but in the larger sense both serve as instruments of popular control. President and Congress are both popularly elected, are both legitimate transmitters of popular attitudes. Even when they compete, they both serve the end of political control of public administration. Richard Neustadt has urged the politicians to unite, the President and Congress to see their joint stakes in controlling the bureaucrats, who are ready enough to rule without subjection to political influence. "Bureaucracy has brought a new contestant into play: the great prospective struggle is between entrenched officialdom and politicians everywhere, White House and Hill alike."[4] Whether or not executive and legislative politicians form the alliance that Neustadt calls for, we can insist that when they subject administration to political influence, in fact they do work together, to borrow from Robert Frost, whether they work together or apart.

LEGISLATIVE CONTROL

The Legislative Reorganization Act of 1946 gave to the standing committees of Congress responsibility for maintaining "continuous watchfulness of the execution by the administrative agencies concerned of any law the subject matter of which falls within the jurisdiction of such committee," and provided strengthened committee staffs to pursue that goal. A leading scholar of the subject has found that, in fact, " . . . Congress exercises the greatest degree of direction and control of administration found in any major democratic country."[5] If Congress has seemed in the last generation to be less and less important in the legislative function, it has been increasing its control over administrative processes, intensely developing methods of legislative surveillance. Lack of executive or party control over the legislature and heavy reliance on committees form the basis for its control of the bureaucracy, but they result in extreme specialization and dispersion of knowledge and power within the legislature. Committee, subcommittee, senior members, or chairman may, in the name of Congress, exercise great influence over an agency or program.

Methods of legislative control, formal and informal, include influence over: (1) program, (2) procedures, (3) funds, (4) personnel, (5) organizational form, and (6) specific decisions.

(1) Constitutionally, administrators may conduct only those programs authorized by legislation (though the courts have sustained vague standards as a sufficient guide to administrators) and may not conduct activities forbidden by legislation. Congress can directly forbid a program or indirectly block it by refusing funds or abolishing the agency. It can grant powers with varying specificity: a wider range of discretion may be granted to administrators for crisis programs; for programs with strong political support and wide consensus, whose officials have won the confidence of Congress; or where Congress cannot agree on just what it wants done. Administrators learn the will of Congress not only from legislation but in less formal ways, and "many administrative officials now receive a great deal more day-to-day guidance from Congressmen

than they get from the President."[6] Great detail in a statute may impede sensible development based on experience; daily intervention means control by one or a few legislators; but broad grants and infrequent intervention mean large discretion for administrators.

(2) Congress regulates not only the substance of programs, but procedures. The Administrative Procedure Act of 1946, discussed in the previous chapter, did this for a whole range of agencies concerning rule making and adjudication. Statutes regulate fiscal, personnel, contract, purchasing, and other procedures, for all or many or particular agencies. Detailed restrictions, often adopted in reaction to an instance of apparent waste or bad administration, may block needed discretion and flexibility. There is too much red tape in American public administration in part because legislatures have focused on preventing mischief and securing uniformity, sometimes at the expense of asking whether programs are effectively meeting public needs.

(3) (a) After careful study, Joseph Harris affirms the conventional view that control over expenditures is "perhaps the most important single control over the departments," indeed "the cornerstone of legislative control of administration."[7] Appropriations subcommittees are at the core of congressional control of expenditures. Their recommendations are usually accepted by the full appropriations committee, and the whole house inclines to accept the reports of its appropriations committee. Subcommittee members and staff have developed long tenure and considerable detailed knowledge of the agencies with which they deal. The relationship between the appropriations subcommittee and the agency may include kindly feelings between administrator and congressman, or at least relations may be benevolently paternalistic: subcommittee leaders' preferences are respected and they provide protection and support for those units and programs of the agency that they approve. Budget recommendations prepared by the Office of Management and Budget, working under the President and over and with the departments, go from the President to the House of Representatives. The usual pattern is: the House subcommittees (whose ethos is the need for economy) cut administration requests, the House sustains the cuts, the Senate subcommittees restore a substantial part of the cuts, this is sustained in the Senate, then a compromise is struck in the conference committee. The House subcommittees hold lengthy, detailed hearings on the proposed budget, at which officials (including career officials) justify the needs of their agencies, and in which detailed data are submitted to supplement the oral presentation. (These hearings are later published and, even though somewhat edited, are a rich source of information for students of government.)

Twenty or so appropriations bills are considered each year by Congress.

An appropriations subcommittee can influence administration by its formal action in approving funds for one purpose or another. It can write commands to perform or abstain from some action into the appropriations bill, despite congressional rules against substantive legislation in appropriations bills. For example, agricultural appropriations some decades ago forbade investigations into the allegedly deleterious effect of insect sprays, and the NLRB appropriations prohibited spending money in connection with collective bargaining for agricultural laborers—the not-so-fine rural legislator's hand. The subcommittee can put directives into its report, where they stand as warnings which are normally observed. By questions or demands at hearings, committee members can set policy guidelines, perhaps extorting promises from administrators. Oral or written statements made by officials stand as moral commitments, whose violation may offend committee members. If an agency finds it necessary to spend in significantly different fashion from its estimates or from the strict letter of its appropriation act, it will first check with its appropriations subcommittee, perhaps with the staff on minor items, with the chairman on more important ones. Subcommittees are now turning somewhat less to details and more to policy and program than in earlier decades, and Congress has substantially reduced the specificity of its appropriations. It has, for example, largely stopped voting money specifically for a particular field office, although many state legislatures still use detailed itemization, even specifying salaries for particular officials.

Congressional control through appropriations encounters substantial difficulties. Though subcommittee members have considerable detailed information, they still must be ignorant of much of the internal life of the bureaucracy and much of the reality of programs. Subcommittees usually have but a single clerk to aid them in analyzing the budget of one or more departments or agencies; the Office of Management and Budget has little contact with the subcommittee; and each agency insists that it needs the funds asked for. Some people propose an expanded congressional staff, but this poses the danger of a new legislative bureaucracy to be controlled. Congress as a whole probably knows fairly little about what it is doing when it votes appropriations, and items which do not change much from the previous year's sum will generally be accepted as reasonable. When Congress makes substantial cuts, it often does so in relative ignorance of what the consequences will be. Other limitations on control of administration through appropriations include: carry-over authorization permits spending in any year to be based partly on appropriations in earlier years, which has been a major problem in the Defense Department; much of the budget, evidently over half, is for fixed obligations, such as interest payments on the public debt and veterans' pensions, which cannot be easily controlled; the President on occasion, but not too frequently because it strains relations with Congress, may impound appropriated funds and not permit their use; some agencies borrow money from the Treasury and may lend from a revolving fund, so they do not depend so heavily on appropriations.

Despite all the crudities of the budget-appropriation process, administrators do take account of cues from departmental superiors, the Office of Management and Budget, legislators, and interest groups, as well as their own agency people, in proposing their budgets. It is a politically sensitive process, if not a perfectly rational one. Legislative influence occurs at every stage, in part through anticipation of legislative response to one or another possible lines of action. Nor is the subcommittee completely autonomous, for there is a good deal of informal coordination, taking into consideration the views of other participants in the political-administrative arena. When one realizes that the British Parliament does not change the executive budget at all, that it has not even had a standing appropriations ("estimates") committee through most of its history, one is impressed with the authority vested in the congressional appropriations process.

(3) (b) Auditing by an agency independent of the executive helps assure that expenditures have been properly made. The General Accounting Office (GAO) is headed by the Comptroller General, who is appointed for a fifteen-year term, is ineligible for reappointment (so he need not please anyone), and is removable not by the President but by Congress. The GAO can prescribe accounting procedures and can examine and even disallow specific expenditures of agencies, as violative of statutes or GAO rules. To avoid disallowance, agencies may, if in doubt, clear with the GAO before making an expenditure. The GAO has tended to an excess of vigor and self-righteousness in narrowly interpreting what expenditures are permissible. (The GAO once disallowed an expenditure for an artificial limb as not properly included under "medical services and supplies.") State and local auditors in the United States seldom impose the kind of roadblocks that the GAO sometimes has, nor do business auditors. After much prodding, the GAO is now more cooperative, for example, in no longer requiring that all vouchers be sent to Washington (substituting sampling and field visits) and in working with the Treasury Department and agencies on accounting systems—in general, in paying heed to the needs of administration. The GAO has sometimes shown hostility

to vigorous governmental programs, evidently in deference to congressmen opposed to administration policies. The more limited concept of auditing which commends itself is that the GAO should check for and report on regularity of expenditures and quality of accounting systems, but should not be an autonomous force blocking effective administration. The GAO is presumed to assure that the administration spends money as Congress intended, but congressional-GAO ties seem at best rather informal. In comparison, the British audit admirably touches questions of irregularity, waste, poor financial administration, and the like, without claiming power to disallow particular expenditures, and ties the auditor to a respected legislative committee and to the Treasury, which has been the key executive fiscal-personnel control agency.

(4) Congress influences personnel actions in various ways. Impeachment might have proved interesting, but, with a single exception, has not been used against administrators. Congress can limit presidential removal of quasi-judicial administrative officers, but authority to dismiss is fundamentally an executive authority. Senatorial confirmation of appointments applies to over 100,000 positions, but a good many are routine military and foreign service appointments. Real authority may be asserted by the Senate, with political considerations dominant, concerning such appointments as marshals, collectors of customs, federal attorneys, field office headships, or high-level political executives in Washington. In these cases senatorial confirmation may mean actual control of the appointment by a single senator, for "senatorial courtesy" induces deference by fellow senators to the wishes of a senator of the President's party respecting major nominations of people from his home state. The standard study of confirmation found: "There have been few unfit appointments rejected by the Senate, but appointments of many able men have been denied confirmation for political reasons which would not stand the light of day."[8] In a famous instance, Leland Olds, an extraordinarily vigorous and competent member of the Federal Power Commission, was denied reappointment because oil and gas interests opposed federal regulation of the price of natural gas—though other reasons were used in public debate. There is informal consultation with congressmen on politically sensitive appointments even if they are not subject to senatorial confirmation—even on major civil service appointments sometimes.

Congress can punish and perhaps drive out an administrator by cutting his appropriation, harassing him with endless hearings, abolishing the agency or function, or otherwise indicating displeasure to higher-ups. Some men are passed over for appointment because it is learned that they would encounter trouble with confirmation or in doing business with Congress. Sometimes a committee supports a man against his superiors, and saves his skin. (This happened repeatedly with Admiral Rickover, the "father" of the atomic submarine, who was better loved in Congress than in the Navy.) Evidently a good many federal employees turn to their senator or congressman for help in personnel matters, but presumably they usually get routine, token assistance. From time to time Congress enacts limits to the numbers of federal employees, restricting the filling of vacancies, and it adopts statutes in great number and detail concerning personnel procedures.

(5) Congress can go as far as it wishes in prescribing organizational form or in leaving discretion to the President or department heads. Reorganization proposals often draw intense responses from administrators, interest groups, and concerned legislators, testifying to the apparent importance of organizational form, which may seem to emphasize or degrade a particular program or official or agency. For example, supporters of a new cause typically want their own agency established, rather than adding one more program within a going agency. In some departments the bureaus have traditionally been created by the secretary, in others they are established by statute. Harris found that of 124 bureaus and other major executive units existing in 1960, sixty-eight had been founded by statute, fifty-six by executive action. Even specific posts of importance may be established by statute. When Congress acts on organization, it usually has policy in mind.

(6) (a) Congress can control specific decisions in various ways. Since World War II it has developed a technique of control through the "legislative veto" or "committee clearance." Particular executive decisions must be submitted to Congress as a whole or to a specified committee for a waiting period, usually sixty days, before going into effect. During that period Congress may reject the action, by vote of one or two houses or of a committee, as specified in statute. Evidently the system dates from a provision in a 1932 appropriation act permitting the President to reorganize the executive branch, subject to congressional rejection. In the post-World War II era, when better staffing of committees permits more effective surveillance, the power to reject has usually been vested in a committee, thus formalizing the already substantial informal authority of committees. Committee veto has been used especially respecting public works authorizations and other economic actions of concern to particular constituencies, giving individual legislators a measure of control over activities within their districts or states. This method has stirred considerable presidential hostility, as well as academic criticism, as impinging on constitutionally granted executive powers. A formal legislative veto system for regulations

promulgated by administrators has been more fully developed in Britain than here, but a very small proportion are refused and these usually on rather technical grounds; the results do not especially excite envy. Apart from formal veto provisions, agencies typically consult one or more committees, perhaps especially a House appropriations subcommittee, before moving in an unexpected and possibly controversial direction not outlined when the budget was defended.

(6) (b) Individual administrative decisions are also influenced through "case work"—the intervention by a legislator with an administrative agency at the request of a constituent who seeks political help in securing prompt or favorable action from the agency. Agencies most frequently the object of citizen requests to congressmen are the Social Security Administration, the military, the Veterans Administration, the Immigration and Naturalization Service, and the Internal Revenue Service—agencies that decide many cases involving ordinary citizens. Case work is encouraged in the United States by the weakness of political parties and the dispersion of power, which make each legislator responsible for his own political survival. Congressmen are convinced that case work makes loyal supporters of constituents whom they have assisted and so helps win elections, as diligent committee service may not. It may also give congressmen a sense of energy and power (the legislative role is often frustrating). Some legislators simply ask an agency for information or express interest in the claim; others may apply pressure or appear as counsel for a constituent. If the case work is done with too forceful a hand, it distorts administrative decisions and destroys the lawfulness and impartiality of public administration, for federal administration is "almost perforated by congressmen and their staffs."[9] Legislators and their aides (most case work is actually handled by staff aides of legislators) rarely have the time, energy, or information to give a complaint detailed and objective treatment. Most legislators support constituents' cases irrespective of their merit, but will not press for more than an explanation or prompt action. Speeding up a decision is probably the most frequent consequence.

Case work is very weakly developed in many states, where turnover in legislators is high (over half the legislators may be newcomers at each session), staff is lacking, office space is tight or absent, pay and allowances are low, sessions are short and in some cases biennial, and professionalism is scarce. In some states legislators conceive of their role as including case work; in others they do not, which may betoken a realistically modest view of their potential.

(6) (c) Congressional investigation by a committee or subcom-

mittee (either a regular standing committee or a special committee) into an administrative agency, program, or problem may affect agency action. So may the threat of an investigation with formal hearings, published reports, and substantial publicity. Investigations have increased substantially since the Legislative Reorganization Act of 1946. They are determined largely by committee chairmen, who tend to be somewhat more protective of an administration headed by a President of their party than of the opposition. An agency may go for years without being investigated if no congressman sees need for and gain from one and the affected interests are not in rebellion. The decision to investigate is essentially political. Investigations may serve to uncover corruption or incompetence, to attack and reformulate policy, or to educate those present and the attentive public. Abuse of legislative investigation can easily occur when congressmen are primarily concerned with publicity and personal political advancement or with pushing or impeding particular groups or policies.

State legislative control sometimes seems nothing but a mixture of impotence and mischief making. State legislatures "have only the barest capacity to provide any kind of oversight of the state administration."[10] With Congress, one can easily see the limitations and failures, and legislators themselves are aware of how little they can move some of the bureaucratic monster's limbs. But one cannot conclude that legislative control is a myth. In varied ways, formal and informal, it is genuine, though ranging from ignorance and impotence to detailed knowledge and legislative leadership of a program. Where bureaucratic action or inaction arouses significant political objection, Congress is likely to intervene. Where secrecy is imposed, congressional control may be frustrated or limited to a very few congressmen, perhaps exclusively those sympathetic with the agency. The whole area of political control of the military poses special problems. There are the difficulties of understanding complex issues which constitute only a part of a congressman's responsibilities (and concerning which constructive action may not be especially rewarding politically) and the lure of treating the military primarily as a source of contracts, bases, and jobs for constituents. Additionally, the concern, or susceptibility to the charge, that action critical of the military is a threat to the national defense has dampened legislative efforts to curtail spending or change policies. When the Vietnam War turned sour and the Soviets and Chinese no longer seemed so aggressively intentioned as they once did, congressmen became more willing to take on the military.

If the New Deal seemed to spell executive triumph, the years since 1945 have seen Congress busily developing and utilizing its means of controlling the administration, having decided that if we are to have government by bureaucracy, then Congress will go where the action is. The gravest reservations about congressional procedures of control of administration center on the fragmentation of power within Congress and the consequent use of influence for personal, constituency, and interest group purposes.

EXECUTIVE CONTROL

The President's Committee on Administrative Management (1937) concluded its report—a classic statement of the case for presidential control of administration—with the hope that "the President will have effective managerial authority over the Executive Branch commensurate with his responsibility under the Constitution of the United States."[11] To facilitate executive management, it recommended: expansion of the White House staff; strengthened management arms for the President—budget, personnel, and national resources planning agencies; extension of the merit system; consolidation of all the many administrative agencies into twelve departments, with the President responsible, and granted authority, for carrying out administrative reorganizations; abolition of General Accounting Office authority to disallow expenditures; development of departmental managerial services to permit each Secretary to focus on policy, with the department managed by a career executive. Congress should determine policy, give the President the necessary authority and tools without imposing detailed administrative requirements, and hold him directly accountable for effective administration. Thus, the 1937 Committee argued what became the orthodox doctrine of American public administration: presidential control of administration is the way to vigorous, effective government in the service of democratic purposes.

Where presidential control works well, it can coordinate functions which are placed in different agencies but are interrelated in important ways, can secure certain economies and uniformities of operation, can distribute resources in accord with an overall comparison of costs and benefits that no particular agency can make with any objectivity, can generate political support for controversial programs, and can provide responsibility to the electorate in the form of a highly visible official accountable for governmental performance. But it has been hard to make good the theory. Rossiter described the President's role as manager of the administration as "the one major area of presidential activity in which his powers are simply not equal to his responsibilities"; Neustadt observed that "as between a President and his 'subordinates,' . . . real power is reciprocal and varies markedly with organization, subject matter, personality, and situation."[12] If the President is to succeed in his political goals, he must persuade the bureaucratic agencies to do his will, not theirs.

Authority as co-equal of the legislature is provided to the President by the Constitution; he is independently elected, participates in the lawmaking process, and is specifically charged with executing the laws and with making high-level appointments, with the advice and consent of the Senate. Additionally, he has institutional devices for gaining information and control, notably the Executive Office of the President and the executive budget. If executive control is to work, however, it requires personal sagacity in the chief executive, and energy and love of politics. Also, the President needs political support in Congress, party, and nation, which he can help create but which is partly beyond his control.

When a new President enters office, how can he effectively influence the bureaucracy? Experience in recent presidential transitions suggests he may: (1) gather information and ideas for the new administration, (2) select candidates for top-level jobs, (3) transmit policy directions to the bureaucracy, and (4) organize the presidency itself for these tasks.

(1) Information. The uninformed chief is used by subordinates. Pre- or postinaugural task force reports proposing policy lines, prepared by outside experts with or without participation by government officials, may lessen what otherwise may be the predominant influence exercised by agencies over the President's program formulation. Incoming officials can discuss memoranda provided by private individuals or organizations (such as the Brookings Institution) and can be briefed by departmental political and career executives. The CIA specifically may brief the incoming President and Vice-President on foreign and military affairs and procedures during the campaign, and in more detail after the election. Departments can provide office space, staff, and secretarial help to incoming executives before they formally enter office. The outgoing and incoming Presidents can meet for a briefing, which is publicized so as to set a tone for subordinates of the old administration. Presumably official briefings and memoranda may either indoctrinate incoming officials to agency policy preferences or may provide information needed by a new administration to challenge and change policy.

(2) Personnel. An inventory of key positions to be filled and potential appointees can be prepared before inauguration (even before the election), perhaps by an outside agency such as a management consultant firm. A talent hunt to secure political executives can be organized by associates of the new President. The

new administration will make key personnel changes when it enters office, but holdover political appointees may be used for a brief period to ease the transition.

(3) Policy. The new administration can prepare revised budgets, to reflect its policy preferences. It can assign an observer at the Office of Management and Budget from shortly after the election until inauguration day. The administration can announce policy changes to give clear guides to the bureaucracy and, once in office, can make organizational and procedural changes.

(4) The Presidency. The outgoing and incoming Presidents can designate officials to be in charge of the transition, and the Office of Management and Budget can coordinate preparations for the take-over. The new President can organize headquarters and staff for preinauguration preparations, covered by federal money. With this transition process now increasingly regularized, a new administration has a better chance to make a dent while it still has substantial energy, unity, and claim to a popular mandate.

Over the long haul the President has significant means of influencing the bureaucracy, four important aids to which are: (1) budget authority, (2) staff and auxiliary agencies, (3) reorganization authority, and (4) control of personnel.

(1) Budget authority is a primary means of prescribing what agencies shall do. Since the Budget and Accounting Act of 1921, which established the Bureau of the Budget and the presidential budget system, presidential control over the budget process has developed impressively. The early Budget Bureau emphasis was economy, and it still requires agencies to limit requests, but it now also establishes a kind of priority ranking in federal expenditures and stimulates good management. The President appoints the director without senatorial consent, and he is accountable directly to the chief executive. Though the President's budget is changed by Congress, the changes are generally relatively minor, so the executive budget is the most important influence on actual appropriations. Most budget decisions cannot be made by the President personally, but he will be involved in some overall decisions—how large a budget, the total for military spending or health programs—and some of the tough specifics; he can intervene where he wants. Department heads and lower officials also use the budget to control the scope and content of programs of their subordinate units; at lower levels, detail can be more effectively scrutinized. Budget power is basic to program control, though it is limited by the political strength of agencies and the constitutional position of Congress.

Budget reformers try to improve its use for analyzing program goals, costs, and accomplishments. In 1965 President Johnson announced adoption of a new "planning-programming-budgeting system" (PPBS) throughout the federal government. The system had been first introduced in the Defense Department, where Secretary McNamara and his civilian aides apparently exercised considerable control over the military by requiring agencies to spell out assumptions, projected achievements over time, alternatives, marginal gains from further expenditures, and the whole costs of a program over time, in precise, quantitative form. PPBS seeks to improve and to relate to each other the planning and budgeting processes, and it relies heavily on quantification and systematic analysis. Probably PPBS enthusiasts underestimated the pressure of politics as a limit to rationally planned action in government, the pervasive entry of value questions at every stage of decision, and the difficulty of quantification and prediction in areas other than hardware. The results thus far are modest, especially outside the Defense Department. But PPBS or the like can serve against simple inertia, bureaucratic autonomy, and bureau-committee-interest group control of agency programs. It can clarify, in some cases at least, costs, benefits, and alternatives. PPBS is now of great interest at state and local levels, but most jurisdictions may lack adequately trained personnel to make the system successful even in those operations to which it is best suited.

(2) The staff and auxiliary agencies of control that the President has at hand may be divided roughly between (a) his personal staff (brought in by him directly and personally as his aides, resigning when he leaves), who are grouped especially in the White House Office, and (b) more institutionalized staff, career men in agencies attached to the presidency, grouped especially in the Executive Office of the President, which includes the Office of Management and Budget (OMB), National Security Council, Central Intelligence Agency, and Council of Economic Advisers, among others.

Since 1939, when the Executive Office of the President was created and the Bureau of the Budget (now the Office of Management and Budget) transferred from Treasury to it, the OMB has become so influential that "without its help in both fiscal and administrative affairs the Presidency would long since have sunk without a trace."[13] The OMB's major contribution is budget preparation, which forces a justification of programs, but it has other control functions too. It has central clearance responsibility respecting agency legislative proposals, agency responses to requests from congressional committees for views on bills, and agency recommendations on bills passed by Congress and awaiting presidential signature or veto. The OMB must indicate whether the measure is in accord with the President's program. But the

President may have no program covering the question or, if he does, the line agencies are likely to know it as well as anyone. Where line agencies are in conflict, the Office tries through compromise to avoid a showdown. Apart from an institutional bias toward economy, it is in a disinterested position, able to urge coordination upon agencies with parallel or competing programs. In the Kennedy, Johnson, and Nixon administrations the White House staff (now the Domestic Council specifically) increasingly assumed the clearance function respecting major bills. Thus there has been a decline from the strong position of the 1950's in OMB power in the legislative realm, though the vast majority of bills (if not the most controversial ones) proposed by agencies are still handled by OMB.

President Nixon, by executive order in July 1970, transformed the Bureau of the Budget into the Office of Management and Budget and established the Domestic Council. The Council, chaired by the President, consists of most of the cabinet officers (but not Defense and State) and such other executive branch officials as the President designates. It is intended, with the help of a professional staff, to coordinate policy formation in a more consciously political way than would be appropriate to the career staff of the Office of Management and Budget. Ad hoc committees are to be used for much of the Council's work, drawing on staff support from the various agencies and even from outside government. In its first year a variety of interagency subcommittees were at work under the Council devising policy, notably respecting revenue-sharing and health programs. The Council was conceived as a domestic counterpart to the National Security Council, also located within the Executive Office of the President, whose "function is to advise the President with respect to the integration of domestic, foreign, and military policies relating to the national security."[14] Reports from both Councils to the President are confidential. However the Domestic Council has released various leaflets aimed at persuading the public and Congress to support presidential programs such as welfare reform, revenue sharing, environmental protection, and executive reorganization.

The transformed Office of Management and Budget oversees policy implementation as the President's chief managerial arm. It retains the old Budget Bureau functions, but the President has stated that preparation of the budget is no longer its dominant concern. He reported his need for management tools "particularly in program evaluation and coordination, improvement of Executive Branch organization, information and management systems, and development of executive talent."[15] He planned the new office to emphasize evaluation of program performance and to work on interagency and intergovernmental cooperation outside of Washington. The Domestic Council was to be concerned with "*what* we do," the President said, OMB with "*how* we do it."

President Nixon forecast that his plan would not weaken the cabinet departments, and his aides insisted it would give new policy responsibilities to cabinet secretaries. Observers were skeptical, however, viewing the whole as an effort to strengthen White House control at the expense of agency autonomy. When President Roosevelt sought to reorganize along the lines recommended in the 1937 report of his President's Committee on Administrative Management, he was condemned as a dictator and there was a grand political battle; times change, enabling a fairly conservative Republican administration to chant the litany of executive responsibility for formulation and execution of policy without even blushing.

Paralleling growth of the President's staff, a major development since 1933 has been the growth of the departmental secretary's staff. Formerly, almost everyone in a department was in one bureau or another, leaving the hapless secretary to control the lot with little aid. A larger, better personal and career staff for the secretary has helped in the battle against bureau autonomy, but the auxiliary agencies which have developed since the 1930's may also make the effort of the subordinate unit to carry on its program more difficult. For example, all federal departments and many subunits have a budget officer (since 1921) and personnel officer (since 1938). They assist the department in establishing control over subunits, but are also channels to the Office of Management and Budget and the Civil Service Commission, not simply servants of the department. Providing professional services and implementing uniformity in procedures, they help tie the various departments and agencies into a single federal administration. But such auxiliary agents threaten the necessary authority of line agencies, for their chief commitment may be not to program goals but to economy, regularity, or uniformity. Too often in American public administration we assure legality and propriety in hiring, purchasing, building, or the like, but prevent not only corruption but action prompt and vigorous enough to be effective. A personnel agency that rejects or takes months to approve appointment of someone the line official is anxious to set to work at once, or a purchasing unit that rejects a scientist's choice and prescribes for him what brand of microscope he must buy, is not likely to seem a very useful aid to the line officials. Tension between auxiliary and line agencies is probably incurable. But auxiliary agency controls (bred in distrust of line agencies) that lead in some state and local governments to a near paralysis can be rectified by placing more authority in line agencies to carry out the functions and spend the monies allotted to them.

(3) Authority to reorganize has been recognized by Congress

as a means of executive control over bureaucracy, but one which Congress shares. Minor reorganizations may be made by an executive official. Perhaps the action will be checked out with the congressional appropriations subcommittee. Congress itself creates, changes, and terminates agencies by statute, or authorizes reorganization, perhaps providing guidelines. Since 1932 Congress has enacted a series of statutes authorizing the President to reorganize the bureaucracy, though with varying provisions for nullification by Congress of the presidentially proposed plan, exemption of specific agencies, denial of authority to create and/or terminate agencies, and the term of the grant. Presidential actions under these statutes have included the creation of the Executive Office of the President in 1939 and the Department of Health, Education, and Welfare in 1953. President Nixon's first legislative request, which was granted, was for renewal of the lapsed authority to reorganize. Congress remains uneasy about giving the President this authority, caught between a sense of the President as a manager seeking rational administration and a perception of public administration as a political art. Limits in the reorganization statutes, congressional rejection of various presidential reorganization plans, and occasional refusals to extend the authority attest to this. An agency and its interest group and congressional allies will wage battle against a reorganization proposal which threatens agency autonomy or is seen in any way to have adverse policy implications. When the Nixon administration in 1971 proposed merging a variety of volunteer agencies into one, supporters of Volunteers in Service to America (Vista—the domestic Peace Corps) denounced the move as an administration effort to abolish a valuable but politically troublesome agency in the name of efficiency.

Reorganization is sometimes fostered by establishment of a special commission, the two Hoover Commissions being well-known examples. While the first Hoover Commission, in the late 1940's, had a spirit similar to the 1937 committee's acceptance of the key role of the President in managing the executive branch, the second (in the flush of Republican victory and anticipation of probusiness, antigovernment policies) reflected a conservative, antiexecutive perspective and entered boldly into policy questions. It sought to cut the scope of government, rather than simply to increase its competence. Well over half the states established reorganization commissions around 1949–1951. In general these supported the governor as manager of the administration, seeking to strengthen his office and buttress it with improved staff and auxiliary agencies. The effects were quite limited as a result of opposition from bureaucrats, interest groups, legislators, and party leaders—opposition reflecting both policy concerns and skepticism about the principle of unified state management under a strong chief executive.

(4) Control of personnel is a key means of executive influence on the bureaucracy. The hierarchical nature of bureaucracy permits a limited number of appointments at the top to have great influence on the tone of administration. Presidential control includes appointment and removal power, but operates under severe limits. Most civil servants have merit appointments and tenure. Persons whom the President does appoint are in most cases relatively unknown to him and not necessarily loyal to him or his party. Senatorial confirmation of appointments and the political need to please various wings of his party or important interests, or at least not infuriate them, sharply limit presidential appointment and removal. It is limited too by the difficulty of finding people who are politically acceptable, competent at governmental administration, and willing to take the job he can offer. The President will want to appoint department heads, regulatory commissioners, and some others, to give policy direction, and agency heads can make a limited number of political appointments and can shift some senior civil servants. The Civil Service Commission, though subject both to legislative influence through statutes and to pressure to act independently of the President, generally responds to presidential wishes concerning the governmental personnel system. He can act to make more effective the entire staffing of the bureaucracy, if his wits, will, and budget permit, or he can seriously impair its morale and functioning.

There is a kind of mutual influence and dependence between bureaucracy and chief executive, though control of a giant, politically fragmented administrative system is at best fitful and spotty. Thus, New York City's mayor "is confronted by a governmental organization too large, complex, specialized, and independent for one man to control in any but the most general fashion," while the Department of Health, Education, and Welfare is "an inherently unmanageable conglomerate of vaguely related social agencies."[16] Even each department or bureau may find its own subunits rebellious, concerned for their own purposes and health, difficult to coordinate.

But, if the President is beleaguered, pity the governors, far less equipped to control administration. Federal grants-in-aid specify state financial contributions, programs, personnel system, organization, and the like for a significant proportion of the state's activities, placing them under supervision of federal agencies. This lessens the authority of state and local chief executives, enhancing control by federal officials, usually career professionals at the daily working level. States vary significantly, but governors are likely to have less authority than the President to appoint chief officials (half the major administrative posts in state government are typically filled by election or by appointment by the legislature or by boards) or to reorganize. They have shorter terms, fewer staff and auxiliary agencies (despite recent improvements) and lack a centralized hierarchy of administrative agencies; some state agencies seem to be little islands, living from earmarked funds no one can touch—state highway departments exemplify this. Formal gubernatorial controls are most developed in the giant, urban states, while in the rural states informal political controls through jobs and expenditures count for more. The governor typically cannot rely on much political party support, and interest groups seem to be especially powerful in state politics. Though variety is great, "few governors have constitutional powers or managerial tools commonly associated with the concept of 'chief executive.' "[17] Even in states with a relatively strong governor, the effect of strengthening the chief executive has been "to give him about an even chance in competing with the legislature for influence over the courses of action taken by state administrators."[18]

ANTIPOLITICAL ORGANIZATION: COMMISSIONS AND CORPORATIONS

The authority of the President over the bureaucracy is based on a shared sense of his legitimate control through hierarchy. Subordinates recognize his legal right to give orders, his moral right to exert influence, even when they resist or subvert. The clearest cases of reservations about a hierarchical national executive are the independent regulatory commissions and government corporations. They are created to get outside the normal control through executive hierarchy. They are anointed with the lubricious promise to take politics out of governmental administration.

Independent regulatory commissions were created to regulate industry. When it was seen that private enterprise did not adequately protect the public and that the courts could not or would not do it, government regulation of banks, railroads, insurance companies, and the like was undertaken through administrative agencies. Viewing regulation as properly unpolitical, deliberative, expert, quasi-legislative and quasi-judicial, and not wanting to strengthen the chief executive, the legislature turned to bipartisan boards, outside the regular departments, with members appointed by the chief executive for long, overlapping terms. State commissions preceded the federal experience, which dates from establishment of the Interstate Commerce Commission in 1887. There are about seven to ten such national commissions, depending on definition. Regulation is also performed by cabinet departments, however, including the Agriculture Department's work on marketing and (in the Health, Education, and Welfare Department) the Food and Drug Administration's regulation of food and drug processing and labeling. The commissions are distinguished from cabinet agencies by their independence from the President, which led the 1937 President's Committee to condemn them as "a headless fourth branch of the government, a haphazard deposit of irresponsible agencies and uncoordinated powers," which "enjoy power without responsibility" but "leave the President with responsibility without power." The President's Advisory Council on Executive Organization in 1971 roundly criticized the performance of the commissions and urged that four new single-headed agencies be established, replacing commissions, to regulate transportation, power, securities, and trade practices.

The commissions have not performed with great distinction. First of all, they have lacked sufficient vigor and independence of the interests regulated really to serve the public interest. Cut off as they are from control by the President and from the political support he might bring them, from popular political influences, and from regular coordination with other agencies, even commissions which begin vigorously are likely to come to define success as acceptance by the industries they regulate. Of course, one cannot much blame commissions for lack of forcefulness if the President has chosen men reputed not to favor energetic regulation and has never indicated that he believes that the public interest requires toughness. (A newly appointed FCC member under President Eisenhower declared himself "one of the strongest free enterprise men on the commission," for "I don't believe in Government regulation.")[19] Adaptation to the demands of the regulated industry is common.

Secondly, commissions fail to formulate policy for the industries they regulate. They become involved in case-by-case decisions, preferring court-like procedure to pragmatic problem solving and policy formulation. Formal hearings may simply be ill-suited to such tasks as planning a rational network of air or train transportation. The policy failure of the commissions must be laid partly to Congress and the President for failing to elucidate policy toward particular areas (transportation, television, and so forth), to which the commissions might conform. But commissions too often fail to act, within the discretion granted them, to clarify policy.

In the third place, by segmenting and isolating different aspects of economic policy into separate agencies, commissions make more difficult the formation of national policy. Forms of organization which impede hierarchical control can exacerbate the difficulties of clarifying and coordinating policy. Commission members serve fixed terms and are not easily dismissed, and commission decisions are generally not subject to presidential approval or reversal. Presidents are not entirely without means of influencing commissions, including appointment, designation of the chairman of almost every commission, and informal provision of policy guidelines. But the direct control and accountability of the President's relation to a cabinet secretary is lacking. There is no simple authoritative means of coordinating the commissions with other governmental agencies involved in regulating the economy.

Finally, commission members have often been mediocre. The multi-member structure seems to call forth less concern for quality. Maybe the sense that the President is not directly accountable for the commissions lessens his concern for the performance of his appointees. And he cannot dismiss those who have performed badly.

In sum, the independence of the commissions has not proven demonstrably advantageous over regular departmental regulation. The most independent of all the commissions has been the ICC, oldest and proudest and least responsive to the President. Has it worked well? Behold the railroads.

Government corporations constitute another effort to lessen political control of governmental operations. Corporations were established especially during the depression of the 1930's and during World War II. They extend credit to private parties (loans for homes or agriculture), provide insurance (on bank deposits), carry on commercial activities (the Panama Canal Company), and deal with emergency production problems (rubber and tin during wartime). The reader will at least be familiar with the Tennessee Valley Authority and the Federal Deposit Insurance Corporation. The Nixon administration urged establishment of the Post Office as a corporation, as a more efficient and less political form, and 1970 legislation created a new United States Postal Service. The President appoints for long terms the board of directors (which sets rates) and a rate-recommending commission, employees continue as civil servants, the Service may sell bonds (to the Treasury if necessary), and there will be an annual subsidy for a good many years. Thus was the most political of departments, mired in patronage and bad management, to be transformed into a businesslike agency.

The justification for use of the corporation in place of a regular agency to carry on business activities is greater freedom from control, especially a financial flexibility which is deemed appropriate to business functions. The 1968 commission's report on the Post Office observed barriers to its efficient operation as a regular department: " . . . its funds are appropriated by Congress, its employees are part of Civil Service, its officials are subject to a host of laws and regulations governing financial administration, labor relations, procurement and purchase of transportation. . . . Congress sets postal rates and wages, governs Postmaster appointments and approves or rejects construction of individual post offices."[20] Government corporations, compared with ordinary government agencies, have had greater budgetary freedom, authority to borrow, and exemption from constricting auditing procedures, though since 1945 they really have been deprived of much of their former freedom from normal controls. Laws set and can change the degree of autonomy that government corporations in general or a particular corporation enjoys. A step beyond the corporation is establishment of agencies such as RAND to do work for the government through the contract device, free of normal salary, hiring, purchasing, appropriations, and similar limitations. Or government may simply choose to contract with or leave the field to established private business firms, rather than provide services itself. The Postal Organization Commission gave some thought to turning the Post Office—the most prominent outpost of the federal government in each community—into a private business, but stopped short of so drastic a reform.

Government corporations and similar devices for providing special autonomy may make coordinated policy more difficult to achieve. To the extent they are freed from legislative and executive control, they are little sovereigns. Furthermore, there is a tendency to judge them by the profit standard, without having established that, for example, government provision of electricity or of loans to small farmers or ghetto businessmen should always be done for profit. The question of how much freedom from political control a governmental agency should have is perennially difficult, as a member of a state university can testify. It takes just the right touch, stronger for some agencies, programs, or issues than others. One of the challenges to European democratic socialism has been how to get sufficient political control over a business so that nationalization brings concern for the public interest into the running of the business, yet not stifle it or lose the value of market competition and the price system. A persuasive case for government corporations or similar relatively autonomous agencies usually is a case against normal public administration as being excessively regulated by statutes, rules, auxiliary agency control, or political interference.

Do we trust our public administrators and politicians enough to relax some of the rules intended to prevent fiscal corruption and partisan spoils in our public administration? Do we need uniformity among agencies or can we encourage greater flexibility and discretion? Proponents of a function may well seek freedom for it if the system of controls over public agencies other than corporations is a stifling one. A 1967 panel recommended to New York's mayor that the city's hospitals and health services be operated by a public corporation to gain freedom from "the constraining regulations and procedures" of the city government.[21] Excessive political interference—"management by legislature," according to the 1968 presidential commission—led to decommissioning of the Post Office Department. When control goes too far, is abused, or petrifies, the response is a revolt against all controls. Is the future with heightened executive control through a clear line of command and competent staff and auxiliary agencies, or is it with decentralization of authority and much agency autonomy, in some cases under local citizen control, in others largely under self-control by bureaucratic professionals?

POLITICAL PARTIES AND PUBLIC ADMINISTRATION

Political parties are a necessary instrument of rule by the many. But when parties touch the civil service, they often enough bring butchers' hands to surgeons' work. Party officials are seldom entirely convinced of the virtues of a merit system, for they want to use the public bureaucracy for party and public purposes which the merit system obstructs. A patronage system is one of appointment to public office at least in part for reasons of party or factional affiliation or personal relationship; a merit system is one of appointment to public office by objective assessment of competence for the particular post or for a career in the system, with certain assurances of tenure and protection against compulsory partisan involvement. Parties may seek advantage from the public service through control of appointments and subsequent personnel actions, such as promotions; securing contributions of money and campaign service from public servants; and—if they have put their partisans in the strategic offices through election or appointment—control of specific administrative actions (a zoning decision, deposit of public funds, grant of a license, award of a contract).

Most federal civil servants today are under the merit system, either the regular classified service or a similar system operated by a particular agency such as TVA or the Public Health Service. They are hired for competence and, after a probationary period, enjoy essentially life tenure, though subject to economic cutbacks and agency terminations or dismissal for bad behavior. The rotation in office which President Jackson eloquently defended as a democratic virtue (" . . . I can not but believe that more is lost by the long continuance of men in office than is generally to be gained by their experience.")[22] had become by the late nineteenth century a crude instrument of the party or faction in power, not clearly related to the virtues of republican government. The landmark reform was the Pendleton Act of 1883, though only about a seventh of federal employees were initially covered by it. The act established a bipartisan Civil Service Commission and provided for open competitive examinations with appointment from among those earning the highest grades, a probationary period for new appointees, and protection for civil servants against pressure to make campaign contributions or engage in political activities. Over the years, Presidents have brought most of the federal service under merit, and the extent of federal patronage has shrunk, though with ups and downs. Sometimes a lively scandal led the President to place a group under merit, other times he thought well to extend merit tenure to his partisans who had been noncompetitively appointed.

There is not a great deal of worthwhile federal patronage. In recent changes of administration, there have been an estimated 5000–6500 patronage jobs which are of some attractiveness and importance, including probably 1000 or fewer significant policy-making leadership positions. Republicans in the 1950's estimated they could fill but one tenth of 1 percent of federal positions by patronage. Post Office and Justice were reputed to be especially patronage prone. Contemporary Presidents are more concerned to use appointments to secure able men who will support their policy and effectively administer it, and to trade appointments for legislative and political program support, than with running a large-scale partisan employment service. Purely partisan federal patronage is mainly in the field, where congressmen seek appointments for constituents, with an eye to elections. In Washington the political appointments relate more to personal loyalty, program commitment, administrative talent, except for a limited number of places for defeated congressmen and similar needy partisans. For a real patronage system, see the courts at every level of government. A 1964 study of the national party committees concluded of patronage that it is not of much significance to presidential or congressional politics. "Compared with the importance and consequences of patronage in some states like Pennsylvania and Massachusetts, the spoils system of the federal government is very small indeed."[23] At least for the national parties and presidential contests, patronage cannot maintain a party or bring it electoral success, the study concludes. Patronage is not a significant cause of either electoral success or administrative incompetence in the federal government today.

What of the states? Frank Sorauf argued in 1960 that the

triumph of merit over patronage, nearly complete at the federal level, was coming at other levels too, with far less need for patronage than there was only fifteen or twenty years earlier. The boss, the machine, and patronage were declining, as a politics of issues, national level focus, and mass media replaced that of personalism, locality, and patronage. The middle classes supply volunteers in response to issues and candidates, interest groups supply personnel and money. Patronage is dying because social conditions have changed. Yet remnants of patronage survive, mainly at the local level, more for the Democrats (dependent on the urban, poor, ethnic groups), more in some states than others, and of more importance to congressmen and governors than to the President.

State and local civil service varies from high quality professional systems to old-fashioned patronage operations. Pennsylvania has been described as having some 50,000 positions available to the party in power, having only 20 percent of state employees in the civil service system, with state employees assessed a portion of their salary to support the party. Massachusetts has a civil service system, but it is so politically riddled that a 1965 commission reported the service suffering from political interference and the "deep infiltration of patronage" and a special commission warned in 1967 that politicians and administrators must "restrain the exercise of power for personal or partisan ends" if the service is to do the job.[24] In California and Wisconsin, in contrast, patronage is negligible. Even in patronage states, the more important jobs are often filled with thought to merit, while the less important go for simple patronage. Much state and local administration before the New Deal was surprisingly amateur, and much still reflects and reinforces local politics.

Social Security Act amendments in 1939 required states to establish a merit system as a condition of receiving federal grants for employment security and public assistance programs, later extended to other federal programs. This federal intervention has been an important wedge for merit systems in the states. The Office of State Merit Systems, in the Department of Health, Education, and Welfare until transferred to the Civil Service Commission in 1971, is responsible for assuring that states comply with these merit requirements (federal aid has never been cut off under the provisions). The office provides assistance in the operation of a merit system, especially the examination process. Some tensions have recently arisen as the office has shifted from emphasis on strict impartiality toward urging state agencies receiving federal grants to recruit minority group members, with less emphasis on formal experience and objectivity.

The most striking fact about patronage in the United States is the diversity, reflecting the heterogeneity in our political history, culture, groups, and institutions. Some states have a formal merit system but cheat or bungle; some lack a formal system but develop customary merit within one-party politics; some have merit only for federal grant-in-aid programs; some are, like the federal government, basically merit with pockets of patronage; some are formally and truly merit throughout. Similarly for cities: some council-manager cities are strikingly pure merit, most large cities have a system, while lesser cities may limit civil service to police and fire departments. No wonder that of three reputable observers, one reports a decline in patronage during this century as a trend "at all governmental levels, national, state, and local"; another notes that "except in a handful of states," there are still "the persistent, scarcely yielding traditions of patronage"; while the third observes: "We have no accurate information as to the extent to which 'merit systems' have replaced patronage in the state administrative services."[25]

Patronage is defended as performing functions necessary to the political health of our society, serving (1) the party system, (2) the chief executive, and (3) the less privileged members of society.

(1) The party is necessary to modern political democracy, and patronage helps sustain the party by rewarding those who work for it. Jobs for humble party workers, defeated legislators, or candidates who at personal sacrifice made a race, secure the necessary efforts and strengthen loyalty and morale. It helps the party when prominent members of ethnic, religious, or other groups are given appointments that have symbolic value, just as a spot on the election ticket does. Appointments help deal with factional divisions within a party, soothing conflict. A payroll tax levied by a party or contributions based on promise of a job provide funds which free the party from total dependence on corporate wealth. Parties need jobs to give, it is argued.

(2) Patronage gives the chief executive a means of shaping the public service. When the governmental system itself is uncertain or threatened, as under Washington or Lincoln, patronage may be used to recruit men loyal to the regime. When the public service seems to be composed overwhelmingly of people from certain segments of the population, patronage may be used, as it was by Jefferson and Jackson, to build a more representative service. When merit civil service is routine and rigid, patronage (whether or not the appointees are party loyalists) may be used to recruit men who are vigorous, imaginative, and committed to administration programs. (A 1954 observer judged that, though the President showed relative respect for merit procedures, the quality and role

of the federal service were then declining, but "were moving rapidly upward during the days when President Roosevelt was apparently disregarding or even doing violence to civil service criteria.")[26] Often legislators unofficially choose the men who will fill positions; in such cases patronage can have great value to the chief executive as a resource in making a trade for legislative support for his program. If we remove patronage, it is argued, we deprive the chief executive of a key tool.

(3) Patronage is defended as providing opportunities for groups which cannot win jobs through civil service tests. Whose interest does merit or patronage serve? Merit reform has been interpreted as a presidential, centralizing weapon in a struggle against Congress and local party leaders. The post-Civil War civil service reform movement was attacked as a middle-class, business movement, and merit reform may be a tool of those who are hostile to politicians, to the common man, or to the current holders of power.

Now it is especially black Americans who argue that civil service tests discriminate unfairly, reflecting white, middle-class culture, and that education, experience, and nonarrest requirements hurt slum youths. Many governments used to maintain two separate registers of eligible candidates according to color. A 1969 report on employment of Negroes in state and local government found "frequent evidence that a merit system in itself does not guarantee equal opportunity for minority members."[27] The truth is a mixed verdict. Some jurisdictions with and some without a merit system have a relatively high proportion of black employees, others a relatively low proportion. The mechanics of merit can be manipulated to hurt Blacks or, alternatively, to help them into the service; the specifics of the civil service laws and especially the intentions of officials in the civil service and line agencies are crucial. Except where there was deliberate effort to exclude them, the merit system helped Negroes (and women) enter the federal civil service. Thus Catholics, Jews, and Negroes entered the New York City civil service in numbers and rose through objective examination systems at times when private corporations sniffed at their names and faces. Some jurisdictions are now experimenting with such modifications as awarding points for coming from a poverty area or limitation of employment in certain antipoverty jobs to local residents. But much antipoverty agency staffing is being done entirely outside the merit system (with occasional hints of personal and ethnic patronage), giving jobs to local ghetto-dwellers who might not meet formal civil service requirements. Whatever its impact on earlier disadvantaged groups, the strict merit system, emphasizing formal education and competitive examinations, is under attack as alien to the culture of the contemporary ghetto. Merit is middle class, the argument goes; don't ask poor people to love it.

Opponents of patronage see in it the use of public office for personal and partisan ends, with defects concerning (1) competence and integrity, (2) democratic politics, and (3) utility to parties.

(1) The merit system is the foundation of competence and integrity in the modern public service. Merit contributes to competence by recruiting through methods which discriminate according to ability and that alone, and by assuring reasonable tenure, for the employee is not turned out with each change of administration. Patronage makes unneeded jobs, provides unqualified workers for even modest jobs, promotes lack of respect for skill or good work, and makes the public service unattractive to young people of talent. It is presidents who fight for merit, while legislators and party officials, lacking responsibility for running a government, think party loyalty a sufficient recommendation. Our history testifies to the superior honesty of merit over patronage employees. During the rapid growth in highway building in the 1950's, for example, serious management failure and flagrant corruption were confined to "states traditionally practicing a high degree of political patronage."[28] If you prefer pirates to burghers, go with patronage.

(2) Patronage is not necessarily a democratic phenomenon; it has gone with all sorts of regimes, giving those in power some leverage over would-be and actual officeholders. Merit accords with the democratic spirit of equality and liberty, impartially judging men by objectively demonstrated ability. The nineteenth-century civil service reformers viewed the merit system as a political rather than an administrative reform, being concerned with clean politics rather than technical efficiency. In patronage politics the winning of elections turns on the hope of jobs and the use of jobholders, at the expense of serious concern with policies. Under merit, the jobholder is freed from bondage to the party and the citizen is freed from mistreatment by a public official seeking partisan or personal gain from the office. Politicians benefit too, being freed from job seekers' debilitative, distractive, corruptive pressure. Consider the flourishing period of federal patronage: in 1841 the President was "besieged and taken prisoner in the White House itself by a crowd of office seekers."[29]

(3) Parties do not need patronage. Some states manage without it, as do foreign democracies, and federal congressmen have very little. The decline of patronage has not led to decay of parties, which still vigorously compete in elections. What of evidence of a decline in party loyalty, an increase in independent voters? That

may reflect sophistication about the lack of both policy stands by the parties and party discipline among elected officials. It may reflect resentment against the policies and personalities of leading party figures in recent times. Party loyalty is based on tradition, candidates and officeholders, and issues, not jobs.

Elections today depend heavily on mass media campaigns rather than voters herded to the polls by party precinct workers. It was the unassimilated urban groups, economically insecure and lacking involvement in the political tradition and issues, with whom patronage was especially effective in rounding up large numbers of obedient voters. Immigrant assimilation, the vast growth in the middle class, general English literacy, universal education, and the impact of television outmode patronage as an election-winning device. (But what of Puerto Ricans and Mexican-Americans? What of Blacks in the northern cities?) As for campaign managers, persons with skills useful to modern electoral campaigns would hardly be attracted to the typical low-pay, no-tenure patronage job.

If the local, boss-controlled, tightly disciplined party faction is not what it was, the cities may be better governed for the change. The patronage boss in too many cases used his resources to maintain an organization whose primary end was to secure patronage, not to clarify public issues or to govern effectively. At best patronage serves local leaders in struggles against central leaders of broader vision. Policy patronage for top posts is sensible; employment patronage for a wide range of ordinary jobs is outmoded, argues the merit supporter.

Attitudes toward patronage often reflect one's membership in a group, a subculture, with some groups attached to and gaining from patronage while others identify with and use the merit system. There is in addition a sort of esthetics of patronage *vs.* merit. One side is repelled by the personalism of patronage, its lack of objectivity, its emphasis on secrecy, favors, friends and relatives, parties and elections, amateurism, and irregularity. The other takes kindly to these phenomena, but rejects the cold routine of merit system, diplomas and objective examinations, forms with fine print and little spaces to write your life, no man owing another a favor in return. Calling it an esthetic implies rules of craftsmanship for each system, though there is finally an element of taste. It should be possible to admire both the skillful use of patronage and the high-class merit system, whatever one's preference as a citizen in any particular instance.

A second aspect of the relation of civil servants to political parties is the question whether civil servants should participate in partisan politics. To protect civil servants from coercion by elective politicians or by politically appointed administrative superiors and to protect the citizenry from coercion by civil servants, federal and state governments have adopted statutes to keep civil servants out of partisan politics. The Pendleton Act of 1883 provided that no merit system civil servant may be threatened or punished by his superior for refusing to make a political contribution. A 1907 executive order forbade classified civil servants to take any "active part in political management or in political campaigns." The Hatch Act of 1939, reflecting congressional resentment at President Roosevelt's use of patronage and fear that the President would use public employees to build his own machine, strengthened the restrictions and extended them to nearly the entire federal service. The Civil Service Commission has interpreted such statutes and executive orders to forbid convention membership, service on party committees, helping to get out the vote, distributing campaign literature, and so forth, but to permit civil servants to attend party meetings, contribute money, vote, and the like. The second Hatch Act (1940) extended political prohibitions to state and local employees whose employment is financed from federal funds. By the late 1960's this covered more than 1.5 million of the approximately 8 million state and local government employees. The Civil Service Commission is responsible for enforcing antipolitical activities regulations on merit employees. It acts basically on complaints it receives (often from candidates who object to an administration's use of civil servants for politics). In the years 1939–1967 it instituted some 1000 cases, with Pennsylvania (184 federal and 37 state employees) having the distinction of accounting for over a fifth, while Illinois ran a poor second. In the decade 1957–1967 some 180 cases were instituted, resulting in twenty-two removals of federal employees and twenty-four of state employees, plus various more numerous suspensions from duty. Most states (forty-one by recent count) have some laws of their own limiting political activities of public employees (generally more lenient than the Hatch Act, but varying greatly); regulations are often unclear as to what is permitted, and one must guess that there is plenty of nonenforcement.

Political participation statutes may unduly limit freedom of political expression of civil servants. The courts have generally permitted the federal and state governments to impose severe restrictions on public employees, on the grounds that public employment is a privilege; if one does not like the terms imposed, one can work elsewhere. In the absence of clear guides to legitimate modes of political expression, the route generally followed is that federal employees "play it safe and resolve the uncertainties in favor of silence."[30] In 1966 a bipartisan commission was created by statute to study federal laws which limit or discourage participation by federal or state officials in political activities. The Commission on Political Activity of Government Personnel, in its 1968 report, recognized two objectives to be accommodated: encouragement of citizen participation in politics and assurance of integrity and impartiality in public administration. It was impressed to find that about half of a sample of federal employees questioned favored liberalizing the rules for political participation, some 30 percent answered that they had refrained from certain political activities because of restrictions, and about 40 percent predicted they would be more active if the law were changed. The Commission found virtually no evidence of federal supervisors putting pressure on subordinates for political contributions or campaign work or to persuade them how to vote. It recommended expanding the right to political activity, through clarifying and specifying what forms of political behavior are permitted and prohibited and strengthening the prohibition against coercion of public servants, so that truly voluntary activity can be more flexibly allowed. It would permit a federal employee to hold any local office which is not full-time and compensation for which is nominal—presumably excluding thereby most local offices of significance to political parties. The Commission split evenly on allowing federal employees to be party ward or precinct committeemen.

Democratic governments respond variously to the question of political participation by civil servants. The recent European tendency is toward liberalization. European civil servants generally can be candidates in local elections, and in some countries can run for parliament, subsequently resigning, receiving a leave of absence, or even serving in both jobs simultaneously. Britain has divided the service into three groups. Those holding the least significant positions are free for politics. A middle group must use discretion respecting participation, secure departmental approval for certain activities, and not run for Parliament. Those at the top of the service are barred from most national political activities. The U.S. Supreme Court in 1947 specifically refused to limit the Hatch Act prohibitions to holders of top policy-making positions (a mechanic in the mint had claimed the right to engage in politics), but new court or congressional action could make distinctions of the sort Parliament adopted. We hesitate for fear that public employees may use (or even seem to use) their positions for partisan purposes or that politicians may hide coercion of public employees behind "voluntary" participation. Should one who works for government have to barter his constitutional rights of political expression for a job? Courts have lately been less sure the answer is yes. The question is ripe for reconsideration.

CAREER AND POLITICAL EXECUTIVES

At the highest levels of governmental bureaucracy it is necessary to provide not only technical competence but policy control. The old question of the policy-administration relationship suffuses the problem of bureaucratic chiefs. Top executives can be recruited from career people already within an agency or transferred from other agencies, people knowledgeable in the agency's program area who transfer from nongovernmental careers, or people identified with the party or candidate who transfer from partisan activities or private life into agency management. At least a limited number of transfers, promotions, and retirements of career people and also appointments and dismissals of politically appointed noncareer figures will be used to change the tone of the administration when a new President enters. The simplest approach might be to bring in people committed to the party or President, but administrations have difficulty recruiting good political executives and keeping them. There is a scarcity of persons with the necessary political-administrative talents and a lack of any routinized training for such positions. The posts are unattractive to many already successful persons who fear political sniping and serious financial losses of salary, pension, or promotion in business. So civil servants are asked to fill many of the command slots.

The British higher civil service has strongly attracted American public administration scholars and governmental reformers as a model for our own. It has an "administrative class" of rigorously selected civil servants who typically enter fresh from the university into a career as managers of the service. They scrupulously serve either Labour or Conservative governments. They abstain from partisan identification or participation in legislative politics; rather, they manage the department and advise the Minister confidentially. The line between political officials in administration (who are few indeed—they are Members of Parliament) and administrative (career) officials is sharp and clear. The temptation is strong to achieve a similar clarity of politics-administration separation in the United States. However, critical observers of the British higher civil service question its social bias toward the upper classes, its political bias toward conservative attitudes, and its lack of innovative qualities. It is weak in technical specialists, social science knowledge (including economics), and professional managerial competence. Also criticized are its great centralization of authority in the Treasury Department and in departmental Permanent Secretaries, its substantial policy influence over busy and uninformed ministers who lack political staff aides, and its commitment to secrecy and a corporate spirit of mutual protection. Critical Britons agree that their civil servants have impressive integrity and personal decency, but scoff at the notion that theirs is the proper model for a modern higher civil service.

The second Hoover Commission's Task Force on Personnel and Civil Service (1955) emphasized the problem of top management personnel for the federal government and proposed a solution, stirring controversy which has still not subsided. It urged an increase in the number of political executives (high administrators chosen from outside the civil service, without merit examination selection procedures or career rights) and a new "senior civil service" under these political executives. The basic assumption of the Task Force was that the functions of political executives and of top career administrators are distinct and cannot properly be combined or interchanged. Political executives should represent the policies of the President, speak for the general public, and provide leadership in developing policy. Career executives should provide a reservoir of knowledge, managerial competence, and understanding of the peculiarities of governmental administration. The functions of the two types of officials have become mixed and confused, the Task Force complained.

It would have allotted some 755 positions to political executives and some 4000 to nonpolitical career executives. The political posts included heads or deputy or assistant heads of agencies or departments, heads of departmental information offices, and political aides to political executives. The career posts included administrative assistant secretaries, heads of budget and personnel offices, bureau and assistant bureau and division chiefs, and regional and district office directors. Generally career officials should head bureaus, political executives should manage departments. Political responsibility and authority should focus at the departmental level only; bureaus should be clearly subordinate units, whose problems and functions are mainly technical and administrative, not political. The Task Force asked that congressmen and others recognize the proposed distinctions and limit their political dealings to the departmental level, avoiding the normal congressional and interest group practice of dealing directly with bureaus. This change should be aided, it thought, through invigorating departmental control of subunits by a strengthened core of departmental political executives and improvements in management techniques.

In fact, the line between career and political functions has not been clear. Given the separation of powers and absence of party discipline, agencies often lack clear policy guidelines or firm political support. They must get their own political backing, which requires making policy that will win congressional and interest group support. The question is more one of our political, constitutional system than a technical one of organization of the civil service. Bureau chiefs and like positions exemplify the ambiguity of posts that are neither partisan nor purely nonpolitical. Partisan and interest group concerns affect some appointments, though the trend is toward professionalism in "a semipolitical category of federal executive positions" filled by men with professional competence, dependent on interest groups for support but not partisan, "who nevertheless engage actively in public and legislative advocacy of policies and programs within their special field of interest."[31] The line is yet further blurred because political appointees sometimes are blanketed into the career service and career appointees accept policy-political appointments. Some bureau and agency chief positions are limited in practice to persons in a particular profession (medicine, forestry, a scientific discipline) or even to a career professional rising in the agency itself. Of 531 jobs identified for the incoming President in 1952 as the most strategic posts in Washington, half were fully under civil service and fewer than a fourth were completely exempt from civil service protection. In new or more controversial programs, political considerations go lower down the appointment ladder. Late in an administration, as political executives leave and recruitment to a sinking or dull ship falters, career appointees are brought more and more into higher positions. No clear line between career and political executives exists in law, regulations, policy, or tradition.

Schedule C of the federal civil service institutionalized a mixed political-administrative service. When the Republicans entered in 1953 they found a scarcity of available patronage jobs, were dubious about the neutrality of the civil servants (most of whom had been appointed by and served only under Democrats, after all), and suspected that Democratic presidents, including the departing one, had been overgenerous in moving once partisan employees into the competitive service. By executive order President Eisenhower promptly created Schedule C, outside the regular civil service rules of appointment and tenure, for positions of a policy-forming or confidential nature. Often the incumbent was retained when a job was moved into C, and toward the end of the administration over 40 percent of holders of C jobs had come from the competitive service, fewer than 20 percent from outside government. Despite initial alarm and the ravenous hopes of some Republican politicians, Schedule C was no rape of the civil service. It provided flexible means by which an administration can move either civil servants or outsiders into top level positions or, a more questionable need, into lower level confidential positions (about a third of the somewhat more than one thousand Schedule C posts were at the clerical level). That the Civil Service Commission refused about half the agency requests for transfer of positions into C suggests how difficult the drawing of lines was.

The senior civil service recommended by the 1955 Hoover Commission's Task Force would have been a corps of "commissioned" senior civil servants, starting at about 1500 and growing to 3000. On the model of military or foreign service officers, they could be shifted from one job or place to another, with an obligation to serve where needed, and subject periodically to being "selected out" (fired). A special senior civil service board would be created to advise on placements. Throughout was the intention to broaden career patterns of top managers through easy movement among agencies, between Washington and field offices, and between staff and line work. Appointments and promotions in the service would be approved by the President, to lend dignity. Senior civil servants would be unpolitical; they would not defend policy before Congress or the public, as career officials often do now. These proposals raised the question: should the career system "move toward more promotion from within and more 'managed' executive selection, placement, and development; or should our present rather freewheeling system relying on individual motivation and choice, lateral entry, and utilization of all kinds of talent be maintained and strengthened?"[32]

A corps of interchangeable higher civil servants implies a single executive function. Neither the literature of organization theory nor actual governmental experience settles the question whether a man who can administer one function or agency can do as well elsewhere, but reflection and experience lead to a sense of limitations. Some kinds of specialists presumably can move more easily than line officials. As the Hoover Commission plan was developed by the Civil Service Commission subsequently, the possibility was introduced that certain areas would be designated within which a man would have a career broader than an agency career but narrower than a universal administrator career: research and development, insurance-retirement, natural resources, economic regulation, or management services. This still leaves the question of the importance of the knowledge and acquaintanceship that a person builds within a narrower area of operation. What scope is necessary for most higher civil servants to make their best contribution? Should public agricultural research be a career, or public research administration in general, or public administration as such, or research administration, or simply administration?

Many top federal government administrators have a background in a particular profession or program area within which they have gradually developed management experience and skill.

(A 1969 Civil Service Commission report placed nearly half the top executives in mathematics, science, medicine, and engineering.) Various recent studies of top civil servants show half or more making their entire federal career within a single agency, more than three fourths in no more than two agencies, with movement between bureaus (not to mention departments) uncommon after the first years of the career—5 percent changed bureaus after the first ten years in service, in one study. Those who change departments are likely to be experts in administration itself, especially in auxiliary and staff services, rather than persons committed to a particular program area or profession. More than half the executives in the 1969 report had experienced some career outside the federal service, but two thirds had twenty years or more of federal service behind them, only one twentieth four years or less. The report found that in the largest agencies between 62 and 94 percent of the top-level appointees came from within the agency. Senior civil servants do not move much between agencies. Reformers insist this is simply a defect of our current system.

The Hoover Commission largely accepted its Task Force's recommendations for a senior civil service, but a dissenting congressman warned: "A corps of career officials potentially 3000 strong with personal-rank status, ready to move from agency to agency, job to job, region to region, is somewhat fanciful."[33] Congressmen were concerned too that the special board might become a protective organization or have partisan overtones, or that the career executives might themselves gain control of the higher civil service. Maybe they retained their old fear of the President's gaining complete control of personnel at the expense of congressional influence—a recurring battle in this nation. They disliked what they felt were elitist overtones of the proposal and were concerned over adverse reaction that developed within the civil service. Civil service unions and top career officials opposed the plan, which seemed to threaten job security and traditional civil service organization and procedures, offering the menace of service wherever assigned and "selection out." For all its talk of a nonpolitical service, the plan invited political attention to these top officials, and the combination of nomination by agency head, approval by a special board with White House links, and appointment by the President (eventually with senatorial confirmation?) threatened politicization. The bad feeling between the early Eisenhower administration and the career civil servants whom Republicans had been denouncing heightened distrust of administration intentions.

Although President Eisenhower supported the senior civil service proposal, congressional opposition killed it. In a modest step toward a senior service, the Civil Service Commission in 1961 established a roster of career executives. An executive assignment system instituted by executive order in 1966 included a computerized inventory of top-level officials (over 30,000 by 1971), from which agency heads might draw names in filling some 10,000 top posts. In the spirit of the Hoover Commission, the system sought, according to the Civil Service Commission, "greater identification on the part of career executives with the overall purposes of the Government, rather than the single agencies or programs with which they may be associated at any given time," and a clear distinction between career and noncareer executive assignments, the former limited to management and professional duties, the latter involved in political policy making.[34]

Early in 1971 President Nixon recommended to Congress the establishment of a new Federal Executive Service. The Civil Service Commission, after a study of the existing executive manpower management system, had concluded that "the problems in the present system were too basic to be remedied by further patching, and that an entirely new start was needed."[35] The proposal presumes increased emphasis on use of talent files within an agency, a government-wide basis in making top appointments, managerial and professional development of executives, and effective executive appraisal; but these do not require new legislation. The proposed Federal Executive Service would include some 7000 persons. Rank would be in the person, not in the executive jobs, thus facilitating movement among jobs. For example, one would not have to put a GS-16 person into a GS-16 job, as at present. A Qualifications Board, with members appointed from within and outside the Federal Service, would have to approve a person's initial appointment as a career executive. Fifteen to twenty such boards of experts in various occupations would operate throughout the government, specialized by occupational areas. Career appointments would be for three-year terms, renewable by the agency. For those not reappointed, pension or a lower-rank job would be provided. An obligation to accept geographical transfer is involved in a career executive appointment. The Civil Service Commission, in collaboration with the Office of Management and Budget, would manage the system and would be an appeals body for career executives with grievances against the operation of the system. Present top-level personnel would be exempt from various provisions, and could retain their present position or enter the career service, as they preferred (a prudent provision, in view of staff reservations about earlier such plans).

There would be two categories of executives in President Nixon's proposal: career and noncareer, with at least 75 percent in the former group, which is approximately the current ratio and that of recent administrations. Noncareer executives would not be subject to the provisions described just above; they would be appointed and removed at the pleasure of the agency head. The Civil Service Commission explained: "New agency heads perceive that many of their key subordinates are 'locked in,' and that they have no control over who does what work."[36] Further, they "cannot appoint new men because they cannot easily establish new positions," and they lack confidence in their inherited subordinates, "especially where career employees have been placed into political jobs and political 'types' into career jobs." In order to build a unified, loyal management team, agency heads should be able to appoint a reasonable number of their own men, the Commission argues, but present personnel systems do not adequately permit this. Under the proposal—unlike earlier senior civil service plans —assignments will not be designated as career or noncareer, for the Commission now remarks on the difficulty of distinguishing the two types of jobs or distinguishing policy making from policy administration jobs. There will be career and noncareer executives, not positions. Each agency would have a ratio, authorized by the Civil Service Commission, of career to noncareer executives; this may vary among agencies, though the government-wide limit will be 25 percent noncareer. There would thus be "a mix of career and noncareer executives throughout the top organizational structures of agencies." With a more realistic view of the political-administrative mix in the executive function than the 1955 proposal, the quest for a better system of top federal executives continues.

Bureaucratic responsiveness might be encouraged through appointing politically active party loyalists to top administrative jobs, but our national parties are amorphous at best, anemic at worst. The largest single source of political executives (appointments to top-level positions which are not under civil service) during the Roosevelt, Truman, Eisenhower, and Kennedy administrations, according to a 1933–1961 analysis, was men who had had careers in public service, mostly in appointive positions. Nonelective government officials provided over one fifth of the Eisenhower political executives (in an administration entering after twenty years of Democratic administrations), and over two fifths of Truman political executives. Elective officials contributed but 2 to 5 percent of the political executives in these four administrations. Patronage appointments "via the intercession of congressmen and political party organizations in the recruitment process, have to a great extent atrophied, in part because secretaries and administrators largely supervise their own staffing efforts and often set greater store on relevant experience than on political dexterity."[37] Congressmen, party officials, and interest groups operate less to select candidates than to veto those who are objectionable. Political leaders of an administration use a good many career administrators in top posts, because they are convinced that they will bring loyalty to policy goals, administrative competence, and political tact.

A psychological study of 257 federal career and political executives found that the two groups are similar psychologically: both are cooperative sorts of people who tend to accept legitimate authority and have a high sense of purpose about their public service.[38] If the picture sketched by Warner and his associates is even roughly correct—and it makes sense—the federal executives are reliable, public-spirited subordinates, marked by professionalism, loyalty to the organization and superiors, and demands on themselves for integrity and service. (Of course people tend to identify what is good for their unit as also good for the whole organization.) This is not the sort of person who is likely to sabotage an administration for partisan reasons. The mixture of career administrators and outsiders in high executive posts which are not sharply differentiated as to their political or administrative character has been our pragmatic solution to the management of political bureaucracy. An administration can, in fact, have an impact on the bureaucracy through a very limited number of appointments, whether they be career or political people, if selection is made with an eye to personal competence and policy commitment, and if vigorous political leadership is provided from the very top.

INTEREST GROUPS, BUREAUCRACY, AND POLITICS

Political scientists in the 1950's and 1960's gave much attention and much credit to interest group organizations. Students of politics had seen how little the general public, even the comparatively interested and sophisticated public, can know about what is going on in each of the policy areas of government. National government today is not simply a bigger small town, where a good many people can reliably know the characters and the problems. Neither can the President or congressmen be familiar with and control the whole administration. Government is fragmented into policy areas, most of which are dominated by one or more bureaus, one or more congressional committees or subcommittees, and one or more organized interest groups.

In contrast to reformers' attacks on pressure groups as distorters of the public interest, students of interest groups have tended to argue that persons most involved in each segment of governmental policy properly have the most influence. The community is always disunited and there is no policy which serves all, the interest group theorists insisted. There is, thus, no public interest of all. The public interest exists less in the substance of particular policies (none of which is true or false) than in the peaceful process of winning citizens' consent to policies most directly affecting them, it is argued. The:e are safeguards against abuse of power by interest groups: each group will be opposed by others, governmental agencies will resist corruption, all participants are believers in the general rules of the game of American politics, group members do not give loyalty solely to one group and so will set limits to their organization's actions, and new groups will arise if important values are violated.

The interest group became the "realist's" substitute for public opinion, President, Congress, or courts as controller of the administration. The legislature balances competing interests, and it passes responsibility to and accepts solutions devised by the bureaucracy, so long as the major groups consent to the solutions. The traditional governmental mechanisms were seen as somewhat formal, legalistic, unpolitical, and far less sophisticated means of keeping administration responsive than interest group action. Satisfaction of the key groups in each policy area is as much as the general public can expect in most cases. Insistence on public officials' striving for the public interest opens a platonic Pandora's box, in which a government official decides what is good for everyone, interest group theorists warned, rather than letting people themselves express their goals and discontents through politics. Government has some responsibility for protecting the least vocal interests, presumably, but interest group theory typically views the public as highly organized and politically active in protecting its various interests—most groups are organized and influential, most interests are protected.

There is a good deal of truth in the interest group writings. Many governmental actions are determined largely by a kind of negotiation between bureau leaders, interest group leaders, and congressional committee leaders. What emerges is an equilibrium, in the sense that Congress, President, and the most powerful interests accept the solution. No one playing the game loses his political life from the decision, the stability of the political system is preserved, peace reigns among organized participants. Change is possible, but ordinarily is gradual, peaceful, and legal, reflecting consensus among active participants. Instead of solutions imposed by bureaucrats in the interstices of vague legislation, we have solutions hammered out by those most directly and deeply involved. Bureaucrats play a part, sometimes little more than passively accepting what the dominant interests and their congressional supporters demand, sometimes shaping a policy that all can live with. So much for the virtues of interest group theory. It has serious defects.

Enthusiastic interest group theorists have argued that there are simply group interests, no overall public interest, or that "a satisfactory criterion of the public interest is the preponderant acceptance of administrative action by politically influential groups."[39] Critics of interest group theory insist on the reality of the public interest—the validity of the concept—however difficult it is to know the correct policy to achieve it in a particular instance. We have common interests and long-run community interests that, in a lucid moment, might be perceived and respected even by one whose own immediate interests run in a contrary direction. Interest group organizations, founded and maintained to advance the interests of a limited group—and only some of their interests, usually economic—are ill suited to discerning and supporting action in the public interest. Interest group politics loses sight of the public interest, which involves substantive policies as well as peaceful procedures. The public interest seems to this author to mean justice to the various members of the community in the allocation of punishments and rewards, and the fostering of the best qualities in the citizens and the society. We can disagree as to what constitutes the public interest in a particular instance without rejecting the concept of the public interest as absurd.

Interest group politics is not likely to give all citizens a just, proportionate reward. Though there are some public-spirited organizations which seek no interest of their own, and which make real contributions to our politics, most politically active organizations are business connected, Schattschneider has shown.[40] Many subgroups of the community simply are not organized, many public needs are not fought for by an effective group. Even among the organized farmers or businessmen, the poorer are far less likely to be members of organizations. Organizations tend to be oligarchical, with the leadership comfortable, stable, and noncompetitive to a greater degree than governmental leadership. Organizations fail to represent a good many public needs and a good many poor people; they overemphasize the economic needs of middle- and upper-class groups. And because it is generally both in their interest and easier for political groups to block than to induce governmental action for change, the interest group system may inherently operate to preserve the status quo and to discourage shifts in policies and in distribution of rewards. Interest group politics penalizes the poor, the uneducated, the unorganized.

Bureaucrats may, from a sense of professionalism and public spirit, strive to achieve the public interest. But if they are left to live with organized groups without political supervision, they may find it impractical, politically dangerous, and finally unnecessary and uncivil to define the public interest in ways offensive to the most active, powerful, even cooperative participants.

Intervention in the bureaucracy by political officials can broaden the considerations affecting governmental decisions beyond the claims of organized, professionally represented, economically plush, continuously active interests. Formal politics—parties, elections, presidential action—tends to recede in interest group theory, becoming (in the case of legislation, for example) little more than the proclamation of outcomes determined by the play of interests. Yet the formal governmental institutions and electoral politics offer advantages in the search for the public interest, in action toward justice for the weak. Interest groups are not bound to talk or even to think in terms of the public interest, the just action, as fully as are those who act more publicly, especially in the role of public official. The difference is not in the inherent virtue of the different persons, but in their roles; the elective official is better placed to balance claims of special interests than are the special interests themselves. The claims of special interests are a legitimate part of politics and will have real influence even where President and Congress participate, but interests will lose their monopoly if decisions are forced into a wider arena. Their own definition of the good will be matched against the definitions of more groups and of comparatively disinterested officials.

One who argues that a broader politics than interest group politics will help the poor must recognize that presidential, congressional, and other politics may also be middle- and upper-class oriented. These classes produce money, votes, and political officeholders, in quantities disproportionate to their share of the population. This is one possible basis for arguing that bureaucrats should be left alone to discover a public interest more sympathetic to the needs of the poor. But in many policy areas, to leave the bureaucrats alone is to leave them under the watchful eye of the wolves. Typically those with a stake in a particular area will be the only active participants and will have too much commitment to an outcome to discern objectively what serves the public interest or the needs of the dispossessed. While the poor may well be less politically influential than the economically comfortable, at least in the politics of elections there is more chance for participation on equal terms, universal influence, and the power of numbers, than in the closed politics of interest group organization-congressional committee-governmental bureau policy making, where concentration of power, money, and expertise may predominate. A politician seeking power may appeal to the poor, the consumer, the Blacks, and so forth, if he sees the possibility of votes among these groups. American parties have been agents of expansion of the right to participate in politics. Organized interests will normally oppose expanding issues or participants, for they prefer the system as it operates at the moment, freezing out those not currently participating effectively and avoiding the raising of new issues. Interests of the weakest groups and the unobserved needs of the many will have to be pressed by government in one or another of its institutions. While it is tempting to think that bureaucrats can do that, and they will sometimes really try, the general rule is that cut off from political support, bureaucrats lose political battles.

Interest group theory has both descriptive and prescriptive evaluative elements. Much of the descriptive element is helpful, though it apparently exaggerates the extent to which all individuals and groups are organized and fit for political combat. One insight we can accept from interest group theorists is the important role of bureaucratic agencies in shaping governmental policies. The older notion of a sharp policy-administration distinction disappears. Bureaus influence the President's proposals, and the action of Congress in legislating and appropriating, and the shape of the program as it actually develops from abstract legislative language into action. Also interest group theory avoids some of the more bizarre warnings against the bureaucracy as a ruling class. Bureaucrats are important to policy making not as a unified new class, but in more or less segmented policy areas, and some bureaucrats infinitely more so than others. They are neither homogeneous nor unified.

There is no gain from exhorting bureaucrats to stop being influential. What can be asked is that students of politics not assume that bureaus, interest groups, and congressional subcommittees should be left alone to make policy in a particular area, on the assumption that the policy which emerges is in the public good. Policy intervention by high-level officials, career or political, up to the President, should be seen as legitimate and necessary, though of course not in every case substantively wise. Involvement by congressmen who have not become part of the policy-making consortium in a particular field can be helpful in revealing and influencing what would otherwise be left to the small policy-making group. The press is also crucial in revealing what is going on; good reporting opens up the little policy groups to larger considerations, to outside criticism. Partisan disagreement on issues helps expose assumptions, operations, and goals. These opening-up processes of bringing new considerations to policy making, including spokesmen for groups normally excluded, are necessary to administration in the public interest.

Political control is necessary. Bureaucrats are not especially evil and cannot be made powerless. They can and must supply continuous professional concern with policy areas, but should not be left to themselves or to pressure groups. That blocks the democratic process of popular influence, distorts the policies of government in ways not reflective of the good of the whole community. Bureaucrats, elective officials, interest group leaders, the press, and others make policy contributions, and probably bureaucrats more than most. But properly the final decision is in the hands of elective politicians who, however crudely and with whatever failures of mechanism and purpose, represent the entire community and strive for the public interest.

Hearings of the Senate Subcommittee on Constitutional Rights in 1971 raised the specter of uncontrolled surveillance of citizens by government agencies, including the Army.[41] Information gathered may be used against the citizen by the collecting agency or possibly by other agencies, politicians, the press, or business firms to whom the information may leak. The very presence of the surveillance and information filing system, with computer aid to facilitate rapid accessibility of large amounts of information, may lessen the spirit of free, vigorous political expression. (Loyalty investigators often seem to have narrow conceptions of what are "legitimate" views.) Surveillance might potentially serve governmental repression. If the legislative and executive politicians support and use the snooping of the bureaucrats, freedom is threatened; if they respond to the threat to constitutional rights, the politicians can rein in the bureaucrats. As long as the Attorney General of the United States is opposed to legislation to curb the government's information-gathering activities, he urges reliance on precisely what seems to have failed—"self-discipline on the part of the executive branch."[42] But the failure is not simply one of bureaucrats—it is a failure of elective and appointive political officials. Mechanisms of control are needed, but alone they never save freedom; the good character and goals of the political participants are essential. The value of political control of government bureaucracy depends finally on the quality of the political officials.

CHAPTER FOUR

Beyond Political Bureaucracy?

It is extraordinarily difficult for a student of politics to know what is simply part of a current bubbling and what signifies a long-range basic trend. Historians are very good at that, picking out centuries later the document or action that signaled great change, but political scientists are challenged to hear a sigh in the midst of a storm. (1) Does the future hold the deterioration of constitutional democratic government with a responsible bureaucracy into an administrative state ruled by bureaucrats? (2) Or does the future hold essentially a continuance of government in which bureaucrats play a significant role but are subject to control by law and politics? (3) Or does it hold the promise of more power for and better service to the poor and the Blacks? Will there be a change in the composition of governmental bureaucracy toward one significantly more representative of the public served? Will there be advocacy administration in which governmental bureaucrats effectively speak for the needy? Will there be citizen participation through more effective advisory committees, community action programs governed by local citizen boards, or decentralization of cities into neighborhood government? (4) Does the future hold a new, democratic form of large-scale organization, more equalitarian and dignifying for its members than current bureaucracy?

THE FUTURE: RESPONSIBLE GOVERNMENT OR BUREAUCRATIC RULE

Many students of politics see us marching toward the bureaucratic state, the administrative rather than the political state. Real power, actual decision making is centered in the bureaucracy. The need for continuity, professional expertise, and authority—the very virtues which Weber attributed to bureaucracy as the characteristic phenomenon of the twentieth century—seems to rule out a decisive role for politicians. They will orate, they will have their occasional, temporary, well-publicized triumphs, but they will not govern. Bureaucrats will do that. Neither legislators nor the chief executive and his minions nor the stern courts can really control the power of the bureaucrats to govern, probably in lawful and decent fashion, but still to govern us. Bureaucratic government behind democratic rituals. If we are not there yet, are not all the signs pointing that way—toward more professionalism and reliance on self-control rather than control by elected officials, decline of patronage even at state and local levels, growth in size and complexity of government at every level, decisions made secretly in committee, slender public respect or self-respect for legislators and all elective officeholders? Whatever their errors of detail or their simplifications, were Weber and Burnham and all who intuited that we are living in or moving toward an administrative age really wrong?

Yet one need not be quite so pessimistic. Accepting a good deal of the argument about the growth and importance of bureaucracy, one may challenge the assumption that it is uncontrollable. There are a good many housewives, factory workers, and farmers in this world, and we can testify to their crucial role, but are they really the power elite? So for bureaucrats. Of course we need them but perhaps we can control them, for the performance of a necessary social function does not automatically bring the exercise of great political power. Let us concede that in many small matters and occasional large ones, bureaucrats may quietly decide. The preceding chapters suggest, however, ways in which the bureaucrats can be and are challenged and controlled. Two traditional forms of control of bureaucracy are basic: control by the rule of law (providing impersonal objectivity and constitutional continuity and justice) and control by politicians (providing democratic responsiveness and adaptation to change). Are these sufficient or can they be improved to sufficiency? Can other forms consonant with constitutional democracy supplement or supplant them: professional self-control or community control of administration?

The rule of law is not a mere formality. Careful procedures within agencies can usefully limit bureaucratic discretion and assure the citizen a fair decision; an American public official is no oriental potentate. The courts exist for important abuses, and we are learning to use them to help the poor better than we have in the past. Administrative units of investigation or grievance enable bureaucrats to restrict other bureaucrats. We may experiment with specialized administrative courts and with ombudsmen-type officials. The steady, cool, even-handed influence of the objective rule of law is a guarantee deeply appreciated by any freedom-loving person who has lived under a totalitarian system. To take this for granted is like taking for granted a bed of peonies or a kindly friend, simply because they speak softly.

Political controls are also not so puny as critics claim. If parties seem to be in disrepair, individual politicians and interest groups flourish. If Congress as a whole flounders about, subcommittees quietly hone their weapons of control. If chief executives seem hopelessly distracted by the range of their responsibilities, when they do move on a particular front they bring to bear much authority over bureaucrats. Politics permeates our governmental bureaucracies; if a good deal of sheer technical competence leaks out through the political-administrative seams, much popular influence seeps in. It is a highly political bureaucracy.

Nor is self-limitation in use of power to be dismissed. Our bureaucrats represent no special caste, they embody much variety —geographic, ethnic, social-economic class, educational and career background. The identification with career and profession and the relative safety of most bureaucrats from dismissal or punishment by politically powerful figures provide a perspective emphasizing the doing of the job well and justly. Even the military and the CIA, which seem to possess substantial power that is hard to control, really give no evidence of desire to subvert our political system. Our generals want bigger armies, they occasionally deceive others and as often deceive themselves, and sometimes appear too ready to deal with international problems by military means, but they do seem quite docile before political control, ready to follow orders from the President, committed to constitutional democracy. Our bureaucrats, being not much different from the rest of us, believe in public administration under the control of politics and law, so they do not try to subvert those controls—except, presumably, occasionally.

In sum, one can reasonably argue that the future of American public administration is seen clearly in the present. The bureaucracy will be a major participant in our governing process, both in formulating and in carrying out policy. But this will be done under controls. The bureaucrats will have no monopoly of power and will not make the major choices of direction for our society. In large measure they will carry out policies whose general outlines at least are approved by political officials, though their task will require energy, judgment, political sensitivity, and professional competence. Bureaucrats are much more than merely clerical, but perhaps Weber was right to emphasize the honor-seeking of the politician and the docility of the bureaucrat. The future may lie with more professionalism, improvements in our ways of enforcing the rule of law, continued formal and informal political controls, a bureaucracy increasingly representative of the whole society. May not responsibility be achieved through bureaucracy which is controlled and representative?

Those who see present trends culminating in a more professionalized civil service may rejoice at the competence and virtue of bureaucrats, as contrasted with politicians, or despair at administrative tyranny. Moderate optimists see controlled bureaucracy as a major participant in governing, but not the chief. Some among the hopeful emphasize the mechanics of control, the importance of courts and legislative committees and hierarchy, while others stress self-control and representativeness within a context of responsiveness to legitimate authority. Joseph Tussman, in a book not primarily concerned with public administration, seeks to synthesize control and self-control in a conception of the public official as agent.[1] He likens the agent to one who, faithfully interpreting the will of another, discovers a not fully articulated will. Analogous is the architect who builds the house you want, even though you cannot fully describe it. The translator of poetry might serve as an example, for the task requires much talent and learning, originality and daring; yet if it is done truly it requires submission to the will of the original poet. The good bureaucrat in a constitutional democracy may have to do that at times—go off on his own, yet truly seek to do what he understands was asked of him by those who could not fully know how to achieve their ends. Have you ever done something for a friend in just the way you think he would have wanted you to, could he have been there to see the problems which had arisen and were not accounted for in his original directions? Tussman's ideal may sound too abstract or ambiguous, but it is a challenging conception of the bureaucrat's role when he has to act beyond clear directions. Some mixture of explicit, deliberate external controls and this kind of self-control may be a realistic goal.

THE BUREAUCRATIC LIFE

Objections to governmental bureaucracy and hopes to replace it with a better system reflect both reluctance to being a bureaucrat and hostility to being ruled by bureaucrats. Frequent objection by young people to the bureaucratic aspects of large educational institutions appears to be but one manifestation of a widespread resentment against bureaucratization. The innocent IBM card has become a symbol of oppression. An existentialist cry for freedom, to be truly a person making one's own life, resounds through our society. Pity him to whom the mermaids have not sung. Of the philosophers we say nothing; we observe that the young people feel in their bones at least a vulgate version of Buber and Marcel demanding that man not give himself entirely to bureaucracy, that students are tasting and praising Eastern and other antirationalist traditions. But the condemnation of bureaucracy is as old as the celebration of bureaucracy, for Weber's nonacademic writings movingly warned against the soulless official as the typical modern man.

To respond to this plea for a life free of bureaucracy, might we alter bureaucracy so that its members find dignity in their work? For the moment let us turn to the bureaucrats themselves, not the citizens outside, subject to the governmental bureaucracy. At this point we will consider matter-of-fact reforms—civil service rules and unions—later, more radical change. Government employment has frequently been robbed of dignity by the concept that holding a government job is a privilege, not a right, and therefore the government can attach any terms to the employment which courts will accept as reasonable. The doctrine of the sovereignty of government strengthens the idea that the employee has no rights, the employer has all. Actions based on this theory of public employment as a privilege have included prohibitions against collective employee action in labor relations, prohibitions against political participation, and mean-spirited loyalty-security programs in the 1950's.

The loyalty-security programs of the post-World War II era had a significant debilitating impact upon the public service. Carried out without the sort of procedural guarantees used in the courts or in careful administrative regulatory agencies and in a climate of harsh publicity and great hostility to political or personal unorthodoxy (for example, homosexuals became a special target for security searches), the programs discouraged able people from entering the public service, caused the discharge of others from it, and frightened into bland caution a good many public employees, to the detriment of the public service. With the softening of the Cold War, the termination of the political career of Senator Joseph McCarthy and some other right-wing politicians, and court actions striking various loyalty oaths as unconstitutional (in 1969 the Federal Civil Service Commission dropped the loyalty oath requirement for new employees), the issue has ceased being of major consequence to the public service, at least for the time being. It may still be true that various able young people who have engaged in radical activities either are denied government jobs or, just as likely, assume that they would be so do not apply. And the Justice Department and Civil Service Commission, expressing concern over membership in "terrorist revolutionary" organizations, have been considering tightening security requirements for federal employees.

When objections are raised to the theory that public employment is a privilege to which a government may attach any restrictions it wishes, the ready answer, and one which the courts have frequently accepted, is that there is a constitutional right to political participation, but not to government employment, so a choice must be made. In the 1950's for example, the courts would not support the claim of constitutional rights to protect civil servants from administrative dismissal in loyalty-security cases. A case can be made for limiting government employees' rights to partisan participation, to strike, or to hold a sensitive job without a security check. But we can hope that a pragmatic sense of the needs in each case—what would be the practical consequences of granting particular rights to a particular group of employees—is replacing a vague claim of illimitable governmental power. In the 1960's the Supreme Court did question the claim that public employment may be conditioned on surrendering constitutional rights. In areas such as political expression, labor relations, and loyalty-security, a more analytical and balanced approach to government's needs and employees' rights does seem to be developing.

Statutes or civil service rules provide guarantees against various arbitrary actions, such as racially discriminatory hiring or dismissal without cause, so the civil servant is hardly at the mercy of hierarchical superiors. Protections against disciplinary dismissals or lesser penalties are typically very strong in civil service systems; the firing of an employee who has survived the probationary period can be accomplished, but it takes a determined boss with a plausible case to go through the necessary proceedings.

Unionization, the least romantic reform today, provides important additional guarantees against abuse by superior officials or neglect by the legislature and elected executive. An act of 1912 guarantees the right of federal employees to organize and to affiliate with outside labor unions. A 1962 executive order, (which set an example important at state and local levels as well), affirmed the right to join unions and the right of unions to be consulted and to negotiate agreements with agency management on working conditions. Government employee unions were the fastest growing component of organized labor in the 1960's and have nearly a tenth of total union membership. States and most medium and large cities have one or more public employee unions. Over two and one half million state and local employees are organized into professional associations (such as the National Education Association); craft unions (such as the Metal Trades Councils); and industrial unions, which include varied occupations within a department or governmental jurisdiction (especially the American Federation of State, County, and Municipal Employees, with over 400,000 members). About a million federal employees were in unions (largely affiliated with the AFL-CIO) in 1969. Blue-collar workers in the postal service (whose rank and file employees are almost totally unionized) and Defense Department have been especially ready to join. More than half of all federal civil servants are represented by, whether or not they are members of, unions with exclusive recognition rights in federal agencies. In public employment as in private, unionization tempers the authority of those at higher levels and contributes economic strength and job security to those at the bottom.

Occasional strikes in big cities—especially of employees such as teachers, policemen, firemen, transit workers, or sanitation men, whose work directly touches many citizens—arouse great anxiety and get much publicity. The language of some unions has become militant. But the tradition thus far has been against strikes of public employees, and, with rather limited exceptions, strikes have not been a major problem. Strikes of private employees may cause more inconvenience or hardship than those of public employees. The rate of time lost due to strikes in the 1958–1961 period was over 250 times as great in private employment as in government. Federal government strikes are rare (postal employees did strike in 1970, however), and strikes of local public employees usually are brief affairs, largely spontaneous. They usually deal with economic issues, though sometimes with problems of union recognition or working conditions. While both federal law, and court decisions or statutes in a good many states prohibit strikes by government employees, striking employees are usually taken back without punishment, as a practical response to a labor relations problem.

What is the strike toll in a single year? In 1970 there were, among others, strikes or "sick-outs" (large-scale absenteeism with false claims to illness) by the following public employees: (1) postal employees were out for about a week, apparently the first time in our national history for this group, concerning wage claims mixed with problems of legislative politics and the presidential plan to convert the postal service to a public corporation; over 200,000 employees were out at one time and reservists and National Guard troops were called out to help with the mail; (2) federal air-traffic controllers were out over pay and working conditions and equipment, in a sick-out by perhaps 15 percent of the controllers but concentrated heavily in particular cities, which disrupted normal air service and lasted about three weeks; it was preceded by a six-week slowdown in 1968 and a three-day sick-out in 1969; (3) sanitation employees were out in Cincinnati, Philadelphia, Seattle, and Tacoma; (4) various city employees in San Francisco and Atlanta; (5) police in Pittsburgh; and (6) teachers in Newark, Jersey City, and other Jersey communities, Philadelphia and Scranton, various Connecticut cities including Hartford, New Haven, and small cities and towns, Toledo, Hammond and Gary, East St. Louis, San Francisco and Los Angeles, Butte, and Kentucky and Michigan (state-wide). Some were brief flare-ups, some involved only part of the employee group, others were comparatively long and bitter. Many must have involved hardship or discomfort, and teachers' strikes were too widespread not to cause concern. Yet in total they seem neither an alarming sign of a country coming apart at the seams nor necessarily a graver problem than strikes in the private sector. A wage dispute that causes a few days' walk-out is generally easy to live with (even with police and firemen, supervisory personnel generally do what is crucial). A prolonged strike of school teachers involving questions of race relations and community control of schools, as in New York City in 1968, however, both reflects and exacerbates basic social problems whose resolution is a primary public concern.

Some unions or associations (notably social workers, teachers, and black policemen) have been taking public or bargaining positions on policy questions lately, for example, on client rights, on appropriations adequate to support a vigorous program, and on maximum workloads to permit good service to clients. This is closely related to good working conditions for themselves, but unlike the more traditional employee demands. Government employee unions, like other economically based associations, have often protected their own members' interests without much evidence of concern for the good of the clientele served. It is possible that socially aware government employee associations will increasingly try to serve member needs and clientele needs simultaneously, but it is unlikely that the interests of both will always be identical. Unions will probably continue primarily to add to the security and dignity of the employees, but not to lessen our society's bureaucratic spirit, for bureaucracy is quite compatible with the sort of security and employee rights that unions seek. Public employee unions afford useful protections to their members, but they sometimes press for constraints against openness of the bureaucracy, against political controls to reshape policy, and against citizen demands for influence on the bureaucracy. Struggles involving the public school teachers' union in New York City against community groups seeking to influence the schools have dramatized the claims and challenges to professionalism and career rights. Apart from any question of simple self-interest, a legitimate concern for the dignity of public employment and for disinterested, professionally sound public service may run counter to efforts at popular control of government.

Beyond the protections of civil service rules and unions, what can be done to ameliorate the bureaucratic life? Perhaps methods of making jobs more complex, and therefore more interesting and demanding, can be devised for government bureaucrats; political participation rights might be extended, and the doctrine of government employment as a privilege might be qualified. Perhaps some kind of ombudsman within the agency or for all employees in a jurisdiction will be common. Perhaps new forms of consultation with employees by higher officials may be worked out. Perhaps employees will win a kind of elective representation in agency governance that we can scarcely describe at this point. Some people see self-coordination by experts replacing the purely administrative line of command, but the actual potentialities of self-coordination are uncertain. The obvious problem is that attempts to change the authority system of bureaucracy may run into the need for hierarchy, if bureaucracy is to be effective and responsible. These next decades may well see many attempts to lessen the authority system within bureaucracy. If nothing else, a relatively equalitarian style—already characteristic of American bureaucracies as compared with those of most other times and places—will likely mark the governmental bureaucracy of the late twentieth century.

REPRESENTATIVE BUREAUCRACY

The history of the public service in America is not a straight-line development from patronage to merit system, but we can fairly say that the twentieth century has been marked by a substantial triumph for the merit system of nonpolitical management of civil service, with recruitment based on objective evaluation of candidates' qualifications. The personal element increasingly disappears from appointment to the civil service. One could easily be led to predict that even the most reluctant and benighted localities would join the movement, that testing or other objective evaluation of qualifications would everywhere predominate in hiring and promoting. There is now a strong countermovement, however, which protests that the merit system has produced an unrepresentative public bureaucracy, and that ethnic considerations should be taken into account. The point of concern may be the whole service, particular agencies, or more particularly the higher civil service.

The problem is not limited to the United States. In nations freed of colonial rule after World War II, one encountered "Africanization" policies. In the case of "Nigerianization" this meant the accelerated replacement of higher-level European officials with native officials, along with concern to give adequate representation in top civil service posts to the northern region, large and populous but less urban, westernized, and educated than the south. In Switzerland civil service appointments are based in part on preserving a certain balance between elements of the population, paying attention to the canton, political party, religion, and language (French or German) of those appointed. In Western Europe the problem of representativeness of the higher ranks has been raised primarily concerning economic class—a recent examination of the best posts in the French civil service found less than 1 percent of the incumbents from families of industrial workers or agricultural laborers. The composition of the civil service as a whole or of the choice higher posts reflects inequalities in the society, especially differences in access to and cultural affinity for higher education. Along with efforts to open higher education more widely, since World War II Europeans have tried to ease promotion from lower to upper civil service "classes"; admission to these classes is closely related to the educational level completed.

In the United States, traditionally one who started at the bottom encountered no such formal barriers to promotion to top jobs as European civil service classes imposed, and a good many federal officials have risen from humble starts. This openness has been a real virtue of the American civil service. American federal executives are surely as a group more male, white, and educated than the population in general, but there is no tradition of a caste or elite quality about our top civil servants. Though federal executives come disproportionately from families of business executives and professional men, the fathers of the career service executives in a recent major study were in nearly one fourth of the cases laborers (mostly skilled workers or mechanics, it is true). This research on business and government executives led to the conclusion that "American society is not becoming more caste-like."[2] Rather, our society is more open than it used to be, with more opportunity for men to gain access to education and use it to rise socially. Inherited social position still helps, but less than it did a generation ago. Bureaucracy respects and rewards ability impartially, to the extent that ability can be demonstrated in ways that the society judges valid.

Compared with European civil services, we have granted less prestige to the career officials, lacked a clear higher civil service, and had opportunities to rise to the top of the service far more open to those without elite university education. Therefore, the question of the social composition of the higher civil service has been of less interest here than in European nations. And we have lacked the experience known to other continents of a professionalized European civil service administering a non-European state. It has taken the black revolution and the women's liberation movement in America to bring the question of social composition of the civil service into sharp focus.

What of the "minority" that is not a minority?[3] In 1971, according to an unofficial study, 1.6 percent of the top (nearly 4000) policy-level federal jobs were held by women. The Civil Service Commission has established a Federal Women's Program (directed by a woman) and is endeavoring to prevent discrimination against women. It is insisting on the right of women to be considered for almost all jobs. One of its major areas of concern seems to have been the right of women to work in security guard-law enforcement type jobs traditionally considered man's work. The Commission condemns "preconceived attitudes" about the ability of persons of one sex to perform better on the job than those of the other. In the spirit of greater sensitivity to women's rights, the State Department in 1971 adopted a policy against asking women candidates for Foreign Service jobs whether they are or intend to be married (affirmative answers may have hurt opportunities for employment in the past) and to permit a woman employee who marries abroad to continue her career. Despite such beginnings, the best jobs in the civil service, as in other American institutions, are filled predominantly by males.

Is the civil service open to Blacks? In November 1969 almost one fifth of federal employees were minority group members, including 15 percent Negroes.[4] However, minority group employees constituted some 55 percent of those paid under $5,500 per year, about 8 percent of those paid $10,000 to $18,000, and under 4 percent of those paid more than that. Minority group employees in a mid–1970 count constituted a diminishing proportion of each of six ascending groupings of pay grades: 27 percent of employees in grades 1–4, 17 percent of grades 5–8, and so on until 2 percent of the top grades, 16–18. A 1966 study showed that Negroes constituted a significantly greater share of wage board (industrial type) and postal employees than of the white-collar pay group. Even among wage board employees they constituted over 43 percent of those earning below $4,500 per annum but under 3 percent of those earning over $8,000 yearly. Though the Negro proportion in top jobs is still low, the proportions in the highest quartile of each major pay system grew strikingly from 1962 to 1966, and the growth was not related to larger numbers or percentages of Negroes in the federal service. Variation among departments in employment of Negroes and in proportion at higher grades is substantial—while Interior and Agriculture had in November 1969 between 5 and 6 percent Negroes, HEW and Labor had over 20 percent and over 26 percent respectively. In sum, federal employment is genuinely open to nonwhites; nonwhites are still concentrated strongly in lower-level jobs, but they have moved significantly into the middle and higher ranks in recent years, presumably through a mixture of deliberate federal effort and general changes in educational and other opportunities for and attitudes toward nonwhites in our society.

Local governments are especially important potential employers of the poor, because they are, in total, a large and growing employer, they deal with the local neighborhoods, and they include substantial work that persons with limited training may be able to perform well. A report published in 1969 by the U.S. Commission on Civil Rights studied a group of state and local governments in seven metropolitan areas.[5] Negroes held nearly a fourth of the full-time jobs in these jurisdictions, but were clustered in the lower ranks of the occupational structure. In nearly all these jurisdictions, however, Negroes were employed at higher levels and in white-collar jobs in greater proportions than in private employment. There is much variation among agencies; hospitals and welfare departments, for example, are heavy employers of Negroes, fire departments largely exclude them. (A 1966 report in Massachusetts found no minority group members among the 550 employees of the state police.) Proportions in better rank jobs vary among agencies similarly. Some menial jobs are filled almost entirely by Blacks. For some attractive new kinds of jobs, as with civil rights agencies, Blacks are actively recruited and given authority. Blacks have a solid place in public school teaching—even with segregation, black teachers were needed to teach black children. The agencies that employ high proportions of Blacks tend to be either heavy users of menial labor or those dealing largely with the black community.

The case for representativeness in the civil service, and in the various ranks and agencies, rests on: (1) the idea that everyone in the working force should have a chance at the best job he can manage, with no exclusion based on race, class, or the like; (2) the fact that bureaucrats make policy, and their social background influences the kind of policy they make, especially if they all share the same background; (3) the belief that social-economic-ethnic background affects the way people treat each other, so treatment of citizens by bureaucrats may be influenced by the background of the bureaucrats, especially if members of an agency are rather homogeneous; (4) the psychological identification of the population with the bureaucracy, an element of government by consent, requires a representative bureaucracy. (Inner-city Blacks have been attacking firemen, an apparently irrational action, perhaps in part because there are very few black firemen.) These propositions argue for personnel reflective of the cultures and needs of all groups in the society. The difficulty in achieving representativeness is not blatant discrimination, but that the society is not equalitarian throughout, especially with respect to the distribution of education and professional skills. This distribution, in turn, may hinge on objective opportunities and on the values of the various subcultures of the society. Within particular agencies, special factors are at work, of course; it would be surprising if the Labor Department were not more Catholic and urban than the Agriculture Department, the Interior Department more western than Justice. But those cases are not problems of the exclusion of minorities from major opportunities in American life.

As indicated in the discussion of patronage (Chapter III), a merit system does not in itself guarantee even formal equality of opportunity for minority groups, but neither is it necessarily the enemy of minorities; it depends how the system is used. Efforts have been made recently to cope with the charge that the civil service excludes minorities by rewarding white middle-class values. The law is now squarely on the side of no punitive discrimination because of race, but the more recent efforts have been toward positive redress of the balance. Examples of such actions that harmonize with merit include: recruiting at Black and Mexican-American schools and neighborhoods, establishing entry-level positions which do not require a high-school diploma, programs combining work with training or education, creation of summer jobs for poor youngsters, checking examinations to see whether they are comprehensible to persons of inner city background and whether they are really related to competence at the job or career, giving certain examinations in Spanish as well as English, and making job training available to minority group members. The U.S. Civil Service Commission includes a new Office of Federal Equal Employment Opportunity, one of whose responsibilities is to facilitate upward mobility for minority group employees in low-paying jobs—an office whose first director appropriately is a black man who has risen during his career from a lowly GS–3 post to a top-level position.

Some modifications of merit will win mixtures of praise and concern. In 1968 the New York City Human Resources Administration announced that a limited number of low-paying clerical jobs would be filled through civil service examinations, requiring a minimum score of seventy, but with impoverished persons receiving five free points plus five points if they lived in a poverty area plus two points if they were fifty-five to sixty-three years old. The Federal Civil Service Commission in 1968 developed a worker-trainee examination for low-level jobs which gives negative scores for experience and education, while it seeks to reward motivation and need. Some public agencies are seeking to promote into professional positions, such as social worker, persons who have served successfully as aides but lack the normal education and certification. The Civil Service Commission in 1971 announced a policy of having agencies adopt numerical "goals" for employment of minority group members (in agencies or localities recognized as problem areas requiring progress) and timetables, with plans for their achievement within the merit system. But it rejected "quotas" which, it held, restrict employment opportunities of other groups, and thus are contrary to the merit system.

Conflict with merit system principles is apparent if a program sets up a quota for minority group members irrespective of examination rankings or allocates a position to a minority group to the exclusion of others. The justification offered for such actions may be: the particular post requires a person who can deal with a particular community, and ethnic background is an important factor (for instance, a black principal or police captain in a black neighborhood); the civil service must be brought into better ethnic balance; employment must be found for minority group members; past injustices against Blacks and other minorities must be compensated for; examinations and degree requirements are essentially artificial devices not related to good work on the job; satisfactory performance is all we need for most jobs, rather than the best-qualified person; the merit system is not sacred and never was thought so by ethnic groups that, having entered government service and risen, now use the merit system to block Blacks. In brief, we are called to balance the strict merit system, based on impersonality and formally objective qualifications, against the demand for a more representative civil service. Merit system proponents must provide convincing answers to critics who charge that examinations and required qualifications often bear no demonstrable relationship to the job to be done, but simply reward the talents nurtured in middle-class white culture. The reader is invited to decide, for example, whether a high-school or college education would generally make one a better public servant in a clerical post. As a teacher, executive, or engineer? Police departments, for example, are being exhorted simultaneously to hire men with college training and to hire Blacks, yet the two preferences may work against each other in practice.

Paraprofessionals in the public service seem to combine qualities of professional competence, permitting them adequately to serve the true interests of the citizen, and representativeness of the population served, permitting them to embody the same social characteristics as the citizenry. Paraprofessionals are persons without the normal educational background and certification to perform as professionals. The job of the professional is split into components, and those which can be well done by a nonprofessional are sorted out to be performed by a paraprofessional. It is argued, for example, that case aides chosen from among mothers on public welfare will not only do work that releases the professional public welfare worker for other tasks, but may do the welfare job better than the professionally trained social worker, and will provide a sympathetic citizen-government bond. Teacher aides and mental health aides chosen from the local community are also being used. Citizens deeply concerned with the quality of services provided in the central city, not to mention persons looking for jobs or power, may prefer representative public servants to professional ones, if a choice must be made. But paraprofessionalism holds out the promise (a false promise, some professionals argue) of technical competence combined with representative experience, attitudes, and characteristics, to permit citizen-bureaucrat mutual identification.

Important conflicts over the nature of jobs and careers, talent and training, are involved in the effort to recruit a representative bureaucracy. There are sometimes severe strains between those identified with professionalism, merit system, or civil service unionism and those working to enlarge opportunities for ethnic groups and poor people. Civil service bureaucracy is thus being challenged in the name of representative bureaucracy.

ADVOCACY ADMINISTRATION

Bureaucracy is not always seen as a neutral tool wielded by elected politicians. Public administration has recently been marked by vigorous advocacy, that is, the passionate commitment of those with professional skills and official standing to use these assets on behalf of the least powerful and wealthy members of the community. Three sorts of advocacy may be distinguished: first, advocacy from outside government directed at the public agencies, as in advocacy planning; second, advocacy from within a government agency established to act in a manner adversary to other public agencies and programs, as in the Office of Economic Opportunity advocacy law program; and third, advocacy by program officials within agencies servicing and/or regulating the poor, as in public welfare.

The concept of advocacy planning (in which the planner pleads for his client) borrows from the legal practice of advocacy. Planners cannot be value-free technicians, it argues; their plans for a neighborhood or city always serve one goal or another. There should be alternative plans, representing diverse group interests, not a unitary official plan only. Through contention among supporters of competing plans, the value premises and social-economic consequences of plans would be made clear.

Advocacy planning attempts to combine representation of the disadvantaged citizens and professional competence, through persons outside government countering the allegedly elitist influence of public officials. It seeks to provide a professional urban planning staff for the use of local citizens who want to oppose "the system," including especially the municipal and other bureaucracies. The new breed of advocate planner, himself probably a middle-class professional, is on the side of the poor people and mistrusts middle-class professionals, especially government officials. He assumes that there are neighborhood interests, or interests of particular groups within a city, that are not identical with the interests of the city as perceived by the mayor and the municipal planning and service agencies. Advocacy planning presumes frequent conflict especially between what the poor black neighborhood wants and needs and what the mayor and the urban renewal agency think is good for the city. Advocate planners reject the view that, through technical skill, planners can achieve a kind of platonic good of the whole community. They see planning as pluralistic, partisan, and political, and urge a fair chance for the least advantaged members of the community.

Advocate planners seek to assist poor citizens in articulating their views in technically sound fashion and to speak for them in the various phases of negotiations among city agencies and outside sources of money and rules (federal agencies notably). The combination of community organizations (with support from law, regulations, and federal agency action) and advocate planners offers a measure of voice and power to the poor. From the organization of the community comes the claim to speak for "the people"; from the planners come technical and bureaucratic skills. The effect is to lessen outside direction of governmental agencies within poor neighborhoods, and to heighten the responsiveness of their programs to poor people's wishes. Even within a poor or black neighborhood, however, are varied groups with competing interests, so it is not always easy to speak for a neighborhood.

Direct citizen action with professional planning support is evident in the revolt against highways since about 1959. The planning processes used by the federal Bureau of Public Roads and state highway departments have been attacked by citizens' groups as serving the highway interests and the highway bureaucracies, at the expense of the neighborhoods. Engineering studies and cost-benefit analyses left out too many human values and the desires of too many groups. In the 1950's the state highway departments typically held the federally required public hearings only after the site had been chosen and the major design decisions made. Neither the Bureau of Public Roads nor the state highway department was required to take the public hearing seriously, and citizens were ill-prepared to tackle the highway professionals. By 1969, however, there were significant changes in the law and in the attitudes of some highway officials. Advocate planners have helped in this area, especially in aiding poor, black, dilapidated urban neighborhoods to resist the highways. There is now in the federal Department of Transportation far more sensitivity to the social problems of urban highways, and a two-hearing requirement permits citizen objections to have real effect on the location of roads. Citizen influence is no longer purely myth and social effects are genuine considerations. In sum, the highway bureaucracies represent more diverse values and groups than they did fifteen years ago, thanks to the efforts of aroused citizens with help from activist planners critical of official policy.

Advocates of the poor against the governmental bureaucracy may come into the bureaucracy itself. Office of Economic Opportunity lawyers, under the Economic Opportunity Act of 1964, are the clearest example, such as in their instituting a suit against a public welfare department on behalf of recipients. They find the law biased in content against the poor, in favor of property. They find the bureaucrats administer the law to treat the poor either harshly or paternalistically; even when the law is in the service of the poor, they find it administered passively and ineffectively. And the poor typically lack lawyers or good lawyers who give good service. Advocacy lawyers can help force administrative agencies to act on behalf of the poor in areas such as housing codes and civil rights, and can help develop law and administrative procedures and policies more favorable to the poor. This is done by providing representation of the poor on the governing board of the legal service office itself, accessibility of service in the poor neighborhood, and moral commitment of the staff to the need to press aggressively the claims of the poor.

Apart from poverty lawyers, can the public bureaucrat be the advocate of the poor client, as well as or rather than the official representative of an agency? Many vigorous young public administrators would like to be advocates for the poor. Public welfare agencies, for example, are attracting dedicated middle-class white advocates of the poor black recipients' needs and rights. They tend to be highly critical of their own agencies. The paradoxical difficulty that may arise is that advocate attitudes may lead to paternalism by the young worker, or something between fraternalism and paternalism. Yet the recent court cases are rather against agency paternalism, supporting the rights of the client against the agency officials. These decisions push the agency toward formality, legality, and client representation by counsel in formally contested adversary relationships. Unless public officials never make a decision contrary to the claims of clients in programs such as public welfare or public low-rent housing (and organized clients may push bargaining claims greater than they really expect to win), they may find that the clients regard them as the adversary. Especially as one advances into more responsible administrative positions, it may be difficult to say yes always, given agency rules, statutes and court precedents, shortage of funds, political pressures, demands from hierarchical superiors, occasional scoundrels among the clients, and the like. Recent moves among public welfare agencies to tighten measures against recipient fraud are an example. Most agencies, and perhaps most public administrators, may finally discover that despite their intentions and hopes, the poor people, the Blacks, the clients want to press their claims and defend their interests through other means, with the public agency as the sometimes hostile other party rather than as the advocate of the poor.

The advocate administrator challenges civil service neutrality as his proper guide. He challenges hierarchical control and ultimate responsibility to elected government officials as the source of goals. A new breed of young public administration teachers and practitioners is arguing vigorously for public administrators (especially in local service agencies) to act on strong personal commitments to justice for the poor, rather than on hierarchical obedience and professional neutralism. The public administrator should represent the dispossessed, they argue. Justice for the poor is the goal, and advocacy, not neutral competence and subservience to duly constituted authority, is the proper mode.

CITIZEN PARTICIPATION IN PUBLIC ADMINISTRATION

Community action programs, seeking maximum feasible participation by local citizens in antipoverty programs, express the new spirit of amateur administration. This actually has shades of the old warning of Andrew Jackson against officials who stay long in office and think they have a right to it. Let any man of common sense do the job. Even if the job is more complex today, it can be argued that college degrees and professional experience are demanded for many jobs that require only common sense, and that the ends a public official seeks to serve are more important than the elegance of his means. We are probably going to be living with a conflict—whose form, focus, language, and participants may vary—between local citizen control and professional career competence in the years ahead. At the very moment that universities proclaim new professionalism in city planning, urban studies, and the like, local poor people articulate a distrust of experts and a desire to run programs themselves. The conflict also pits professional politicians, who claim to speak for the public, against local people's leaders outside the formal party-politics, city-wide elective system of authority. These local leaders ("poverty politicans") write off the old-style politics as irrelevant. The new leaders tend to lump the bureaucrats with the rejected old leadership, and want to control and use the bureaucratic machine themselves where it cannot be dispensed with. How far will citizen administration replace or transform bureaucratic administration?

CITIZEN COMMITTEES

Citizen participation is not an entirely new theme or practice, if its meaning is not limited to poor urban neighborhoods. A variety of citizen boards has been used in American public administration. Especially respecting agricultural policies, there is a substantial history of citizen (farmer) participation, including a national network of some 30,000 elective farmer committees. Often this participation seems to have suffered from one of two faults: (1) the amateur officials, serving on a committee advisory to a full-time administrator and perhaps meeting infrequently, have no real influence, even if they have some authority—they are show pieces; (2) the amateur officials represent a particular group or class (ranchers, successful farmers, white farmers), may remain in office for a long while (voter turnout rates are low in election of committeemen), and protect their own interests at the expense of the least privileged farmers or of the general public interest.

Farmer committees have helped decentralize agricultural policy making, when they have successfully exercised influence, but there have been losses as well as gains in this transfer of power from the department to the localities. Local politics and local citizens can be as thoughtless of poor people as are national politics and career federal bureaucrats. Local farm organizations, to work with agricultural extension agents in bringing scientific information or assistance programs to farmers, and local elected committees, to administer agricultural commodity price supports, have provided a cadre of distinctly political farmers, shaping the local administration of national policy and working in interest group fashion to shape national farm policy. A 1939 study of the agricultural extension agent, who then seemed a prime example of a locally responsible government expert, concluded that he ignored the lower third of farmers. The agent was formally responsible to local, state, and federal governments, but county control and ties to local farm bureau organizations (farmer associations) were typical. "The necessity of pleasing the dominant economic and political leaders because of dependence upon county appropriations as well as the natural tendency to conform to social and economic patterns has resulted in service by the county agent primarily for more prosperous farmers."[6]

Similarly, stockmen serve on advisory boards; these control grazing of privately owned livestock on public lands, under the Department of Interior. Interior has been weak and the local advisory boards strong, a situation that "has acted to minimize the possibility of real federal control and has buttressed the old system of local control of the range by rural elites."[7] Farmer administration, like citizen administration in general, has an essentially political meaning, serving some interests at the expense of others. Local control in agricultural administration often serves the well-established, not the poor farmers.

The wide use of industry advisory committees in government is open to similar questioning. The objections, moreover, raise questions about the basic organizational structure; they do not relate to bad or cynical people abusing power. They touch the problems, first, of who speaks for farmers or businessmen (in reality doesn't each of these categories contain diverse groups with differing and sometimes antipathetic interests); and second, of whether the interests of the group directly concerned (farmer, businessman) are identical with or compatible with the interests of the whole community? One can argue that those most deeply involved, e.g., farmers in farm policy, should have more than numerically proportional consideration and that it is difficult to define the public interest. But the urgency of seeking justice for the weakest groups and of pursuing the public interest persists. Concern about members of advisory committees using their position to advance their own business interests led to a presidential order in 1962 to limit the use and regulate the procedures of advisory committees. Securing consent from key clientele through advisory committee membership may simply exaggerate already severe differences between the haves and the have-nots.

Revelations respecting pollution control boards heighten distrust of citizen committees. A survey by the *New York Times* in 1970 of state boards responsible for air and water antipollution programs found that most of them "are markedly weighted with representatives of the principal sources of pollution."[8] These air and water pollution boards, established under state laws, are part-time citizen panels appointed by governors to set policies and standards for pollution abatement and to oversee enforcement. Federal officials cite the composition of these boards as a serious barrier to pollution abatement (especially respecting water pollution), pointing out that members often represent corporate, agricultural, and local governmental polluters, and have policing powers over their own areas of activity. Pressure group politics often resulted in state laws assuring places on these boards to industry, agriculture, and municipalities, and representatives of major polluters have frequently been appointed to the boards. State officials on such boards are generally from departments tied to industry and agriculture, not conservation. Such heavily polluting industries as steel and other metals, chemicals, and paper are well represented on state boards.

The selective service system has been administered with a good deal of discretion—authority, not simply advice—vested in local volunteer draft boards. This has meant in some cases rather harsh (if not unconstitutional) local interpretations, reflecting patriotic white middle-class community, or at least draft board, hostilities to certain kinds of young men. Even where economic interests are not involved, then, local citizens are not necessarily generous to and understanding of one another, nor even constitutionally circumspect in their use of authority over compatriots.

One response to criticism of citizen administrative or advisory committees may be that the wrong people (the well-to-do) have been put on the committees; now it is the poor people's turn. We have seen, for example, establishment of committees of public welfare recipients to advise the welfare department, replacing committees of the "good people" and professionals of the community. The recipients' experience (their suffering from the problem, living in the neighborhood, being clients of the agency), their keen knowledge of what they want and their willingness to fight for it, is held to be more valuable than the education or technical competence of old-style board members. A board may include both sorts of members, of course, but there may be controversy over the proportions of each. But if some advisory committees have much power (for example, committees of scientists advising federal agencies on research grants), most have rather little. They have difficulty shaping bureaucratic policy because they meet only occasionally, are insufficiently familiar with details of what is going on and what the law permits and requires, and they lack authority.

The part-time amateur seldom beats the professional at his own game. So there are demands from spokesmen for the poor for more than advice to bureaucrats.

COMMUNITY ACTION PROGRAMS

"Community action" refers to control of one or more governmental functions (education, urban renewal, public health, job training, etc.) within a neighborhood by a board representing the community's residents, rather than control by city-wide political and bureaucratic officials. There have been two major intentions or justifications. (1) Community action or citizen participation is a means of improving the mental health of the citizens and the social-organizational quality of a neighborhood. A high rate of juvenile delinquency is a typical sign of community failure. A poor neighborhood is seen as suffering from personal (psychological) and social (inter-personal relations and joint action) failure. Giving responsibility to citizens of the poor neighborhood will help cure this sense of impotence and failure. (2) Community action is a means of redistributing political power and, consequently, changing the allocation of resources by government. If the poor or the black (or the poor black, commonly) are given new power through placement in positions of influence, their neighborhood will receive more money and consideration than it did when middle-class Whites made the decisions. What is to be cured is not an illness of a neighborhood which is sick within a healthy society, but a fault of the society, which cheats its weakest segments to aid its strongest.

Justification of community participation has utilized both approaches, but the latter is the prominent one today. It is politically more radical, less paternalistic, and focuses on the state of public and private services within central-city ghettoes. Citizen participation through community action programs is a political issue, affecting who has political power, what goals and interests power serves, and how economic resources and electoral offices are distributed.

Community action programs offer citizen participation in and control of public administration. Local neighborhood representatives are held to be more truly spokesmen of the disadvantaged citizens, of the spirit of the local community, than the politicians of city hall and city council. Alongside this control by responsive, typical citizens is a good deal of direct doing by local citizens rather than by professionals in the public service recruited from outside the neighborhood, the ethnic group, the local culture. Citizen control of public administration is clearly of more than administrative intent and significance.

Citizen control of local schools (personnel, curricula, budget, buildings), for example, has mixed intentions and justifications. These touch upon: the quality of the schools, as seen in student test performance and drop-out rates; teacher attitudes to students; curriculum relevance to the life experience and ethnic identification of the students; community control of institutions as a means of fostering community pride or as an opening wedge toward locally controlled neighborhood physical renewal; parental responsibility toward and participation in school matters; jobs and contracts for local people. Varied ways of justifying local control of schools raise questions of political power, of neighborhood versus city, and of race relations. In one perspective, local control of schools is a question of (a) city-wide bureaucracy, highly certificated and enmeshed in strict rules to assure objective relations, under central contol, versus (b) smaller local organizations, relying more on presumed competence and enthusiasm for the task at hand, under boards composed of people who are culturally, ethnically, and politically quite different from city-wide board members. The question is whether to debureaucratize the schools. Resulting school systems might more closely resemble those of suburbs or towns, where the personality, ideology, and life style of students and teachers can be taken into account. The big-city school system has generally relied on tests and tenure and standardized curriculum, rather than adjusting teachers and studies to local conditions.

Though there has been trouble with teachers' unions and resentment from white citizens who distrust black-controlled public schools, experiments at school decentralization are being made. New York City in 1970 decentralized its vast school system (900 schools, 60,000 teachers, over one million pupils) into thirty-one districts, each headed by a community school board elected by neighborhood residents. Though the city-wide Board of Education continues, community school boards have at least qualified authority to employ a district superintendent, hire and fire all employees within the limits of union agreements with the central board, choose teaching materials, and operate the buildings. Soon such decentralized control of city schools may seem the obvious thing to do. Presumably there will be real central-local tensions, and some neighborhood school boards will use their power well and have good schools while some will not.

The federal government has supported community control of public administration, though its support has been qualified by divided counsels and evident grave doubts. The Economic Opportunity Act of 1964 called for community action programs "developed, conducted and administered with the maximum feasible participation of residents of the areas and members of the groups served." The Model Cities legislation of 1966 provided for "widespread citizen participation in the program"—deliberately more limited than the OEO 1964 provision, for the 1966 act intended to support local municipal authorities as a key to coordinated action on the problems of the cities. Daniel Moynihan, in a book which is critical of community action agencies, concedes them to be an established part of our governmental scene at this time. He is skeptical of the social science explanations which were used to justify them. He asks about the actual local support for the programs, since small proportions of eligible people voted for community action board members (5 percent or less in various large cities). In addition, he wonders about the desire to pit citizen groups against the Democratic party of the big cities and cautions against turning governmental functions and monies over to non-governmental agencies, which lack the responsibility and controls of the established governmental bureaucracies. Yet he sees these community action agencies as a way of reaching the poor, the Black, and the usually politically inactive but now hostile citizens; as a source of federal money to the cities; and as a means of administering a variety of neighborhood programs. The purpose and justification of the community action programs may still be in contention when the agencies themselves are a regular part of our governmental landscape.

The community action programs were based on the belief that existing public agencies, staffed and supported by the white middle classes, suffered from bureaucratic introversion—inflexibility, insensitivity, preoccupation with maintaining their own organizational structure, a hardening of the arteries that blinded them to the needs of those they served. The answer was a new, more responsive, and more representative kind of organization. But efforts such as the antipoverty program raised the problem of "simultaneous commitment to two different conceptions of democratic accountability. From whom were the projects to take their lead, elected government or those they served?"[9] The federal Office of Economic Opportunity, promoting "maximum feasible participation" of the poor, sought a majority on community action boards for persons elected by residents of the poor neighborhoods. But mayors saw this as a threat to their own authority. More recently the OEO has curtailed its support for organizing the poor to gain power, in the face of hostility from city political and bureaucratic officials. The Nixon administration has argued that mayors, city councils, and county executives, not community action program boards, represent the people. The urban government bureaucracies have been major opponents of community control, for they see it as threatening their own careers and the very significant degree of autonomy which they have achieved in their various realms (public schools, police, fire, sanitation, etc.). Public school personnel have been prominent critics (local group versus teacher hostilities resulted in a bitter strike in New York City in 1968), but other urban bureaucrats may be expected to react with at least equal vigor if they are threatened with local control of their particular function.

If community action agencies claiming to speak for the poor (who almost always have little political power) seem to pose a threat to others in the community, then they may suffer political defeat. If you declare war on the middle classes, the elective politicians, the governmental bureaucracies, and the local power structure, what are your chances of winning? Can political support, bureaucratic expertise, and control of their own neighborhoods by the poor be successfully combined? Can the third goal be achieved without the first two?

Effectiveness of control of governmental agencies by neighborhood representatives evidently depends on very many factors such as: the degree of legal authority possessed by the community action board (to decide or merely to advise, to initiate, to veto projects) and the strength of the statute or the administrative regulation which establishes citizen participation; whether board members are elected or chosen by a government agency, and with whom elected local residents share power on the board; the existence of a veto or initiatory power in other groups, e.g., the city council or a bureaucratic agency; the attitude of local government officials and agencies seeking to repress or encourage; and whether or not the federal government insists on a real role for the board as a condition for its grants or for priority in competitive grants, or instead places confidence primarily in the municipal government. It will also make a difference if the board controls a budget; if it has authority in employment of the staff; if it has planning, legal, and other technical resources at its command; if board members are paid for their time; if organized community groups support the neighborhood representatives, hold them accountable, and compel them to pay attention to issues, and if there are competing candidates for the offices. Further, one must determine whether poor people's representatives are actually chosen and controlled by political forces outside the neighborhood; whether there is experienced poor-people leadership, used to dealing with governmental agencies and recognized within the community as legitimate; whether racial, class, or other conflict within the neighborhood is severe, or there is relative homogeneity or harmony; and whether the board controls a single function or program or a varied and possibly changing set of activities. Neighborhood councils in some programs have had no authority and little influence; in others they have had much to say about the conduct of programs, both goals and means. Only by going behind the name or the mechanisms can one know whether citizen participation is really significant in decision making in any particular program or place.

NEIGHBORHOOD GOVERNMENT

Citizen participation in administration may take varied forms and may have more or less ideological content. Moynihan objected that what began as a relatively modest proposal to assure that the least privileged groups get some of the benefits of a program turned into a method of organizing the poor to seize political power. Neighborhood authority or even autonomy may develop as a goal connected with the experience and ideas of community action programs. (It is nourished by other intellectual currents as well.) An eloquent argument is made by Milton Kotler for local control of neighborhoods within cities, based on popular assemblies open to all. He condemns control of neighborhoods by outsiders (downtown business interests, the state, or the national government). Political liberty requires authority in and deliberation by the people of the community; only the small territory has the capacity for "deliberative democracy." Kotler seeks neighborhood governments with political autonomy plus representation in larger units; the city would be a federation of neighborhoods. Centralized bureaucratic rule is the enemy of liberty, and bureaucrats will resist the transfer of public authority to the localities, he warns. A book such as Kotler's goes far in urging replacement of urban bureaucracy with decentralized citizen administration, in the name of the poor.

Political officials may encourage recognition of neighborhoods, as Mayor John Lindsay of New York City did through various statements and actions.[10] He installed an Office of Neighborhood Government in the Mayor's Office. Pledging to give neighborhoods the responsibility for charting the course of their own communities, despite objections from Democratic city officials who regularly defeated the item in the Lindsay budget, Mayor Lindsay established some neighborhood "little city halls" (local complaint and inquiry offices) beginning in 1966. City councillors in New York City are elected from districts in partisan elections; they preferred that citizens come to them with complaints (and become indebted to them for help), rather than to a governmental agency identified with the mayor—at that time a Republican mayor. Little city halls in a city with a strong tradition of political clubhouses looked too much like potential Lindsay political clubhouses. In Boston, on the contrary, a more hospitable political climate and structure permitted Mayor Kevin White to establish Neighborhood Service Centers in the late 1960's without major political objection. The fifteen centers appear to be essentially outlets of the mayor's office and to some extent of the city and state bureaucracies, rather than instruments of neighborhood political expression. They answer questions and refer complaints and problems to regular city agencies. Typical problems concern inadequate provision of local public service (including failure to require private landlords to provide service), such as lack of heat or hot water in a building, garbage- or trash-littered lots and streets, or water or sewer difficulties. Complaints deal especially with housing, so the Housing Inspection Department works closely with the centers. Though the Boston program has not encountered the vigorous political opposition that the New York City proposal did, it has met with considerable hostility from long-term city employees, who evidently see it as a complaint generator and watchdog. The control of Neighborhood Service Centers in Boston has been in the mayor's office rather than the locality; the centers provide information and service, not local political control.

Despite difficulties thus far encountered, little city halls may prove more attractive to American city governments than the ombudsman as a method of dealing with citizen complaints. They can handle fairly large numbers of problems, go right into the locality, and provide relatively comprehensive advice on dealing with governmental bureaucracy. Community multiservice centers combining various health or welfare functions in one place similarly affirm the importance of the neighborhood. These centers may include a local committee with more or less authority or influence over the operation. The goal of better service probably predominates over the goal of local control generally, but both are present in contemporary efforts to establish multiservice centers, whereas the neighborhood information center aims almost solely at better service.

A step beyond local control of particular functions is true neighborhood government. In June of 1970 Mayor Lindsay proposed a decentralized system of neighborhood government through the creation of sixty-two community boards. The plan would utilize sixty-two existing Community Planning Districts as the Neighborhood Government Districts, and would seek to bring city, state, and federal program district lines within the city into conformity with these districts—something now lacking, as each agency sets its own administrative boundary lines. Each community board would consist of twenty-four to thirty unpaid members, appointed by the mayor, borough president, councilman, community school board, and any local community corporation board or model cities advisory committee. The local boards would make annual evaluations and recommendations on municipal services, hold hearings on capital budget and other district projects, work closely with officials of city agencies in their districts (attending regular community cabinet meetings with officials of all the municipal agencies in the district), and have direct access to an office of neighborhood government in the mayor's office. The mayor would appoint a salaried community director for each neighborhood from a panel of five names submitted by the board. The director would have a small staff. This plan to add a dimension of communal representation in the control of administration received a more sympathetic welcome than the earlier Lindsay proposal to make administration more responsive to citizens through little city halls.

The composition and manner of selection of the community boards was the most controversial aspect of Mayor Lindsay's neighborhood government plan for New York City. A good many people who expressed views felt that the plan left the appointment of the community directors too much in the mayor's hands. Among the existent groups which claimed that they should play a basic role in any new neighborhood government were: civic associations; community planning boards appointed by borough presidents; community councils drawing representatives from local groups such as civic associations, block associations, precinct councils, and fraternal and religious associations; three Model Cities Advisory Committees elected by residents of the Model Cities areas; popularly elected Community Corporations operating in twenty-six designated poverty areas; Block Associations in certain densely settled areas of the city; local political clubs; and vigorous religious organizations. Viewing the variety, the Mayor's Executive Assistant for Neighborhood Government recommended choosing community boards differently in different neighborhoods, to reflect current neighborhood institutions.

Neighborhood government in a large city encounters questions of defining the boundaries of each neighborhood and establishing governmental institutions which genuinely represent the local people in what is likely to be a fairly large and varied area. (Suzanne Keller concluded from her study of the literature that in cities today there are increasingly fewer "neighborhoods that are self-contained, distinctive, and relatively stable."[11] Nor is it clear that modern urbanites want or should have the stability (physical and social) and the limited variety and opportunity which basic commitment to an urban neighborhood may imply. It has been some of the dreariest working-class neighborhoods—where inhabitants needed each other's help and companionship for lack of private or governmental resources—that have most fostered neighborliness, but these communities are not ones that we would lightly try to reconstruct. Occasional communes (urban or rural) for those in whom the need for togetherness is dominant we may certainly have; a communal life style for the great majority of people in a secular, industrialized, technologically sophisticated, socially mobile, individual-oriented culture seems unlikely. Today institutions are specialized and geographically scattered; the small town of imagined memory combined work, religion, politics, sociability, recreation, education, social standards of propriety—one's past, present, and future. How many urban neighborhoods promise that? Who wants so limited a universe? If the urban neighborhood has little reality, why expect neighborhood government to be a vital institution? Is the revival or invention of city neighborhoods as significant social-governmental units a romantic dream? Even if most areas of most cities hardly qualify as communities, where black leaders (or others) with some real local support demand that governmental power be vested in the locality, does not a species of neighborhood government for that area make sense?

Do community action and neighborhood government threaten the effective governing of cities? Don't cities need better central bureaucracies, stronger mayors, and more effective coordination—the classic twentieth-century American prescription for improving the public service? In cities where black control of the highest elective offices is unlikely, if there is a substantial and concentrated black neighborhood black control of the neighborhood may seem urgent. A former regional director of HUD Model Cities programs and OEO community action programs suggests that what is now emerging is "an 'adversary' relationship, where two separate authorities exist,"—the black neighborhood group and the city government—"each with the independent right to block policy development or program action."[12] The conception of governmental bureaucracies as acting for the entire community is thus eroded by growing animosities within the society. Some mayors who are committed to change find the city bureaucracy a major burden. Alliances may even evolve between big-city mayors and the groups pressing for local control, each anxious about control of the municipal bureaucracies and each rejecting the idea of neutral competence as the test of bureaucracy, because neutrality means ossification and/or autonomy.

Will there be losses in competence, if citizen control and neighborhood autonomy are instituted? Will patronage replace merit? Will civil servants suffer personal abuse or loss of career security? Will the municipal legislature and municipal elections and politics lose meaning? Will the integrative, conflict-resolving functions of city-wide politics be lost, and, if so, what will be the consequences? Will parochialism, although praised as local democracy, prove oppressive? Will problems requiring city-wide and multi-city metropolitan action grow ever more difficult to cope with if the city government loses vitality? Will racial separatism increase and racial integration be mocked as a liberal myth not worth pursuing? Will fiscal corruption of government increase? Will the evenhanded application of the law diminish? Questions of this sort, and the list is obviously limited to grim forecasts, can scarcely now be answered, when community action is so tentative a development. Perhaps it will truly save the cities, making citizens out of subjects. Paradoxically, community action may betoken both the despair of the city's poor with governmental performance and the emergence of governmental units, leaders, and programs in which the poor believe. Where integration of neighborhoods and schools has been sought by Blacks and resisted by Whites (including suburbanites in white communities with local control of local governmental institutions), Whites are in a weak position to object to community control of institutions in black neighborhoods.

Community control may vary in form from function to function as well as among places. In an impressively thoughtful study, Alan Altshuler suggests that "one might reasonably judge that community influence over the police should be less than that over the schools, or that supervision of the police from above with respect to fiscal probity should be greater than that with respect to determining tolerable levels of street disorder."[13] Citizen control of administration seems most suitable for essentially local activities. One can conceive of "the new federalism" in some communities consisting of the interrelated functioning of: (1) a highly professional, assertive federal bureaucracy, (2) a patronage-ridden, routine-bound state administration, with pockets of real competence, and (3) a combination of amateur and highly professional, citizen-controlled and self-controlled local administration.

Community control may contribute to responsive local bureaucracy, but much governing is not properly local. In the whole realm of conservation of resources, for example, there is a question about the wisdom of local control. Local groups typically take the short-run view on local resources. Does the federal government have a responsibility, and can it feasibly act, to preserve and even to some extent restore the environment? How will we get smog control, clean water, limits on pesticides that remain in toxic form for long periods after application and through various passages, preservation of wilderness areas, of marshlands, of redwoods, of animal and bird species? Is this a realm for professional competence in science and in governmental regulation, dedicated citizen support, and vigorous governmental action, in the face of real opposition by affected local interests and apathy by many citizens? If we fail to act, will we leave the next generation a ruined earth, and must that be weighed against local option? All this without mentioning population control. What is true respecting natural resource control is also true of the economy; local efforts may be pretty unavailing if there is a national economic slump. In sum, local control will not cure everything. Physically, ecologically, economically, historically, culturally, politically—in how many ways!—we are more than a group of potentially autonomous neighborhoods.

The realm in which nonprofessional, citizen administration seems least likely is the area of military-foreign affairs. The Vietnam War has raised in vivid fashion the question whether the military and civilian bureaucrats are subject to effective control in the making of foreign policy. The President has real power, but the career officials have great influence. There is a widespread feeling that neither the average citizen nor the courts—nor even Congress —can much influence the course of American military policy, which in turn affects the economy, the gap between young and old, and the whole spirit of the day in the United States. The career bureaucrats hardly look as if they are about to be displaced by nonprofessional citizens in military-foreign affairs. Can the citizen have a modicum of influence, much less take over administration, in the age when "military-industrial complex" is a cliché?

THE DEMOCRATIZATION OF PUBLIC ADMINISTRATION

Even where community control in the style of antipoverty agencies is not tried, old-style public administration may be subject to significant "citizen" and "personal" influences. The widespread rejection of bureaucratic authority in the name of the personal and passionate, the spontaneous and idiosyncratic, the small, equalitarian and communal—surely this will affect public administration and the bureaucratic life. Residents of inner-city black neighborhoods will likely make demands for a responsive public administration; so will college-educated middle-class young people. The authority of an official may count for less, as may the majesty of government. The clientele of an agency may demand clear procedures and rights, perhaps kinds of representation within the agency, perhaps new grievance techniques. Any hint of agency paternalism may be resented and attacked. Local citizens may organize, demonstrate, sit-in, and demand rights. Neighborhood offices may regularly be established, with significant decentralization of authority from the central office.

The democratization of administration will affect bureaucrats. Preferential hiring, training, and/or promotion of minority group members may change the composition of and attitudes within the civil service. These practices will likely excite great tensions among civil servants or others who see themselves victims of "reverse discrimination" or who fear departure from merit principles of objectively ranking all applicants. The use of paraprofessionals may be common. And these persons—local residents, poor, often black people—may demand kinds of treatment which bureaucracies have not typically accorded to their lowest members and may import into government agencies the influence of community organizations and angers. Agencies may have to cope with demands, supported by community groups, that paraprofessionals' practical experience and their empathy with the neighborhood be recognized, while the professionals in the agency fear erosion of their own position. Established bureaucrats, professionally committed and dedicated to public service, but on the defensive, may resort increasingly to collective action to protect their interests against the community spokesmen's demands for local control and against the paraprofessionals' demands for scrapping educational requirements, certification, testing, and seniority. Young, radical Whites in the agency may line up with the black neighborhood, demanding commitment to basic social change and challenging hierarchical authority within bureaucracy.

Warren Bennis, a change-oriented organization theorist, sees a more humanist-democratic form coming into being: "Adaptive, problem-solving, temporary systems of diverse specialists, linked together by coordinating and task-evaluating executive specialists in an organic flux—this is the organizational form that will gradually replace bureaucracy as we know it."[14] Reich, more radically hostile to contemporary bureaucracy, sees modern (Consciousness III) persons, who will become a majority, rejecting authority and hierarchy, seeking genuine community, demanding a role in decision making, and insisting on "personal responsibility and true personal equality."[15] Will change really amount to so much, or will the bureaucratic system assimilate new attitudes and forms?

The rebel within us and among us argues that bureaucratization is neither inevitable nor good. Too often the proponents of bureaucracy assume that life must be bureaucratic, without proving the case. If life does not have to be monarchic or despotic or segregated by race or lived in poverty, asks the critic, why does it have to be bureaucratic? Human institutions can be changed and discarded by human will. The future must provide self-control by local people in small, cohesive groups, he argues, at least for those functions suitable to the local area. Where professionalism is required, it must be accompanied by citizen participation. The evil is not governmental bureaucracy, says the rebel, it is the bureaucratization of life. Bureaucracy corrupts our culture, denying us a more personalistic, voluntaristic ethos. Love and community must replace authority and hierarchy. Enough of the fallen nature of man and the praise of ordered rule, enough of the present as child of the past, and the skeptic's saying what cannot be done.

But, answers the skeptic, even if change is inevitable, there is little reason to expect a utopian outcome. Despite a host of qualifications, it is still true that bureaucracy is a necessary means toward goals which we select through a democratic political system—tasks as diverse as diplomacy and national defense, enforcing public health regulations and providing hospitals, inspecting banks and insurance companies and food and drug companies, purifying air and water, enforcing civil rights statutes and regulations, and providing police, fire, and school services to great cities. Some governmental functions now conducted through large formal organizations may be decentralized and perhaps be performed in nonbureaucratic fashion at the local level. For example, in 1970 a Tenant Management Corporation began a pilot program under Boston Housing Authority auspices with OEO funding to show how a group of public housing tenants, mostly black in this case, can manage their own buildings. Bureaucracies may change, becoming more equalitarian, more open to participation by local citizens, or in other ways more attractive. But to expect that local, spontaneous, equalitarian, nonbureaucratic governmental administration will be characteristic of late twentieth-century America is to hope for much indeed. We shall have to work through and watch over our bureaucracy.

When governmental bureaucracy is unresponsive or is oppressive, we must arouse or subdue it vigorously, lest bureaucrats exercise too much power with too little supervision or suffer from insufficient energy or competence. If bureaucracy is at times merely annoying, however, one might recommend a measure of self-control, cooperation, and submission to legitimate and reasonable authority. We must have bureaucracy because we must have government; our task is to make bureaucracy competent in its work, decent to its members, and responsive to political control. The ideal is a governmental bureaucracy of technical and administrative competence and fiscal integrity; of democratic predisposition, accountable hierarchically and responsive to elected public officials; committed to the rule of law and citizens' rights and controlled by the courts as to fairness; scrutinized by press, parties, and interest groups; representative in composition, open to talent, challenging to its members, and lawful and humane in its treatment of them.

Being but a human institution, the American public service falls short of the ideal. The need to be vigilant, critical, and innovative is unceasing if we do not wish to be governed by a bureaucratic state. Yet the quality of the public service is no mean achievement. Compared with governmental bureaucracies elsewhere or in other times, it achieves an impressive record combining competence, dignity, and responsibility. The variety in quality and style of American public administration is incredible, the worst is admittedly bad, but a fair amount is quite decent and the best is impressively good. In a world so bungled, whatever of worth has been achieved merits a restrained word of praise.

FOOTNOTES

CHAPTER ONE

1. Gabriel Marcel, *The Philosophy of Existentialism* (New York: Citadel Press, Inc., 1956 by the Philosophical Library), p. 10.
2. Karl Jaspers, *Man in the Modern Age,* trans. Eden and Cedar Paul (Garden City, N.Y.: Doubleday & Company, Inc., Anchor Books, 1957), p. 51.
3. H. H. Gerth & C. Wright Mills, trans. & ed., *From Max Weber: Essays in Sociology* (New York: Oxford University Press, Inc., 1946), p. 214.
4. Chester I. Barnard, *The Functions of the Executive* (Cambridge, Mass.: Harvard University Press, 1938), p. viii.
5. The quotations are provided by J. P. Mayer, *Max Weber and German Politics; A Study in Political Sociology* (London: Faber & Faber, Ltd., 2nd ed., 1956), pp. 127, 128, respectively.
6. William H. Whyte, Jr., *The Organization Man* (Garden City, N.Y.: Doubleday & Company, Inc., Anchor Books, 1957), p. 3; the following phrase is from p. 4.
7. Robert Townsend, *Up the Organization* (New York: Alfred A. Knopf, Inc., 1970), p. 9.
8. Brian Chapman, *The Profession of Government; The Public Service in Europe* (London: George Allen & Unwin Ltd., 1959), p. 307.
9. This list is a modification of one suggested by Paul H. Appleby, *Policy and Administration* (University, Ala.: University of Alabama Press, 1949), pp. 32 ff.
10. Quoted by Richard H. Rovere, "Eisenhower Revisited . . . ," *The New York Times Magazine,* February 7, 1971, p. 54.
11. U.S. President's Committee on Administrative Management,
Report, *Administrative Management in the Government of the United States* (Washington: Government Printing Office, 1937), p. 5.
12. Leonard D. White, *Introduction to the Study of Public Administration,* 4th ed. (New York: The Macmillan Company, 1955), pp. 23–25, quotation from p. 23. In the 3rd edition (1948), White had suggested that the essence of our system lay in a balance between competing Federalist and Democratic (Hamiltonian and Jeffersonian) ideals of public administration.

CHAPTER TWO

1. John Dickinson, *Administrative Justice and the Supremacy of Law in the United States* (New York: Russell & Russell Publishers, 1959), p. 30.
2. U.S. Attorney General's Committee on Administrative Procedure, *Administrative Procedure in Government Agencies,* Senate, 77th Congress, 1st Session, Document No. 8 (Washington: Government Printing Office, 1941), p. 13.
3. Lloyd D. Musolf, *Federal Examiners and the Conflict of Law and Administration* (Baltimore: The Johns Hopkins Press, 1953), p. 46. Re the Administrative Procedure Act as a code, Heady agrees with the general view that "the federal act has not had a far-reaching impact on the adjudicatory practices of the federal agencies"; state acts, going less far in spelling out detailed procedural requirements, "have for the most part merely attempted to codify procedural practices already imposed by specific regulatory statutes or by the courts," and have not much changed adjudicatory proceedings. (Ferrel Heady, "State Administrative Procedure Laws: An Appraisal," *Public Administration Review, XII* [Winter 1952], p. 14.)
4. *Ibid.,* p. 19.

5. The Attorney General's comment is quoted by Kenneth Culp Davis, *Administrative Law and Government* (St. Paul, Minn.: West Publishing Co., 1960), p. 30.

6. Peter Woll, *Administrative Law: The Informal Process* (Berkeley: University of California Press, 1963), p. 170; cf. pp. 166–170. Winston M. Fick claims the proposed ABA code was "a rather moderate proposal," and points to sharp change in the ABA viewpoint as significant acceptance of administrative procedure. ("Issues and Accomplishments in Administrative Regulation: Some Political Aspects," *Law and Contemporary Problems,* XXVI [Spring 1961], p. 288, fn. 16.) Clark Byse is quoted as charging ABA with still seeking to "upset the compromise embodied in the Administrative Procedure Act," U.S. Congress, Senate, Committee on the Judiciary, Subcommittee on Administrative Practice and Procedure, 90th Cong., 1st Session, *Administrative Procedure Act,* Hearings, March, April, May, 1967 (Washington: Government Printing Office, 1967), p. 344. See the testimony of ABA spokesmen, pp. 12–20, 349–359, and testimony of Frank Wozencraft, Asst. Attorney General, pp. 20–29, 323–348.

7. *L. P. Steuart & Bro., Inc. v. Bowles,* 322 U.S. 398 (1944).

8. *In re Groban,* 352 U.S. 330 (1957).

9. H. W. R. Wade, *Towards Administrative Justice* (Ann Arbor, Mich.: The University of Michigan Press, 1963), p. 10. Emphasis supplied.

10. Davis, *Administrative Law and Government,* p. 156.

11. Henry J. Friendly, *The Federal Administrative Agencies; The Need for Better Definition of Standards* (Cambridge, Mass.: Harvard University Press, 1962), pp. 5 ff.

12. Louis J. Hector, "Problems of the CAB and the Independent Regulatory Commissions," *Yale Law Journal,* LXIX (May 1960), p. 942.

13. Davis, *Administrative Law and Government,* p. 77.

14. Nathaniel L. Nathanson, "Central Issues of American Administrative Law," *American Political Science Review,* XLV (June 1951), p. 353.

15. *Turner v. Fisher,* 222 U.S. 204 (1911).

16. *In re Groban,* 352 U.S. 330 (1957).

17. *Universal Camera Corp. v. NLRB,* 340 U.S. 474 (1951); cf. *FCC v. Allentown Broadcasting Corp.,* 349 U.S. 358 (1955).

18. Woll, *Administrative Law,* pp. 28 ff.

19. Walter Gellhorn, "Administrative Procedure Reform: Hardy Perennial," *American Bar Association Journal,* XLVIII (March 1962), p. 248.

20. Martin Shapiro, *The Supreme Court and Administrative Agencies* (New York: The Free Press, 1968), p. 13, for the lower estimate; Davis, *Administrative Law and Government,* p. 5, for the higher.

21. *Ibid.,* p. 463.

22. Shapiro, *Supreme Court and Administrative Agencies,* p. 266.

23. *Oestereich v. Selective Service System Local Board No. 11,* 393 U.S. 233 (1968); *Breen v. Selective Service System Local Board No. 16,* 396 U.S. 460 (1970).

24. *Camara v. Municipal Court,* 387 U.S. 523 (1967); *See v. Seattle,* 387 U.S. 541 (1967).

25. *Colonnade Catering Corp. v. U.S.,* 397 U.S. 72 (1970).

26. *Parrish v. Civil Service Commission of County of Alameda,* 57 Cal. Rptr. 623, 425 P 2d 223 (1967).

27. *King v. Smith,* 392 U.S. 309 (1968).

28. *Goldberg v. Kelly,* 397 U.S. 254 (1970); *Wheeler v. Montgomery,* 397 U.S. 280 (1970).

29. *Wyman v. James,* 400 U.S. 309 (1971).

30. Kenneth Culp Davis, "Ombudsmen in America: Officers to Criticize Administrative Action," *University of Pennsylvania Law Review,* 1961, reproduced in U.S. Congress, Senate, Committee on the Judiciary, Subcommittee on Administrative Practice and Procedure, 89th Congress, 2d Session, *Ombudsman,* Hearing, March 7, 1966 (Washington: Government Printing Office, 1966), p. 305. Cf. Walter Gellhorn, *When Americans Complain: Governmental Grievance Procedures* (Cambridge, Mass.: Harvard University Press, 1966), p. 212: "In general, American administrative adjudication and rule-making are attended by the world's most fully elaborated procedural protections against ill-informed exercises of official judgment."

31. Re the motivation of proponents of procedural requirements, cf. Fick, "Issues and Accomplishments in Administrative Regulation," *op. cit.,* p. 305; Heady, "State Administrative Procedure Laws," *op. cit.,* pp. 18 ff.

32. Charles A. Reich, "The New Property," *Yale Law Journal,* LXXIII (April 1964), p. 768.

33. Re the local level as the most susceptible to abuse of power, cf. Dickinson, *Administrative Justice,* p. 263; J. Roland Pennock, *Administration and the Rule of Law* (New York: Rinehart & Co., Inc., 1941), p. 219. Cf. Bernard Schwartz, "Crucial Areas in Administrative Law," *George Washington Law Review,* XXXIV (March 1966), pp. 401–402.

34. Reginald Heber Smith, *Justice and the Poor,* The Carnegie Foundation for the Advancement of Teaching, Bulletin No. 13 (New York City, 1919), p. 83.

35. Richard A. Cloward and Richard M. Elman, "Poverty, Injustice and the Welfare State; Part I: An Ombudsman for the Poor?" *The Nation,* CCII (February 28, 1966), p. 232. Cf. Gellhorn, *When Americans Complain,* pp. 170–195, re police departments and the poor.

CHAPTER THREE

1. Paul H. Appleby, *Policy and Administration* (University, Ala.: University of Alabama Press, 1949), p. 24; the following quotation, *ibid.*

2. Herbert A. Simon, *Administrative Behavior; A Study of Decision-Making Processes in Administrative Organization,* 2nd ed. (New York: The Macmillan Company, 1957), pp. 57 ff. and 197, respectively. For a detailed criticism of Simon's book, cf. Herbert J. Storing, "The Science of Administration: Herbert A. Simon," *Essays on the Scientific Study of Politics,* ed. Storing (New York: Holt, Rinehart & Winston, Inc., 1962), pp. 63–150. Further sources of Simon's views include: James G. March and Herbert A. Simon, *Organizations* (New York: John Wiley & Sons, Inc., 1958) and, respecting the potentialities of computers in management, Herbert A. Simon, *The New Science of Management Decision* (New York: Harper & Bros., 1960).

3. John Stuart Mill, *Representative Government,* chap. 5.

4. Richard E. Neustadt, "Politicians and Bureaucrats," David B. Truman, ed. (The American Assembly) *The Congress and America's Future* (Englewood Cliffs, N.J.: Prentice-Hall, Inc., 1965), p. 119.

5. Joseph P. Harris, *Congressional Control of Administration* (Washington, D.C.: The Brookings Institution, 1964), p. 5.

6. Charles S. Hyneman, *Bureaucracy in a Democracy,* (New York: Harper & Bros., 1950), p. 159.
7. Harris, *Congressional Control of Administration,* pp. 8, 46, respectively.
8. Joseph P. Harris, *The Advice and Consent of the Senate* (Berkeley: University of California Press, 1953), p. 397.
9. Walter Gellhorn, *When Americans Complain: Governmental Grievance Procedures* (Cambridge, Mass.: Harvard University Press, 1966), p. 124.
10. Joseph A. Schlesinger, "The Politics of the Executive," Herbert Jacob and Kenneth N. Vines, eds., *Politics in the American States* (Boston: Little, Brown and Company, 1965), p. 228.
11. U.S. President's Committee on Administrative Management, Report, *Administrative Management in the Government of the United States* (Washington: Government Printing Office, 1937).
12. Clinton Rossiter, *The American Presidency* (New York: Harcourt Brace Jovanovich, Inc., rev. ed., 1960), p. 19; Richard E. Neustadt, *Presidential Power; The Politics of Leadership* (New York: Science Editions, Inc., 1962), p. 43.
13. Rossiter, *The American Presidency,* p. 247.
14. *United States Government Organization Manual, 1968–69* (Washington: Government Printing Office), p. 58 ff.
15. This and the following quotation are from the President's March 12 message, *The New York Times,* March 13, 1970. The President's message, the reorganization plan, and the Executive Order re OMB and the Domestic Council are reprinted in "Reorganization Plan No. 2 of 1970," *Public Administration Review,* XXX (November/December, 1970), pp. 611–619.

16. Wallace S. Sayre and Herbert Kaufman, *Governing New York City: Politics in the Metropolis* (New York: Russell Sage Foundation, 1960), p. x1, and John Osborne, "The Nixon Watch: Saving Bob Finch," *The New Republic* CLXII (June 20, 1970), p. 10, respectively.
17. Committee for Economic Development, *Modernizing State Government,* A Statement on National Policy by the Research and Policy Committee (July 1967), p. 45.
18. Deil S. Wright, "Executive Leadership in State Administration," *Midwest Journal of Political Science,* XI (February 1967), p. 13.
19. *The New York Times,* January 31, 1954, quoting Commissioner Robert E. Lee.
20. U.S. President's Commission on Postal Organization, Report, *Towards Postal Excellence* (Washington: Government Printing Office, 1968), p. 1.
21. *The New York Times,* December 16, 1967.
22. The relevant portion of Jackson's first annual message is reproduced in Leonard D. White, *The Jacksonians; A Study in Administrative History, 1829–1861* (New York: The Macmillan Company, 1954), p. 318. Cf. chaps. XVI–XVII, re rotation in office.
23. Cornelius P. Cotter and Bernard C. Hennessy, *Politics Without Power; The National Party Committees* (New York: Atherton Press, Inc., 1964), p. 147.
24. Commonwealth of Massachusetts, Massachusetts Crime Commission, *Comprehensive Report and Appendices (Fifth Report),* Senate No. 1080, May 17, 1965, p. 31; Massachusetts, Commonwealth of, Special Commission on Civil Service and Public Personnel Administration, *Report,* House No. 5100, June 15, 1967, p. 51.
25. The quotations are, in order,

from Harvey C. Mansfield, "Political Parties, Patronage, and the Federal Government Service," Wallace S. Sayre, ed. (The American Assembly), *The Federal Government Service* (Englewood Cliffs, N.J.: Prentice-Hall, Inc., 2nd ed., 1965), p. 136; Harry W. Reynolds,Jr., "Merit Controls, the Hatch Acts, and Personnel Standards in Intergovernmental Relations," *Annals of the American Academy of Political and Social Science,* CCCLIX (May 1965), p. 93; York Wilbern, "Administration in State Governments," The American Assembly, Graduate School of Business, Columbia University, *The Forty-eight States: Their Tasks as Policy Makers and Administrators* (Final Edition, Background papers, 1955), p. 129.

26. Herman M. Somers, "The Federal Bureaucracy and the Change of Administration," *American Political Science Review,* XLVIII (March 1954), p. 149.

27. U.S. Commission on Civil Rights, *For All the People . . . By All the People; A Report on Equal Opportunity in State and Local Government Employment* (Washington: Government Printing Office, 1969), p. 64; cf. pp. 63-69 re minority workers and merit systems. Cf. the discussion of representative bureaucracy below, chap. IV.

28. James W. Martin, "Administrative Dangers in the Enlarged Highway Program, *"Public Administration Review,* XIX (Summer 1959), p. 172.

29. White, *The Jacksonians,* p. 304.

30. Dalmas H. Nelson, "Political Expression under the Hatch Act and the Problem of Statutory Ambiguity," *Midwest Journal of Political Science,* II (February 1958), p. 86.

31. Paul T. David and Ross Pollock, *Executives for Government; Central Issues of Federal Personnel Administration* (Washington, D.C.:

The Brookings Institution, 1957, reprinted with Supplement, 1958), p. 144.

32. Paul P. Van Riper, "The Senior Civil Service and the Career System," *Public Administration Review,* XVIII (Summer 1958), p. 194.

33. U.S. Commission on Organization of the Executive Branch of the Government, *Personnel and Civil Service; A Report to the Congress* (Washington: Government Printing Office, 1955), p. 93; cf. pp. 89–96 for two dissents.

34. U.S. Civil Service Commission, "The Executive Assignment System" (November 1966—leaflet).

35. Letter from Seymour S. Berlin, Director, Bureau of Executive Manpower, U.S. Civil Service Commission, February 24, 1971.

36. U.S. Congress, House Committee on Post Office and Civil Service, 92nd Congress, 1st Session, February 3, 1971, Committee Print No. 3, *The Federal Executive Service (A Proposal for Improving Federal Executive Manpower Management),* Recommendations of the President of the United States (Washington: Government Printing Office, 1971), quotations in this paragraph are from pp. 78, 78, 78, 89, respectively.

37. Dean E. Mann, *The Assistant Secretaries; Problems and Processes of Appointment* (Washington, D.C.: The Brookings Institution, 1965), p. 265.

38. W. Lloyd Warner et al., *The American Federal Executive* (New Haven: Yale University Press, 1963), Part VI, pp. 189–250, deals with the personalities of federal executives.

39. Avery Leiserson, *Administrative Regulation; A Study in Representation of Interests* (Chicago: University of Chicago Press, 1942), p. 16.

40. E. E. Schattschneider, *The Semisovereign People; A Realist's*

View of Democracy in America (New York: Holt, Rinehart & Winston, Inc., 1960), chap. II, pp. 20–46.
41. Senator Ervin's Judiciary Subcommittee on Constitutional Rights began hearings on government spying on civilians and government data banks, February 23, 1971. These are reported in the various issues of *Congressional Quarterly Weekly Report.* Cf. especially XXIX, No. 8, February 19, 1971, pp. 425–430, for background information on hearings.
42. *The New York Times,* March 10, 1971.

CHAPTER FOUR
1. Joseph Tussman, *Obligation and the Body Politic* (New York: Oxford University Press, Inc., 1960). Cf. Brian Barry, "The Public Interest," William E. Connolly, ed., *The Bias of Pluralism* (New York: Atherton Press, Inc., 1969), pp. 159–177.
2. W. Lloyd Warner *et al., The American Federal Executive* (New Haven: Yale University Press, 1963), p. 22.
3. Information on women in the civil service is drawn from the *National Civil Service League Exchange,* I, 6 (July 1971), and *The New York Times,* May 28, 1971.
4. Data are based on: Civil Service Commission press releases; U.S. Civil Service Commission, *Study of Minority Group Employment in the Federal Government, 1966,* and *Study of Minority Group Employment in the Federal Government, November 30, 1969* (Washington: Government Printing Office, 1970).
5. U.S. Commission on Civil Rights, *For ALL the people . . . By*

ALL the people; A Report on Equal Opportunity in State and Local Government Employment (Washington: Government Printing Office, 1969).
6. Gladys Baker, *The County Agent* (Chicago: University of Chicago Press, 1939), p. xv.
7. Phillip O. Foss, *Politics and Grass; The Administration of Grazing on the Public Domain* (Seattle: University of Washington Press, 1960).
8. *The New York Times,* December 7, 1970.
9. Peter Marris and Martin Rein, *Dilemmas of Social Reform; Poverty and Community Action in the United States* (New York: Atherton Press, Inc., 1967), p. 215.
10. For information on New York City neighborhood government, I have relied on *The New York Times* and on materials supplied by Mayor Lindsay's office. Re Boston, I have used the *Boston Globe* and valuable information supplied by David Hoeh of Hanover, N.H., who wrote a seminar paper on this topic.
11. Suzanne Keller, *The Urban Neighborhood: A Sociological Perspective* (New York: Random House, Inc., 1968), p. 163.
12. Melvin Mogulof, "Coalition to Adversary: Citizen Participation in Three Federal Programs," *Journal of the American Institute of Planners,* XXXV (July 1969), p. 231.
13. Alan A. Altshuler, *Community Control: The Black Demand for Participation in Large American Cities* (New York: Pegasus, 1970), p. 44.
14. Warren G. Bennis, *Organization Development: Its Nature, Origins, and Prospects* (Reading, Mass.: Addison-Wesley Publishing Co., Inc., 1969), p. 34.
15. Charles A. Reich, "The Greening of America," *The New Yorker,* Sept. 26, 1970, p. 50.

BIBLIOGRAPHICAL ESSAY

The bibliography is organized by topics parallel to the table of contents and the text. Major chapter subheadings also appear in the bibliography, to facilitate easy location of literature on specific topics, permitting referral to and from the text and the bibliography. The introductory phrase of each paragraph in the bibliography indicates in detail the topic dealt with. Cross-references to other sections of the bibliography are provided where appropriate.

Chapter One: Perspectives on Governmental Bureaucracy

THE EVALUATION OF BUREAUCRACY

Criticism of governmental bureaucracy as incompetent is exemplified by: Ludwig Von Mises, *Bureaucracy* (New Haven: Yale University Press, 1944); Harold J. Laski, "Bureaucracy," *Encyclopaedia of the Social Sciences* (New York: The Macmillan Company, 1930), III, 70–74. Specifically re contemporary American government and the Vietnam War, cf. Richard M. Pfeffer, ed., *No More Vietnams? The War and the Future of American Foreign Policy* (New York: Harper & Row, Publishers, Colophon, 1968), especially pp. 44–114, "American Political and Bureaucratic Decision-Making." Re the loss of vitality in large organizations in general, cf. Marshall E. Dimock, *Administrative Vitality; The Conflict with Bureaucracy* (New York: Harper & Bros., 1959); Robert Townsend, *Up the Organization* (New York: Alfred A. Knopf, Inc., 1970). Criticism of bureaucracy as destructive of the human spirit is exemplified by: Gabriel Marcel, *The Philosophy of Existentialism* (New York: Citadel Press, Inc., 1956 by the Philosophical Library) and *Man Against Mass Society* (Chicago: Henry Regnery Co., 1962); Karl Jaspers, *Man in the Modern Age,* trans. Eden and Cedar Paul (Garden City, N.Y.: Doubleday & Company, Inc., Anchor Books, 1957); William H. Whyte, Jr., *The Organization Man* (Garden City, N.Y.: Doubleday & Company, Inc., Anchor Books, 1957); Sheldon Wolin and John Schaar, "Berkeley: The Battle of People's Park," *New York Review of Books,* XII (June 19,1969), 24 ff.; Charles A. Reich, "The Greening of America," *The New Yorker,* Sept. 26, 1970, pp. 42 ff.; Theodore Roszak, *The Making of a Counter Culture; Reflections on the Technocratic Society and Its Youthful Opposition* (Garden City, N.Y.: Doubleday & Company, Inc., Anchor Books, 1969).

Criticism of governmental bureaucracy as politically oppressive is exemplified by: James Burnham, *The Managerial Revolution; What Is Happening in the World* (New York: The John Day Company, Inc., 1941); Milovan Djilas, *The New Class; An Analysis of the Communist System* (New York: Frederick A. Praeger, Inc., 1957) (formerly a Communist hero and vice-president of Yugoslavia, the brave Djilas has spent years in jail as a consequence of his writings); Eric Strauss, *The Ruling Servants; Bureaucracy in Russia, France—and Britain?* (New York: Frederick A. Praeger, Inc., 1961). For an introduction to the debate over who governs America and a multi-influence position, cf. Arnold Rose, *The Power Structure: Political Process in American Society* (New York: Oxford University Press, Inc., 1967). See also items under "American

Public Administration and the Rule of Law," especially re "administrative justice for the poor," below, chap. II in the bibliography.

Items re "criticism of governmental bureaucracy as incompetent" are cited above in the bibliography. Specific questions of competence involve such matters as the functioning of independent regulatory commissions, patronage civil service, and citizen participation, and are dealt with throughout the text and cited at appropriate points in the bibliography.

Sources of writings on bureaucracy by Max Weber include: H. H. Gerth & C. Wright Mills, trans. & ed., *From Max Weber: Essays in Sociology* (New York: Oxford University Press, Inc., 1946), chap. 8; Max Weber, *The Theory of Social and Economic Organization,* trans. A. M. Henderson and Talcott Parsons, ed. Parsons (New York: Oxford University Press, Inc., 1947), part III, especially pp. 324–341; Robert K. Merton et al., ed., *Reader in Bureaucracy* (Glencoe, Ill.: The Free Press, 1952).

Re Weber and his work, cf. Reinhard Bendix, *Max Weber; An Intellectual Portrait* (Garden City, N.Y.: Doubleday & Company, Inc., 1960), especially part III, a useful summary and commentary on Weber's works; S. M. Miller, *Max Weber* (New York: Thomas Y. Crowell Company, 1963), especially chap. 6; Julien Freund, *The Sociology of Max Weber*, trans. Mary Ilford (New York: Pantheon Books, Inc., 1968); Alfred Diamant, "The Bureaucratic Model: Max Weber Rejected, Rediscovered, Reformed," *Papers in Comparative Public Administration,* Ferrel Heady & Sybil L. Stokes (Ann Arbor, Mich.: Institute of Public Administration, The University of Michigan Press,

1962); Martin Albrow, *Bureaucracy* (New York: Praeger Publishers, Inc., 1970), chaps. 2–3; Nicos P. Mouzelis, *Organization and Bureaucracy; An Analysis of Modern Theories* (Chicago: Aldine Publishing Company, 1968), especially part I; Karl Loewenstein, *Max Weber's Political Ideas in the Perspective of Our Time* (Amherst, Mass.: University of Massachusetts Press, 1966), especially pp. 30–40; J. P. Mayer, *Max Weber and German Politics; A Study in Political Sociology* (London: Faber & Faber, Ltd., 2d ed., 1956), a good source for Weber's nonacademic writings; Karl Jaspers, *Three Essays: Leonardo, Descartes, Max Weber* (New York: Harcourt Brace Jovanovich, Inc., 1964); Arthur Mitzman, *The Iron Cage; An Historical Interpretation of Max Weber* (New York: Alfred A. Knopf, Inc., 1970), a psycho-cultural study which is less flattering than Loewenstein or Jaspers, who knew and admired Weber. For an analysis of Prussian history, which helps one to understand Weber's perspective, cf. Hans Rosenberg, *Bureaucracy, Aristocracy and Autocracy; The Prussian Experience 1660–1815* (Cambridge, Mass.: Harvard University Press, 1958). Criticism of Weber's treatment of authority leads to modification of his theory by: Alvin W. Gouldner, *Patterns of Industrial Bureaucracy* (Glencoe, Ill.: The Free Press, 1954); Victor A. Thompson, *Modern Organization* (New York: Alfred A. Knopf, Inc., 1961).

Concepts of organization used in American administration writing are introduced in: Luther Gulick and L. Urwick, eds., *Papers on the Science of Administration* (New York: Institute of Public Administration, 1937), a classic statement; James G. March and Herbert A. Simon, *Organizations* (New York:

John Wiley & Sons, Inc., 1958); Peter M. Blau and W. Richard Scott, *Formal Organizations; A Comparative Approach* (San Francisco: Chandler Publishing Co., 1962). Current articles and book reviews re administrative organization will be found in the journal, *Administrative Science Quarterly.*

Items re selfhood in the bureaucratic life are cited above, re "criticism of bureaucracy as destructive of the human spirit," and below, chap. IV, "The Bureaucratic Life" and "The Democratization of Public Administration?" in the bibliography.

Items re "criticism of governmental bureaucracy as politically oppressive" are cited above; items re "interest groups, bureaucracy, and politics," relevant to the question of political responsibility, appear in the bibliography below, chap. III.

Whether one should emphasize the uniqueness of public administration or the commonness of all bureaucratic administration is a question which seriously divides scholars and to which much of the literature of organization theory and of public administration is probably at least incidentally relevant. For the argument that we need a "general" theory of administration, because the administrative process is essentially universal, cf. Edward H. Litchfield, "Notes on a General Theory of Administration," *Administrative Science Quarterly,* I (1956–1957), pp. 3–29. For an argument sensitive to the uniqueness of public administration, cf. John J. Corson, "Distinguishing Characteristics of Public Administration," *Public Administration Review,* XII (Spring 1952), pp. 120–125. Each of these journals embodies the position argued in the

article it published. Cf. Dwight Waldo, *The Administrative State; A Study of the Political Theory of American Public Administration* (New York: The Ronald Press Company, 1948), re the influence of general administrative theory and of specifically political theory on American public administration.

Political direction of the French civil service is discussed in: Strauss, *The Ruling Servants,* chap. 9, pp. 179–228; Alfred Diamant, "The French Administrative System—The Republic Passes but the Administration Remains," William J. Siffin, ed., *Toward the Comparative Study of Public Administration* (Bloomington, Ind.: Indiana University Press, 1959), pp. 182–218; Herbert Luethy, *France Against Herself,* trans. Eric Mosbacher (New York: Frederick A. Praeger, Inc., 1955), especially chap. 2, pp. 5–27.

PUBLIC V. PRIVATE ADMINISTRATION

Motivation within modern corporations is analyzed in: John Kenneth Galbraith, *The New Industrial State* (Boston: Houghton Mifflin Company, Sentry Edition, 1969). Cf. Frederick Herzberg *et al., The Motivation to Work* (New York: John Wiley & Sons, Inc., 2nd ed., 1959), dealing especially with middle management.

There is a substantial literature on the motivation of production employees in industry. It hardly supports the notion that profit is a key consideration for them. Cf. A. Zaleznik *et al., The Motivation, Productivity, and Satisfaction of Workers; A Prediction Study* (Boston: Harvard University, Graduate School of Business Administration, 1958). The classic study, still useful and fascinating, is F. J. Roethlisberger & William J. Dickson, *Management and the Worker* (Cambridge, Mass.: Harvard University Press, 1961), actually published first over thirty years ago, describing and speculating upon the Western Electric (Hawthorne plant) studies of factory workers.

THE U.S. GOVERNMENT BUREAUCRACY

The history of the American public service is provided in: Leonard D. White, *The Federalists* (New York: The Macmillan Company, 1956); *The Jeffersonians* (New York: The Macmillan Company, 1951); *The Jacksonians* (New York: The Macmillan Company, 1954); *The Republican Era: 1869–1901* (New York: The Macmillan Company, 1958); Paul P. Van Riper, *History of the United States Civil Service* (Evanston, Ill.: Row, Peterson & Co., 1958). Valuable interpretations of the modern American public service are provided by: Paul H. Appleby, *Policy and Administration* (University, Ala.: University of Alabama Press, 1949); Don K. Price, *The Scientific Estate* (Cambridge, Mass.: Harvard University Press, 1965). Re the current structure and functions, cf. U.S. National Archives and Records Service, General Services Administration, *United States Government Organization Manual* (Washington: Government Printing Office), revised annually. Appropriations hearings of the House of Representatives Committee on Appropriations, published annually, provide detailed information on each agency. Annual reports published by agencies are also useful. For continuing information and analysis of American governmental bureaucracy and the literature on it, cf. the journal, *Public Administration Review*, published by the American Society for Public Administration, a coalition of academicians and practitioners.

Comparative public administration makes important contributions to understanding other nations and provides perspectives on American public administration. Cf. Siffin, *Toward the Comparative Study of Public Administration;* Fred W. Riggs, *Administration in Developing Countries; The Theory of Prismatic Society* (Boston: Houghton Mifflin Company, 1964); Heady & Stokes, *Papers in Comparative Public Administration;* Nimrod Raphaeli, ed., *Readings in Comparative Public Administration* (Boston: Allyn & Bacon, Inc., 1967); Joseph LaPalombara, ed., *Bureaucracy and Political Development* (Princeton, N.J.: Princeton University Press, 1963); Brian Chapman, *The Profession of Government; The Public Service in Europe* (London: George Allen & Unwin Ltd., 1963); Ferrel Heady, *Public Administration: A Comparative Perspective* (Englewood Cliffs, N.J.: Prentice-Hall, Inc., 1966), a brief introduction to the subject. Riggs is the key figure in the development of a theory of comparative public administration; cf. his book and his essays in the Siffin and Heady & Stokes volumes. There is also a useful literature on public administration systems of specific nations; a few items on France are cited above, and in chap. II, below, re "administrative courts," and some on Britain are cited in chap. 3, below, particularly re "participation by civil servants in partisan politics" and re "the British higher civil service," in the bibliography. The *Journal of Comparative Administration*, instituted in 1969 in cooperation with the Comparative Administration Group of the American Society for Public Administration, is a useful source for contemporary thinking in comparative public administration.

Chapter Two: Public Administration Under Law

THE RULE OF LAW

The rule of law is discussed in Walter Lippmann, *Essays in the Public Philosophy* (Boston:Little, Brown and Company, 1955). For a brief classic statement, cf. Aristotle's *Politics,* III, 16. With specific reference to public administration, the classic statement is A. V. Dicey, *Introduction to the Study of the Law of the Constitution,* introd. E. C. S. Wade (London: Macmillan & Co. Ltd., 9th ed., 1939). For criticisms of Dicey's analysis, cf. *ibid.,* Wade's introduction; Ivor Jennings, *The Law and the Constitution* (London: University of London Press Ltd., 5th ed., 1959). In defense of Dicey, cf. F. H. Lawson, "Dicey Revisited," I and II, *Political Studies,* VII (June 1959 and October 1959), pp. 109–126, 207–221. Kenneth Culp Davis, *Administrative Law and Government* (St. Paul, Minn.: West Publishing Co., 1960), pp. 47–51, summarizes meanings of the rule of law and implies that the term is of doubtful use. Cf. Brian Chapman, *The Profession of Government; The Public Service in Europe* (London: George Allen & Unwin Ltd., 1963), pp. 182–185, re alternative conceptions of the proper role of law as a limit upon the state. Cf. Franz Kafka, *The Trial* (New York: Alfred A. Knopf, Inc., 1951), for a brilliant fictional presentation of subjection to incomprehensible, uncontrollable authority.

ADMINISTRATIVE REGULATION

The defects of the judiciary as regulator are discussed in: John Dickinson, *Administrative Justice and the Supremacy of Law in the United States* (New York: Russell & Russell Publishers, 1959); James M. Landis,

The Administrative Process (New Haven, Conn.: Yale University Press, 1938), especially pp. 30–46; Davis, *Administrative Law and Government,* pp. 32–39; U.S. Attorney General's Committee on Administrative Procedure, *Administrative Procedure in Government Agencies,* Senate, 77th Congress, 1st Session, Document No. 8 (Washington: Government Printing Office, 1941), pp. 11–18; Wallace Mendelsohn, "Mr. Justice Frankfurter on Administrative Law," *Journal of Politics,* XIX (August 1957), pp. 441–460; Peter Woll, *Administrative Law: The Informal Process* (Berkeley: University of California Press, 1963), pp. 5–8.

The common law v. administrative law conflict is discussed in: Lloyd D. Musolf, *Federal Examiners and the Conflict of Law and Administration* (Baltimore: The Johns Hopkins Press, 1953); Woll, *Administrative Law,* pp. 10–21; Davis, *Administrative Law and Government,* pp. 25–31, 40–47.

The nondelegability of legislative power was discussed, when the issue seemed more alive than now, in J. Roland Pennock, *Administration and the Rule of Law* (New York: Rinehart & Co., Inc., 1941), chap. IV. For the contemporary law on this and other matters in administrative regulation, with relatively brief, but informed and intelligent analysis, cf. Davis, *Administrative Law and Government.* For a fuller presentation of cases and for matters which Davis slights, cf. Walter Gellhorn and Clark Byse, *Administrative Law—Cases and Comments* (Brooklyn: The Foundation Press, Inc., 4th ed., 1960).

The Administrative Procedure Act is: 60 Stat. 237 (1946), 5 U.S.C.A. s. 1001. The text is appended to Davis, *Administrative*

Law and Government and Gellhorn and Byse, *Administrative Law.* For evaluations, cf. Musolf, *Federal Examiners;* Marver H. Bernstein, *Regulating Business by Independent Commission* (Princeton, N.J.: Princeton University Press, 1955), chap. 7; Woll, *Administrative Law,* pp. 20 ff.

Judicialization of administrative procedure was urged by the second Hoover Commission and the American Bar Association (ABA). Cf. U.S. Commission on Organization of the Executive Branch of the Government, Task Force on Legal Services and Procedure, *Report on Legal Services and Procedure* (Washington: Government Printing Office, 1955); U.S. Commission on Organization of the Executive Branch of the Government, *Legal Services and Procedure,* A Report to the Congress (Washington: Government Printing Office, 1955). Cf. Commissioner Holifield's excellent dissent, pp. 97–112. Cf. Woll, *Administrative Law,* pp. 166–170, for criticism of the task force and ABA view of the administrative regulatory process.

Administrative power to punish is discussed in: Ernst Freund, *Administrative Powers Over Persons and Property; A Comparative Survey* (Chicago: University of Chicago Press, 1928); Dalmas H. Nelson, *Administrative Agencies of the USA; Their Decisions and Authority* (Detroit: Wayne State University Press, 1964), and his "Administrative Blackmail: The Remission of Penalties," *Western Political Quarterly,* IV (December 1951), pp. 610–622; James Hart, *An Introduction to Administrative Law, With Selected Cases* (New York: Appleton-Century-Crofts, 2nd ed., 1950), chap. 22; Davis, *Administrative Law and Government,* especially chaps. 3, 4; Gellhorn and Byse, *Administrative Law,*

especially chap. 2, section 1, despite its title; Charles A. Reich, "The New Property," *Yale Law Journal,* LXXIII (April 1964), pp. 733–787; Francis E. Rourke, *Secrecy and Publicity; Dilemmas of Democracy* (Baltimore: The Johns Hopkins Press, 1961), chap. 6, re the sanction of publicity; Herman Goldstein, "Police Discretion: The Ideal Versus the Real," *Public Administration Review,* XXIII (September 1963), pp. 140–148. For a hostile view of administrative authority to punish, cf. U.S. Commission on Organization of the Executive Branch, Task Force on Legal Services and Procedure, *Report,* pp. 242–246. For a comparison, arguing the greater authority of the French administration over the English or American, cf. Bernard Schwartz, *French Administrative Law and the Common Law World* (New York: New York University Press, 1954), pp. 88–107.

ADMINISTRATIVE DUE PROCEDURE

The legislative *v.* adjudicative facts distinction is discussed in Davis, *Administrative Law and Government,* pp. 149–154. H. W. R. Wade endorses the distinction and shows its applicability to tribunals and inquiries in Britain (*Towards Administrative Justice* [Ann Arbor: University of Michigan Press, c. 1963]; chap. 3).

Rule-making procedures are discussed in Davis, *Administrative Law and Government,* chap. 6; Pennock, *Administration and the Rule of Law,* pp. 49–60, re safeguards. Re rule making in the states, cf. Ferrel Heady, "State Administrative Procedure Laws: An Appraisal," *Public Administration Review,* XII (Winter 1952), pp. 11–13.

The need for standards through rules in administrative

regulation is discussed by: Henry J. Friendly, *The Federal Administrative Agencies; The Need for Better Definition of Standards* (Cambridge, Mass.: Harvard University Press, 1962); Landis, *The Administrative Process,* pp. 50–88; Davis, *Administrative Law and Government,* chap. 2; Pennock, *Administration and the Rule of Law,* pp. 31, 49–53; Louis J. Hector, "Problems of the CAB and the Independent Regulatory Commissions," *Yale Law Journal,* LXIX (May 1960), pp. 939–948, re lack of standards; Theodore J. Lowi, *The End of Liberalism; Ideology, Policy, and the Crisis of Public Authority* (New York: W. W. Norton & Company, Inc., 1969), pp. 297–303 and chap. 5, arguing for "a more formal and rule-bound administrative process" (p. 303), in place of case by case adjudication without clear standards. For a defense by the FTC chairman of the creation of policy through administrative adjudication, cf. Earl W. Kintner, "The Current Ordeal of the Administrative Process: In Reply to Mr. Hector," *Yale Law Journal,* LXIX (May 1960), pp. 965–977.

A code of standards of administrative procedure was urged by a minority of the Attorney General's Committee in the 1941 report, and they offered such a code, running some thirty pages. For the Model State Administrative Procedure Act (1946), with a brief commentary and bibliography, cf. Gellhorn and Byse, *Administrative Law,* pp. 1231–1239. Cf. Heady, "State Administrative Procedure Laws," *op. cit.,* warning against carrying code legislation too far.

Admissibility of evidence in administrative adjudication is discussed in Davis, *Administrative Law and Government,* chaps. 14, 15; Wade, *Towards Administrative Justice,* chap.

5. Each writes that the use of extra-record information is of the greatest practical importance but is the least understood of all administrative law questions.

Hearing examiners are discussed in Musolf, *Federal Examiners,* a basic source; Davis, *Administrative Law and Government,* chaps. 10, 11, 13; Robert S. Lorch, "Toward Administrative Judges," *Public Administration Review,* XXX (January/February 1970), pp. 50–55, arguing for independence for examiners from agency control and finality for their decisions.

Informal adjudication is discussed in Woll, *Administrative Law,* a useful source on procedures short of fully formal adjudication; U.S. Attorney General's Committee, *Administrative Procedure,* chap. 3, one of the early documents to recognize informal procedure as crucial. Kenneth Davis has a few reservations, but accepts the role of informal adjudication; Woll has great enthusiasm. Cf. Walter Gellhorn, *When Americans Complain: Governmental Grievance Procedures* (Cambridge, Mass.: Harvard University Press, 1966), pp. 213–215.

The danger of the "privilege" concept is discussed in: Reich, "The New Property," *op. cit.;* Arch Dotson, "The Emerging Doctrine of Privilege in Public Employment," *Public Administration Review,* XV (Spring 1955), pp. 77–88; Davis, *Administrative Law and Government,* pp. 156–182.

JUDICIAL CONTROL OF ADMINISTRATION

Judicial review techniques are discussed in the administrative law texts cited above: Davis, Gellhorn and Byse, Hart. Re the writs, cf. Hart, *An Introduction to Administrative Law,* chap. 1, for a careful discussion. Re trends in judicial review, cf. Foster Sherwood, "Judicial Control of Administrative Discretion 1932–1952," *Western Political Quarterly,* VI (December 1953), pp. 750–761.

The substantial evidence rule in judicial review of administrative decisions is discussed in: Davis, *Administrative Law and Government,* chap. 29; Dickinson, *Administrative Justice;* Landis, *The Administrative Process,* pp. 127–134, re the bad effects of judicial review of "jurisdictional facts"; Pennock, *Administration and the Rule of Law,* chap. VII, re different treatment of different agencies. Cf. Martin Shapiro, *The Supreme Court and Administrative Agencies* (New York: The Free Press, 1968), re the mutually respectful relations between reviewing courts and administrative regulatory agencies.

Administrative courts are discussed in: Chapman, *The Profession of Government,* chaps. 9–11; C. J. Hamson, *Executive Discretion and Judicial Control; An Aspect of the French Conseil d'Etat* (London: Stevens & Sons Ltd., 1954); Schwartz, *French Administrative Law;* Alfred Diamant, "The French Council of State; Comparative Observations on the Problem of Controlling the Bureaucracy of the Modern State," *The Journal of Politics,* XIII (November 1951), pp. 562–588; Lawson, "Dicey Revisited," I and II, *op. cit.*

The recent American debate on the issue of administrative courts is discussed in: Milton M. Carrow, "Administrative Adjudication: Should Its Role Be Changed?" *George Washington Law Review,* XXVII (January 1959), pp. 279–301; Daniel W. Gribbon, "Should the Judicial Character of the Tax Court Be Recognized?" *ibid.,* XXIV (June 1956), pp.

619–636, re the Tax Court, which is formally an executive agency but seems to work well as a court; Robert E. Freer, "The Case Against the Trade Regulation Section of the Proposed Administrative Court," *ibid.,* pp. 637–655, vigorously condemning the Hoover Commission and ABA proposals as dogmatic, uninformed, destructive; Guy Farmer, "An Administrative Labor Court: Some Observations on the Hoover Commission Report," *ibid.,* pp. 656–671, questioning the unreasoned preference for any court over any administrative agency. For the Ash Council (which was sympathetic to effective administrative regulation) recommendation for an Administrative Court, cf. U.S., The President's Advisory Council on Executive Organization, *A New Regulatory Framework; Report on Selected Independent Regulatory Agencies,* January 1971 (Washington: Government Printing Office, 1971).

THE OMBUDSMAN

The Ombudsman is discussed in: Donald C. Rowat, ed., *The Ombudsman; Citizen's Defender* (London: George Allen & Unwin Ltd., 1965); Walter Gellhorn, *Ombudsmen and Others; Citizens' Protectors in Nine Countries* (Cambridge, Mass.: Harvard University Press, 1966), and his *When Americans Complain,* which urges Ombudsmen in America; Stanley V. Anderson, ed., (The American Assembly), *Ombudsmen for American Government?* (Englewood Cliffs, N.J.: Prentice-Hall, Inc., 1968); U.S. Congress, Senate, Committee on the Judiciary, Subcommittee on Administrative Practice and Procedure, 89th Congress, 2d Session, *Ombudsman,* Hearing, March 7, 1966 (Washington: Government Printing Office, 1966).

AMERICAN PUBLIC ADMINISTRATION AND THE RULE OF LAW

The view that American administrative regulation is overjudicialized is supported by: Bernstein, *Regulating Business by Independent Commission,* who makes this a basic theme; Hector, "Problems of the CAB," *op. cit.,* pp. 931–964; Walter Gellhorn, "Administrative Procedure Reform: Hardy Perennial," *American Bar Association Journal,* LXVIII (March 1962), pp. 243–251; Wade, *Towards Administrative Justice;* U.S. President's Advisory Council on Executive Organization, *A New Regulatory Framework.*

Administrative justice for the poor is discussed in: Reginald Heber Smith, *Justice and the Poor,* The Carnegie Foundation for the Advancement of Teaching, Bulletin No. 13 (New York City, 1919); Harry W. Jones, "The Rule of Law and the Welfare State," *Columbia Law Review,* LVIII (February 1958), pp. 143–156; Charles A. Reich, "Individual Rights and Social Welfare: The Emerging Legal Issues," *Yale Law Journal,* LXXIV (June 1965), 1245–1257; Richard A. Cloward and Richard M. Elman, "Poverty, Injustice and the Welfare State; Part I: An Ombudsman for the Poor?" *The Nation,* CCII (February 28, 1966), pp. 230–235; "Part II: How Rights Can Be Secured," (March 7, 1966), pp. 264–268; Gellhorn, *When Americans Complain,* pp. 195–211; T. E. Utley, *Occasion for Ombudsman* (London: Christopher Johnson, 1961), especially chap. 11, re the distinction between benevolent welfare state control and self-control; Jerome E. Carlin *et al., Civil Justice and the Poor; Issues for Sociological Research* (New York: Russell Sage Foundation, 1967), re the difficulties and possibilities of using the law to aid, not harm, the poor; American Public Welfare Association, *Equal Justice* (Chicago: May 1965). Cf. U.S. Department of Health, Education, and Welfare, Welfare Administration, Advisory Council on Public Welfare, *Having the Power, We Have the Duty,* Report to the Secretary of Health, Education, and Welfare (Washington: Government Printing Office, 1966), which devotes attention throughout to the need to assure the rights of welfare recipients; cf. especially chap. VII.

Chapter Three: Public Administration Under Politics

THE POLICY-ADMINISTRATION RELATIONSHIP

Re the politics-administration dichotomy in pre-World War II American public administration writing, cf. Frank J. Goodnow, *Politics and Administration: A Study in Government* (New York: The Macmillan Company, 1900) and *The Principles of the Administrative Law of the United States* (New York: G. P. Putnam's Sons, 1905); Woodrow Wilson, "The Study of Administration" *Political Science Quarterly,* II (June 1887), pp. 197–222; Dwight Waldo, *The Administrative State: A Study of the Political Theory of American Public Administration* (New York: The Ronald Press Company, 1948), the standard study, chap. 7.

For influential discussions of the politics-administration relationship in post-World War II American public administration writing, cf. Paul Appleby, *Policy and Administration* (University, Ala.: University of Alabama Press, 1949); J. Lieper Freeman, *The Political Process; Executive Bureau-Legislative Committee Relations* (New York:

Random House, Inc., rev. ed., 1965); David B. Truman, *The Governmental Process; Political Interests and Public Opinion* (New York: Alfred A. Knopf, Inc., 1951); Fritz Morstein Marx, ed., *Elements of Public Administration* (Englewood Cliffs, N.J.: Prentice-Hall, Inc., 2nd ed., 1959); Harold Stein, ed., (The Inter-University Case Program), *Public Administration and Policy Development; A Case Book* (New York: Harcourt Brace Jovanovich, Inc., 1952). *Public Administration Review* usually reflects the dominant contemporary position. For the "New Public Administration" perspective, cf. Frank Marini, ed., *Toward a New Public Administration; The Minnowbrook Perspective* (San Francisco: Chandler Publishing Co., 1971).

CONTROL BY ELECTED OFFICIALS

Comparison of congressmen and the President is helped by: Andrew Hacker, "The Elected and the Anointed: Two American Elites," *American Political Science Review,* LV (September 1961), pp. 539–549, re senators and corporation presidents; Samuel P. Huntington, "Congressional Response to the Twentieth Century," David B. Truman, ed. (The American Assembly), *The Congress and America's Future* (Englewood Cliffs, N.J.: Prentice-Hall, Inc., 1965), re the provincialism of Congress, as contrasted with the executive branch. Re presidential *v.* congressional politicians, James MacGregor Burns, *The Deadlock of Democracy; Four-Party Politics in America* (Englewood Cliffs, N.J.: Prentice-Hall, Inc., 1963), especially pp. 195–203, 234–264. Also emphasizing presidential-congressional differences, but more sympathetic to

the congressional, conservative position, cf. Willmoore Kendall, "The Two Majorities," *Midwest Journal of Political Science,* IV (November 1960), pp. 317–345.

Re legislative *v.* executive control of the public service, cf. Joseph P. Harris, *Congressional Control of Administration* (Washington, D.C.: The Brookings Institution, 1964), sympathetic to presidential control; Charles S. Hyneman, *Bureaucracy in a Democracy* (New York: Harper & Bros., 1950), sympathetic to congressional control; the landmark case, *Myers v. U.S.,* 270 US 52 (1926), the Court's opinion by Chief Justice (and former President) Taft; Walter Gellhorn & Clark Byse, *Administrative Law—Cases and Comments* (Brooklyn: The Foundation Press, Inc., 4th ed., 1960), chap. II, "Legislative and Executive Control of Administrative Action"; John D. Millett, *Government and Public Administration; The Quest for Responsible Performance* (New York: McGraw-Hill Book Co., 1959); Richard E. Neustadt, "Politicians and Bureaucrats," Truman, *The Congress and America's Future,* arguing the common stake of Congress and President in controlling the administration.

Re legislative control of American governmental bureaucracy, cf. items above re legislative *v.* executive control; Huntington, "Congressional Response to the Twentieth Century," *op. cit.;* Arthur W. Macmahon, "Congressional Oversight of Administration: The Power of the Purse," *Political Science Quarterly,* LVIII (June 1943), pp. 161–190, (September 1943), pp. 380–414, re informal controls by the appropriations committee; Richard F. Fenno, Jr., "The House Appropriations Committee as a Political System: The Problem of Integration," *American Political Science Review,* LVI (June 1962), pp. 310–324; Aaron Wildavsky, *The Politics of the Budgetary Process* (Boston: Little, Brown and Company, 1964); Robert A. Wallace, *Congressional Control of Federal Spending* (Detroit: Wayne State University Press, 1960), a congressional aide's analysis; Elias Huzar, *The Purse and the Sword; Control of the Army by Congress through Military Appropriations, 1933–50* (Ithaca, N.Y.: Cornell University Press, 1950), re the House and Senate subcommittees on military appropriations; Edward A. Kolodziej, *The Uncommon Defense and Congress, 1945–1963* (Columbus, Ohio: Ohio State University Press, 1966) re Congress' use of its power of the purse to influence military strategic policy; Walter Gellhorn, *When Americans Complain: Governmental Grievance Procedures* (Cambridge, Mass.: Harvard University Press, 1966), especially re case work; Kenneth G. Olson, "The Service Function of the United States Congress," Alfred de Grazia, ed., *Congress; The First Branch of Government* (Garden City, N.Y.: Doubleday & Company, Inc., Anchor Books, 1967), pp. 323–364, re case work; John E. Moore, "State Government and the Ombudsman," Stanley V. Anderson, ed. (The American Assembly), *Ombudsmen for American Government?* (Englewood Cliffs, N.J.: Prentice-Hall, Inc., 1968), pp. 70–100, re case work; Seymour Scher, "Conditions for Legislative Control." *Journal of Politics,* XXV (August 1963), pp. 526–551; Edward A. Shils, "The Legislator and his Environment," S. Sidney Ulmer, ed., *Introductory Readings in Political Behavior* (Chicago: Rand McNally & Co., 1961), pp. 85–94; Joseph P. Harris, *The Advice and Consent of the Senate*

(Berkeley: University of California Press, 1953), re confirmation of appointments.

Re secrecy in American government as a barrier to effective control of bureaucracy, cf. Edward A. Shils, *The Torment of Secrecy; The Background and Consequences of American Security Policies* (Glencoe, Ill.: The Free Press, 1956); Harold L. Cross, *The People's Right to Know: Legal Access to Public Records and Proceedings* (New York: Columbia University Press, 1953); Francis E. Rourke, *Secrecy and Publicity; Dilemmas of Democracy* (Baltimore: The Johns Hopkins Press, 1961). For a lively journalistic treatment of American espionage and intelligence, cf. Donald Wise and Thomas B. Ross, *The Invisible Government* (New York; Bantam Books, 1965).

Re civilian control of the military, cf. Adam Yarmolinsky, *The Military Establishment; Its Impacts on American Society* (New York: Harper & Row, Publishers, 1971), especially chaps. 3 and 4 on presidential and congressional control; Leonard S. Rodberg and Derek Shearer, eds., *The Pentagon Watchers; Students Report on the National Security State* (Garden City, N.Y.: Doubleday & Company, Inc., 1970) essays critical of "the National Security State," with useful bibliography; Seymour Melman, *Pentagon Capitalism; The Political Economy of War* (New York: McGraw-Hill Book Company, 1970), re Defense Department management of a vast industrial network; Sidney Lens, *The Military-Industrial Complex* (Philadelphia: Pilgrim Press, 1970), a condemnation of defense contracting; John Kenneth Galbraith, *How to Control the Military* (Garden City, N.Y.: Doubleday & Company, Inc.,

1969), re military views and power and a prescription for regaining civilian control; Harold Stein, ed., *American Civil-Military Decisions: A Book of Case Studies* (University, Ala.: University of Alabama Press, 1963); Samuel P. Huntington, *The Soldier and the State* (Cambridge, Mass.: Harvard University Press, 1957); Morris Janowitz, *The Professional Soldier: A Social and Political Portrait* (Glencoe, Ill.: The Free Press, 1960), a valuable sociological analysis of the professional military; James M. Roherty, *Decisions of Robert S. McNamara; A Study of the Role of the Secretary of Defense* (Coral Gables, Fla.: University of Miami Press, 1970), re executive control; William Proxmire, *Report from Wasteland; America's Military-Industrial Complex* (New York: Praeger Publishers, Inc., 1970), re military spending, by an involved Senator; Huzar, *The Purse and the Sword* and Kolodziej, *The Uncommon Defense and Congress,* re control through the congressional appropriations subcommittees.

Re techniques of control of the administration by a new President, cf. David Stanley, *Changing Administrations: The 1961 and 1964 Transitions in Six Departments* (Washington, D.C.: The Brookings Institution, 1965), a study of the Eisenhower-Kennedy transition; Laurin L. Henry, *Presidential Transitions* (Washington, D.C.: The Brookings Institution, 1960), which covers the period 1912–1952; Norman C. Thomas and Harold L. Wolman, "The Presidency and Policy Formulation: The Task Force Device," *Public Administration Review,* XXIX (September/October 1969), pp. 459–471. Case studies provide a useful antidote to too much confidence in the effectiveness of presidential control. Cf. especially Arthur A. Maass, "The Kings River Project," Stein, ed., *Public Administration and Policy Development,* pp. 533–572.

Re ideas behind the Budget and Accounting Act of 1921 and the responsibilities of the Bureau of the Budget, cf. Fritz Morstein Marx, "The Bureau of the Budget: Its Evolution and Present Role," I and II, *American Political Science Review,* XXXIX (August 1945), pp. 653–684, (October 1945), pp. 869–898. Hyneman, *Bureaucracy in a Democracy* and Millett, *Government and Public Administration* are useful re executive control of the bureaucracy, including budget control. Items re the budget are cited under legislative control, above; cf. especially Wildavsky, *The Politics of the Budgetary Process,* discussion of the Budget Bureau specifically at pp. 35–47.

For various perspectives on PPBS and key Budget Bureau documents, cf. Fremont J. Lyden and Ernest G. Miller, eds., *Planning, Programming, Budgeting: A Systems Approach to Management* (Chicago: Markham Publishing Co., 1967); Symposium, "Planning-Programming-Budgeting System Reexamined: Development, Analysis, and Criticism," *Public Administration Review,* XXIX (March/April 1969), pp. 111–202; Charles J. Hitch, *Decision-Making for Defense* (Berkeley: University of California Press, 1965), a description by a key person of its operation in the Defense Department; Roherty, *Decisions of Robert S. McNamara,* a more critical view of PPBS in the Defense Department; Edwin L. Harper *et al.,* "Implementation and Use of PPB in Sixteen Federal Agencies," *Public Administration Review,* XXIX (November/December 1969), pp. 623–632, emphasizing the limited change in policy analysis from introduction of PPBS.

The legislative clearance function of the Budget Bureau is discussed in: Richard E. Neustadt, "Presidency and Legislation: The Growth of Central Clearance," *American Political Science Review,* XLVIII, (September 1954), pp. 641–671; and a more critical view, Arthur Maass, "In Accord with the Program of the President? An Essay on Staffing the Presidency," *Public Policy,* IV, 1953, A Yearbook, Graduate School of Public Administration, ed. C. J. Friedrich and J. K. Galbraith (Cambridge, Mass.: Harvard University, 1953), pp. 77–93; Robert S. Gilmour, "Central Legislative Clearance: A Revised Perspective," *Public Administration Review,* XXXI (March/April 1971), pp. 150–158, re the declining importance of the Bureau in central legislative clearance.

Re establishment of the Office of Management and Budget, cf. Executive Order No. 11541, July 1, 1970. Cf. the President's March 12, 1970 message to Congress, *The New York Times,* March 13, 1970. This reorganization responds to a specific study group's recommendations; however earlier calls for an enhanced presidential policy staff were found in: Maass, "In Accord with the Program of the President?" *op. cit.;* William D. Carey, "Presidential Staffing in the Sixties and Seventies," *Public Administration Review,* XXIX (September/October 1969), pp. 450–458; Edward H. Hobbs, "An Historical Review of Plans for Presidential Staffing," *Law and Contemporary Problems,* XXI (Autumn 1956), 663–687, a review and analysis of proposals since 1918 for staffing the presidency; George A. Graham, "The Presidency and the Executive Office of the President," *Journal of Politics,* XII (November 1950), pp. 599–621.

Re the distinction between and the function of the "personal" and the "institutionalized" presidential staffs, cf. John R. Steelman and H. Dewayne Kreager, "The Executive Office as Administrative Coordinator," *Law and Contemporary Problems,* XXI (Autumn 1956), pp. 688–709; Edward H. Hobbs, "The President and Administration—Eisenhower," *Public Administration Review,* XVIII (Autumn 1958), pp. 306–313; Richard E. Neustadt, "Approaches to Staffing the Presidency: Notes on FDR and JFK," *American Political Science Review,* LVII (December 1963), pp. 855–864; Lester G. Seligman, "Presidential Leadership: The Inner Circle and Institutionalization," *Journal of Politics,* XVIII (August 1956), pp. 410–426.

Re the important growth of departmental level staff institutions, cf. R. N. Spann, "Civil Servants in Washington. I. The Character of the Federal Service," "II. The Higher Civil Service and Its Future," *Political Studies, I* (June 1953), pp. 143–161, (October 1953), pp. 228–246.

The auxiliary-line agency tension is discussed in a sophisticated textbook: Herbert A. Simon, Donald W. Smithburg, and Victor A. Thompson, *Public Administration* (New York: Alfred A. Knopf, Inc., 1950), chaps. 12 and, most directly, 13. Cf. Marver H. Bernstein, *The Job of the Federal Executive* (Washington, D.C.: The Brookings Institution, 1958): pp. 63–78, 83–89, re the tension in the federal government between agency autonomy and executive coordination. For analysis of Budget Bureau-operating agency relations, based on a set of interviews in 1965, cf. James W. Davis & Randall B. Ripley, "The Bureau of The Budget and Executive Branch Agencies: Notes On Their Interaction," *Journal of Politics,* XXIX (November 1967), pp. 749–767. On the limits to advice from overhead agencies to the Mayor of New York City (for the advice may well be serving the Board of Estimate and the bureaucracies), cf. Wallace S. Sayre and Herbert Kaufman, *Governing New York City; Politics in the Metropolis* (New York: Russell Sage Foundation, 1960), chap. 10.

A political interpretation of reorganization struggles is presented by Avery Leiserson, "Political Limitations on Executive Reorganization," *American Political Science Review,* XLI (February 1947), pp. 68–84. Cf. Harvey C. Mansfield, "Federal Executive Reorganization: Thirty Years of Experience," *Public Administration Review,* XXIX (July/August 1969), pp. 332–345, for a survey of the purposes, methods, and results of federal executive reorganization. On the lively political battle involved in the executive reorganization of 1939, cf. Richard Polenberg, *Reorganizing Roosevelt's Government: The Controversy Over Executive Reorganization, 1936–1939* (Cambridge, Mass.: Harvard University Press, 1966). The political and bureaucratic obstacles to reorganization are illustrated in case studies, including: Stein, *Public Administration and Policy Development,* especially, "The Transfer of the Children's Bureau," pp. 15–29, and "The Office of Education Library," pp. 31–52; Frederick C. Mosher, ed., *Governmental Reorganizations, Cases and Commentaries* (Indianapolis: The Bobbs-Merrill Co., Inc., for The Inter-University Case Program, Inc., 1967).

Both "Hoover" Commissions had the same official name, so one pays attention to the date. For a sense of the two commissions' approaches and recommendations, cf. U.S. Commission on Organization of the Executive Branch of the Government, *General Management of the Executive Branch, A Report to the Congress,* and *Concluding Report, A Report to the Congress* (Washington: Government Printing Office, 1949), and the dissenting statements in *Reorganization of Federal Business Enterprises, A Report to the Congress* (1949), for a reprimand respecting policy entanglements; *Final Report to the Congress* (Washington: Government Printing Office, 1955), including the statement by Commissioner Holifield; for a spirited, sophisticated criticism of the Commission's work, cf. James W. Fesler, "Administrative Literature and the Second Hoover Commission Reports," *American Political Science Review,* LI (March 1957), pp. 135–157. For a sense of the working of the first commission, cf. "The Hoover Commission: A Symposium," *American Political Science Review,* XLIII (October 1949), pp. 933–1000. On state commissions, cf. Karl A. Bosworth, "The Politics of Management Improvement in the States," *American Political Science Review,* XLVII (March 1953), pp. 84–99.

Gubernatorial control of administration is discussed in: Joseph A. Schlesinger, "The Politics of the Executive," Herbert Jacob and Kenneth N. Vines, eds., *Politics in the American States* (Boston: Little, Brown and Company, 1965), which offers comparative measures of governors' potential influence on administration; Deil S. Wright, "Executive Leadership in State Administration," *Midwest Journal of Po-*

litical Science, XI (February 1967), pp. 1–26, reflecting responses to a questionnaire mailed to state agency heads; Committee for Economic Development, *Modernizing State Government,* A Statement on National Policy by the Research and Policy Committee (July1967), chap. 4, whose title conveys its point, "Making Chief Executives of Weak Governors"; York Wilbern, "Administration in State Governments," The American Assembly, Graduate School of Business, Columbia University, *The Forty-eight States: Their Tasks as Policy Makers and Administrators* (Final Edition, Background papers, 1955), pp. 111–137, a fine discussion focusing on administrative integration under gubernatorial control; re the real power of some governors, Robert B. Highsaw, "The Southern Governor—Challenge to the Strong Executive Theme," *Public Administration Review,* XIX (Winter 1959), pp. 7–11; Thomas R. Dye, "Executive Power and Public Policy in the States," *Western Political Quarterly,* XXII (December 1969), pp. 926–939, arguing that weakness of the governor's formal powers may have little effect on policy outcomes.

ANTI-POLITICAL ORGANIZATION

Independent regulatory commissions are referred to in chap. II, above. Sources critical of commissions include: Marver H. Bernstein, *Regulating Business by Independent Commission* (Princeton, N.J.: Princeton University Press, 1955); U.S. President's Committee on Administrative Management, Report, *Administrative Management in the Government of the United States* (Washington: Government Printing Office, 1937); U.S. President's Advisory Council on Executive Or-

ganization, *A New Regulatory Framework; Report on Selected Independent Regulatory Agencies,* January 1971 (Washington: Government Printing Office, 1971); James Q. Wilson, "The Dead Hand of Regulation," *The Public Interest,* 25 (Fall 1971), pp. 39–58. Cf. Robert E. Cushman, *The Independent Regulatory Commissions* (New York: Oxford University Press, Inc., 1941), a basic source, by the author of the study for the 1937 committee; Emmette S. Redford "The President and the Regulatory Commissions," *Texas Law Review,* XLIV (December 1965), pp. 288–321, the case for and against the commission form and independence from the presidency; U.S. Commission on Organization of the Executive Branch of the Government, *Regulatory Commissions, a Report to the Congress* (Washington: Government Printing Office, 1949), generally sympathetic to the commission form, but see the task force report for more detailed information; William L. Cary, *Politics and the Regulatory Agencies* (New York: McGraw-Hill Book Company, 1967), a former SEC chairman defends the commissions as politically responsive; Merle Fainsod, "Some Reflections on the Nature of the Regulatory Process," *Public Policy,* A Yearbook . . . , 1940, ed. C. J. Friedrich and Edward S. Mason (Cambridge, Mass.: Harvard University Press, 1940), pp. 297–323, reflecting critically on assumptions that regulatory agencies are simply pawns of other forces. David T. Stanley *et al., Men Who Govern; A Biographical Profile of Federal Political Executives* (Washington, D.C.: The Brookings Institution, 1967), has information on appointments to commissions, especially pp. 48, 68–72, 135–136, 154–157.

Government corporations are discussed in an intelligent, balanced way by Harold Seidman, "The Theory of the Autonomous Government Corporation: A Critical Appraisal," *Public Administration Review,* XII (Spring 1952), pp. 89–96, and "The Government Corporation: Organization and Controls," *ibid.,* XIV (Summer 1954), pp. 183–192. Cf. U.S. Commission on Organization of the Executive Branch of the Government, *Reorganization of Federal Business Enterprises* (1949), including the dissents; U.S. President's Commission on Postal Organization, Report, *Towards Postal Excellence* (Washington: Government Printing Office, 1968), recommending a government-owned corporation to operate the postal service; Sayre and Kaufman, *Governing New York City,* chap. 9, re special authorities, for a politically sensitive analysis; Lucile Sheppard Keyes, "Some Controversial Aspects of the Public Corporation," *Political Science Quarterly,* LXX (March 1955), pp. 28–56, re Britain, where nationalization of certain industries since World War II has challenged political analysts.

POLITICAL PARTIES AND PUBLIC ADMINISTRATION

Re the British civil service model and innovations to suit the Pendleton Act to American ideas, cf. the insightful discussion: Paul P. Van Riper, "Adapting a British Political Invention to American Needs," *Public Administration,* XXXI (Winter 1953), pp. 317–330. Re the history of the reform movement leading to the Pendleton Act, cf. Ari Hoogenboom, *Outlawing the Spoils; A History of the Civil Service Reform Movement, 1865–1883* (Urbana: University of Illinois Press,

1961); A. Bower Sageser, "The First Two Decades of the Pendleton Act; A Study of Civil Service Reform," *University of Nebraska Studies,* XXXIV–XXXV (1934–1935), on the politics of civil service reform; Ruth McMurry Berens, "Blueprint for Reform: Curtis, Eaton, and Schurz" (M.A. Dissertation, Political Science Department, University of Chicago, 1943) or the *Dictionary of American Biography,* re leading reform figures. A book by one of the key reformers, Dorman B. Eaton, *Civil Service in Great Britain: A History of Abuses and Reforms and their Bearing Upon American Politics* (New York: Harper & Bros., 1880), seeks to show that patronage is not uniquely American.

The extent and value of patronage in the United States are elusive. Re the extent of federal patronage, cf. *Congressional Quarterly Weekly Report,* XXVII (January 3, 1969), pp. 15–31; for a 160-page list of patronage jobs, the "Plum Book" of federal positions excepted from the civil service, U.S. Congress, House of Representatives, Committee on Post Office and Civil Service, 90th Congress, 2nd Session, *United States Government Policy and Supporting Positions* (Washington: Government Printing Office, 1968); U.S. President's Commission on Postal Organization, *Towards Postal Excellence,* pp. 40-43, a valuable account of political control of appointments in the Post Office; re congressional refusal to permit a merit system for an office under patronage since 1789, Rita W. Cooley, "The Office of United States Marshal," *Western Political Quarterly,* XII (March 1959), pp. 123–140; Paul P. Van Riper, *History of the United States Civil Service* (Evanston, Ill.: Row, Peterson & Co., 1958); Leonard D. White's histories of the civil service; an earlier classic, Carl Russell Fish, *The Civil Service and the Patronage* (New York: Russell & Russell, Publishers, 1963), first published in 1904; for the argument that Jackson (like Jefferson) did not radically democratize the public service, at least not in the elite positions, cf. Sidney H. Aronson, *Status and Kinship in the Higher Civil Service* (Cambridge, Mass.: Harvard University Press, 1964). There is a literature dealing with the civil service of particular periods, which can be located through the White and Van Riper volumes. Cf. Cornelius P. Cotter and Bernard C. Hennessy, *Politics Without Power; The National Party Committees* (New York: Atherton Press, Inc., 1964), pp. 138–148, re patronage management by the President and national committee.

Cf. Keith Ocheltree, "Developments in State Personnel Systems," *The Book of the States*, 1966–1967 (XVI), pp. 155–162; a feeling for the variety (e.g., Vermont *v.* New Hampshire, the Midwest *v.* the South) in patronage may be gained by reading books descriptive of politics in particular states or areas, e.g., V. O. Key, Jr., *Southern Politics in State and Nation* (New York: Random House, Inc., Vintage Books, 1949); John H. Fenton, *Politics in the Border States* (New Orleans, La.: Hauser Press,1957); Duane Lockard, *New England State Politics* (Princeton, N.J.: Princeton University Press, 1959). For the case of one city, Sayre and Kaufman, *Governing New York City;* Theodore J. Lowi, *At the Pleasure of the Mayor: Patronage and Power in New York City, 1898–1958* (Glencoe, Ill.: The Free Press, 1964).

Re methods, problems, and limited value of patronage, cf. Frank J. Sorauf, "The Silent Revo-

lution in Patronage," *Public Administration Review*, XX (Winter 1960), pp. 28–34, and "State Patronage in a Rural County," *American Political Science Review*, L (December 1956), pp. 1046–1056; James Q. Wilson,"The Economy of Patronage,"? *Journal of Political Economy*, LXIX (August 1961), pp. 369–380; Daniel Patrick Moynihan and James Q. Wilson, "Patronage in New York State, 1955–1959," *American Political Science Review*, LVIII (June 1964), pp. 286–301; Joseph B. Tucker, "The Administration of a State Patronage System: The Democratic Party in Illinois," *Western Political Quarterly*, XXII (March 1969), pp. 79–84.

Re the advantages and disadvantages of patronage, cf. the excellent essay by Harvey C. Mansfield, "Political Parties, Patronage, and the Federal Government Service," Wallace S. Sayre, ed. (The American Assembly), *The Federal Government Service* (Englewood Cliffs, N.J.: Prentice-Hall, Inc., 2nd ed., 1965), pp. 114–162; Frank J. Sorauf, "Patronage and Party," *Midwest Journal of Political Science*, III (May 1959), pp. 115–126, a vigorous attack on the value of patronage; Pendleton Herring, *The Politics of Democracy; American Parties in Action* (New York: W. W. Norton & Company, Inc., 1965), chap. 26, for a fairly sympathetic view of patronage. For a senior career official's argument that politics and civil service have learned to coexist happily in the federal government, Roger W. Jones, "The Merit System, Politics, and Political Maturity: A Federal View," *Public Personnel Review*, XXV (January 1964), pp. 28–34; for a dialogue on patronage and merit, full of respect for both politicians and civil servants, Leonard D. White and T. V.

Smith, *Politics and Public Service* (New York: Harper & Bros., 1939); for a critique of the quality of the administrative service produced by a merit system, Edward H. Litchfield, "Apostasy of a Merit Man," *Public Personnel Review*, XXII (April 1961), pp. 84–89.

Re the federal contribution to state merit systems, cf. Albert H. Aronson, "Merit Systems in Grant-in-Aid Programs," *Public Personnel Review*, XVII (October 1957), pp. 231–237; Harry W. Reynolds, Jr., "Merit Controls, the Hatch Acts, and Personnel Standards in Intergovernmental Relations," *Annals of the American Academy of Political and Social Science*, CCCLIX (May 1965), pp. 81–93.

Re participation by civil servants in partisan politics, cf. U.S. Civil Service Commission, *Political Activity of Federal Officers and Employees*, Pamphlet 20 (Washington: Government Printing Office, 1966), for a detailed description of prohibited and permitted activities; U.S. Congress, Senate, Committee on Rules and Administration, Subcommittee on Privileges and Elections, 84th Congress, 2nd Session, Document No. 98, *Federal Corrupt Practices and Political Activities* (Washington: Government Printing Office, 1956); U.S. Commission on Political Activity of Government Personnel, Report, *Findings and Recommendations* (Vol. I), *Research* (Vol. II), *Hearings* (Vol. III) (Washington: Government Printing Office, 1968). Vol. I provides a fairly succinct summary, II provides useful research materials and bibliography, III provides a record of lengthy hearings. Cf. Charles O. Jones, "Reevaluating the Hatch Act: A Report on the Commission on Political Activity of Government Personnel," *Public Administration Review*, XXIX (May/June 1969), pp. 249–254. Cf. *United Public Workers of America (CIO) v. Mitchell*, 330 U.S. 75 (1947), sustaining the constitutionality of the Hatch Act. Cf. Pamela S. Ford, *Political Activities and the Public Service: A Continuing Problem* (University of California, Berkeley: Institute of Governmental Studies, 1963), re federal, state and local, and British limitations on political activities.

Cf. Dalmas H. Nelson, "Public Employees and the Right to Engage in Political Activity," *Vanderbilt Law Review*, IX (1955–1956), pp. 27–50, and his "Political Expression under the Hatch Act and the Problem of Statutory Ambiguity," *Midwest Journal of Political Science*, II (February 1958), pp. 76–88, critical of the law of political expression and participation by government employees. Cf. Henry V. Nickel, "The First Amendment and Public Employees—An Emerging Constitutional Right to be a Policeman?" *George Washington Law Review*, XXXVI (December 1968), pp. 409–424, re the more critical view by the courts of government's claims in the 1960's. Cf. Reynolds, "Merit Controls in Intergovernmental Relations," *op. cit.*, pp. 86–88, for criticism of Nelson's position, but argument for some liberalization of the restrictions. For insightful critical analysis of the conception of public employment as privilege, cf. Arch Dotson, "The Emerging Doctrine of Privilege in Public Employment," *Public Administration Review*, XV (Spring 1955), pp. 77–88.

Cf. Mathew E. Welsh, "The Hatch Act and the States," *State Government*, XXXVII (Winter 1964), pp. 8–13, a Governor criticizing Hatch Act limits on political activity of appointive department heads. Re compulsory contributions of funds and campaign efforts, cf. Miller Lee Martin, "Political Activity Restrictions in Louisiana," *Public Personnel Review,* XVI (October 1955), pp. 203–205. Re foreign practice, cf. Commonwealth of Massachusetts, Senate No. 951, Legislative Research Council, *Report Relative to Political Activities of Public Employees* (December 21, 1964), pp. 25–30; re the key differences between the American and British situations, cf. James B. Cristoph, "Political Rights and Administrative Impartiality in the British Civil Service," *American Political Science Review,* LI (March 1957), pp. 67–87; cf. Britain, Cmd 7718, *Report of the Committee on the Political Activities of Civil Servants* (London: HMSO, 1949); W. H. Morris-Jones, "Political Rights of Civil Servants," *Political Quarterly,* XX (October-December 1949), pp. 364–375; "The Political Activities of Civil Servants," *Public Administration,* XXXI (Summer 1953), pp. 163–175, for extracts from Cmd 8783, and comments.

Cf. chap. II, re the privilege doctrine; cf. chap. IV, discussion of bureaucratic life.

CAREER AND POLITICAL EXECUTIVES

Re political and career executives in the United States public service, cf. U.S. Commission on Organization of the Executive Branch of the Government, *Task Force Report on Personnel and Civil Service* (Washington: Government Printing Office, 1955), which opened the question of the higher civil service and political executives to intensive discussion. The Hoover Commission itself largely adopted the Task Force position; its report is much briefer: U.S. Commission on Organization of the Executive Branch of the Government, *Personnel and Civil Service, A Report to the Congress* (Washington: Government Printing Office, 1955). For the antecedents of the proposal and a succinct summary and defense, cf. Leonard D. White, "The Senior Civil Service," *Public Administration Review,* XV (Autumn 1955), pp. 237–243. For a valuable critique of the proposal, cf. Paul P. Van Riper, "The Senior Civil Service and the Career System," *Public Administration Review,* XVIII (Summer 1958), pp. 189–200. For a vigorous, perhaps nasty, attack on critics, cf. William Pincus, "The Opposition to the Senior Civil Service," *Public Administration Review,* XVIII (Autumn 1958), pp. 324–331. A valuable analysis of the questions raised by the Commission is offered by Paul T. David and Ross Pollock, *Executives for Government; Central Issues of Federal Personnel Administration* (Washington, D.C.: The Brookings Institution, 1957, reprinted with Supplement, 1958).

Re the Executive Inventory system subsequently established, cf. U.S. Civil Service Commission, "The Executive Assignment System" (November 1966—leaflet); Executive Order 11315, November 17, 1966, authorizing the Executive Assignment System. The Commission's Bureau of Executive Manpower has issued informal, useful items on top executives and the Inventory. For President Nixon's proposal: U.S. Congress, House Committee on Post Office and Civil Service, 92nd Congress, 1st Session, February 3, 1971, Committee Print No. 3, *The Federal Executive Service (A Proposal for Improving Federal Executive Manpower Management), Recommendations of the President of the United States* (Washington: Government Printing Office, 1971).

Re characteristics of top federal executives, a useful brief statement, "Characteristics of the Federal Executive," *Public Administration Review,* XXX (March/April 1970), pp. 169–180, which is the text of a report from the U.S. Civil Service Commission, Bureau of Executive Manpower, November 1969. Cf. Michael Cohen, "The Generalist and Organizational Mobility," *Public Administration Review,* XXX (September/October 1970), pp. 544–552, re the differences between federal executives who change departments and those who do not. Cf. W. Lloyd Warner *et al., The American Federal Executive* (New Haven: Yale University Press, 1963), a study of the social backgrounds, career routes, personalities, and ideologies of top career and political federal executives. Cf. David T. Stanley *et al., Men Who Govern; A Biographical Profile of Federal Political Executives* (Washington, D.C.: The Brookings Institution, 1967), on the characteristics of appointees to federal political executive positions, 1933–1965. For data on the sources of political executives and their characteristics, cf. Dean E. Mann, "The Selection of Federal Political Executives," *American Political Science Review,* LVIII (March 1964), pp. 81–99. For a fuller version re characteristics of appointees, cf. Stanley, *Men Who Govern.*

Re selection and functioning of federal executives, cf. Dean E. Mann, *The Assistant Secretaries; Problems and Processes of Appointments* (Washington, D.C.: The Brookings Institution, 1965), examining 1945–1951; David T. Stanley, *The Higher Civil Service; An Evaluation of Federal Personnel Practices* (Washington, D.C.: The Brookings Institution, 1964), re careers of federal higher civil servants, sympathetic to increased mobility and steps toward a corps of higher civil servants. Two writers arguing that political appointments are necessary in top posts: Milton J. Esman, "Administrative Stability and Change," *American Political Science Review,* XLIV (December 1950), pp. 942–950; Arthur S. Flemming, "The Civil Servant in a Period of Transition," *Public Administration Review,* XIII (Spring 1953), pp. 73–79. Cf. Bernstein, *The Job of the Federal Executive,* for discussions of higher civil servants, including skepticism re a politically uninvolved career executive corps (especially pp. 40–48, 56–62); re the limited contribution of parties as suppliers of political executives, cf. pp. 169–172.

The classic argument that there is a set of functions common to executives is Chester I. Barnard, *The Functions of the Executive* (Cambridge, Mass.: Harvard University Press, 1950). Cf. John J. Corson and R. Shale Paul, *Men Near the Top; Filling Key Posts in the Federal Service* (Baltimore: The Johns Hopkins Press, 1966), rejecting the notion of a single executive function. For a sophisticated analysis of executive functions, cf. Amitai Etzioni, *A Comparative Analysis of Complex Organizations* (Glencoe, Ill.: The Free Press, 1961), especially pp. 271–280.

Cf. items cited re change of administration, above; useful sources include: Henry, *Presidential Transitions* (especially pp. 727–731 and chap. 37); Stanley, *Changing Administrations.*

Re the British higher civil service, cf. Herbert Morrison, *Government and Parliament; A Survey from the Inside* (London: Oxford University Press, Inc., 2nd ed., 1959), chap. 14, pp. 311–336, re Ministers and civil servants; William A. Robson, ed., *The Civil Service in Britain and France* (London: The Hogarth Press Ltd., 1956), including Clement Attlee's essay; G. A. Campbell, *The Civil Service in Britain* (Harmondsworth, Middlesex, Penguin Books, 1955). Re the social origins and educational background of higher civil servants, cf. R. K. Kelsall, *Higher Civil Servants in Britain, From 1870 to the Present Day* (London: Routledge & Kegan Paul Ltd., 1955). For vigorous criticism, cf. J. Donald Kingsley, *Representative Bureaucracy; An Interpretation of the British Civil Service* (Yellow Springs, Ohio: The Antioch Press, 1944), with useful historical and theoretical analysis; Thomas Balogh *et al., Crisis in the Civil Service* (London: Anthony Blond, 1968), for contemporary criticism. The British journal *Public Administration* is an essential source of information on contemporary developments, official reports, and books re the British civil service.

INTEREST GROUPS, BUREAUCRACY, AND POLITICS

Re interest groups, an influential and useful book, marred by certain analytic defects, is David B. Truman, *The Governmental Process; Political Interests and Public Opinion* (New York: Alfred A. Knopf, Inc., 1951). Cf. Avery Leiserson, *Administrative Regulation; A Study in Representation of Interests* (Chicago: University of Chicago Press, 1942), an earlier defense of group influence on public administration. Cf. J. Lieper Freeman, *The Political Process; Executive Bureau-Legislative Committee Relations* (New York: Random House, Inc., rev. ed., 1965), a case study but also a general statement of bureau-committee-interest group influence in policy making. Cf. Donald C. Blaisdell, ed., *Unofficial Government: Pressure Groups and Lobbies, The Annals of the American Academy of Political and Social Science,* CCCIXX (September 1958); Bernstein, *The Job of the Federal Executive,* pp. 126–136.

Re the superiority of political over purely interest group politics, cf. the stimulating work by E. E. Schattschneider, *The Semisovereign People; A Realist's View of Democracy in America* (New York: Holt, Rinehart & Winston, 1960); William E. Connolly, ed., *The Bias of Pluralism* (New York: Atherton Press, Inc., 1969), for criticisms of the theory of pluralism and interest group politics; Robert Paul Wolff, "Beyond Tolerance," *A Critique of Pure Tolerance,* Wolff, Barrington Moore, Jr., and Herbert Marcuse (Boston: Beacon Press, 1969), pp. 3–52, a useful illumination and criticism of the theory of pluralism; Theodore J. Lowi, *The End of Liberalism; Ideology, Policy, and the Crisis of Public Authority* (New York: W. W. Norton & Company, Inc., 1969), attacks pluralism and interest group liberalism, arguing for strong government serving the public interest; Emmette S. Redford, "The Protection of the Public Interest with Special Reference to Administrative Regulation," *American Political Science Review,* XLVIII (December 1954), pp. 1103–1113, suggesting limits to interest group theory and some positive steps toward administration in the public interest; Allen Schick, "Systems Politics and Systems Budgeting," *Public Administration Review,* XXIX (March/April 1969), pp. 137–151, attacking interest group pluralism through analysis of public budgeting.

Chapter Four: Beyond Political Bureaucracy?

THE FUTURE: RESPONSIBLE GOVERNMENT
OR BUREAUCRATIC RULE
Re professionalism and democratic control of the civil service, cf. Frederick C. Mosher, *Democracy and the Public Service* (New York: Oxford University Press, Inc., 1968); Emmette S. Redford, *Democracy in the Administrative State* (New York: Oxford University Press, Inc., 1969).

THE BUREAUCRATIC LIFE
For critical analysis of limits to political expression and participation by civil servants, cf. Dalmas H. Nelson, "Public Employees and the Right to Engage in Political Activity," *Vanderbilt Law Review,* IX (1955–1956), pp. 27–50; Arch Dotson, "The Emerging Doctrine of Privilege in Public Employment," *Public Administration Review,* XV (Spring 1955), pp. 77–88; and "A General Theory of Public Employment," *ibid.,* XVI (Summer 1956), pp. 197–211, for a critical analysis of the doctrine that public employment is a privilege without rights, and a proposed alternative conception which would recognize public employee rights. Cf. Henry V. Nickel, "The First Amendment and Public Employees—An Emerging Constitutional Right to be a Policeman?" *George Washington Law Review,* XXXVI (December 1968), pp. 409–424, re greater court protection for government employees in the 1960's. Cf. the discussion of political participation by civil servants above, chap. III.
Re the loyalty-security programs of the 1940's–1950's, cf. Association of the Bar of the City of New York, *Report of the Special Committee on the Federal Loyalty-Security Program* (New York: Dodd, Mead & Co., 1956); Eleanor Bontecou, *The Federal Loyalty-Security Program* (Ithaca, N.Y.: Cornell University Press, 1953); Adam Yarmolinski, ed., *Case Studies in Personnel Security* (Washington, D.C.: The Bureau of National Affairs, Inc., 1955); Ralph S. Brown, Jr., *Loyalty and Security Employment Tests in the United States* (New Haven: Yale University Press, 1958); Edward A. Shils, *The Torment of Secrecy; The Background and Consequences of American Security Policies* (Glencoe, Ill.: The Free Press, 1956); Earl Latham, *The Communist Controversy in Washington; From the New Deal to McCarthy* (Cambridge, Mass.: Harvard University Press, 1966), re Communist activities in the federal government, which Latham does not dismiss as a myth, and the in-part hysterical reaction; Hans J. Morgenthau, "The Impact of the Loyalty-Security Measures on the State Department," *Bulletin of the Atomic Scientists,* XI (April 1955), pp. 134–140, a strong condemnation of the program.
Re labor relations in the public service, cf. Advisory Commission on Intergovernmental Relations, *Labor-Management Policies for State and Local Government* (Washington: Government Printing Office, 1969); Willem B. Vosloo, *Collective Bargaining in the United States Federal Civil Service* (Chicago: Public Personnel Association, 1966), a study of labor relations under Executive Order 10988 of 1962; useful symposia in *Public Administration Review,* issues of Winter 1962 (XXII) and March/April 1968 (XXVIII) on collective bargaining in the public service. Cf. Loretto R. Nolan and James T. Hall, Jr., "Strikes of Government Employees, 1942–61," *Monthly Labor Review,* LXXXVI

(January 1963), pp. 52–54, for useful statistics. For current discussion, cf. *Public Personnel Review.* For more theoretical analyses of public employee labor relations, cf. Morton R. Godine, *The Labor Problem in the Public Service; A Study in Political Pluralism* (Cambridge, Mass.: Harvard University Press, 1951); Mosher, *Democracy and the Public Service,* especially chap. 6.

The problem of a worthwhile bureaucratic life is discussed in my "Honor in the Bureaucratic Life," *Review of Politics,* XXVI (January 1964), pp. 70–90. Concerning modes of reaction by organization members to the bureaucratic life, cf. Robert Presthus, *The Organizational Society; An Analysis and a Theory* (New York: Alfred A. Knopf, Inc., 1962), especially chaps. 4–8. For analysis of the incompatibility of adult personality with large-scale organizations' demands (especially in industrial manufacturing), cf. Chris Argyris, *Personality and Organization; The Conflict Between System and the Individual* (New York: Harper & Bros., 1957). Re development of the theory of organization in the direction of professional self-control within bureaucracies at the expense of hierarchical control, cf. Victor A. Thompson, *Modern Organization* (New York: Alfred A. Knopf, 1961). Rensis Likert, *The Human Organization: Its Management and Value* (New York: McGraw-Hill Book Company, 1967) argues for participative management, and provides quantitative data to support his claim that democratic management brings better attitudes and higher output. The counterculture's attack on bureaucratic life is exemplified by two "believers": Charles A. Reich, "The Greening of America," *The New Yorker,* Sept. 26, 1970, pp. 42 ff.; Theodore Roszak, *The Mak-*

ing of a Counter Culture; Reflections on the Technocratic Society and Its Youthful Opposition (Garden City, N.Y.: Doubleday & Company, Inc., Anchor Books, 1969).

REPRESENTATIVE BUREAUCRACY

Re the problem of representativeness in continental civil service, cf. Brian Chapman, *The Profession of Government; The Public Service in Europe* (London: George Allen & Unwin Ltd., 1959), especially part I, but in scattered comments throughout. Re England, cf. J. Donald Kingsley, *Representative Bureaucracy* (Yellow Springs, Ohio: Antioch Press, 1944), the classic indictment of the administrative class of the higher civil service. Re the United States, cf. Paul P. Van Riper, *History of the United States Civil Service* (Evanston, Ill.: Row, Peterson & Co., 1958), especially pp. 549–559; W. Lloyd Warner *et al., The American Federal Executive* (New Haven: Yale University Press, 1963); Samuel Krislov, *The Negro in Federal Employment: The Quest for Equal Opportunity* (Minneapolis: University of Minnesota Press, 1967), including a discussion of compensatory employment, pp. 75–85. Cf. the discussion of patronage-merit above, chap. III, re the relation of merit to ethnic group opportunities. For recent statistics, cf. U.S. Civil Service Commission, *Study of Minority Group Employment in the Federal Government,* November 30, 1969 (Washington: Government Printing Office, 1970); U.S. Commission on Civil Rights, *For ALL the people . . . By ALL the people; A Report on Equal Opportunity in State and Local Government Employment* (Washington: Government Printing Office, 1969), re state and local governments. Re the need for and possibilities of achieving representative government bureaucracy at the local level, cf. Alan A. Altshuler, *Community Control: The Black Demand for Participation in Large American Cities* (New York: Pegasus, 1970), especially pp. 160–173.

ADVOCACY ADMINISTRATION

Re advocacy planning, cf. Paul Davidoff, "Advocacy and Pluralism in Planning," *Journal of the American Institute of Planners,* XXXI (November 1965), pp. 331–338; Lisa R. Peattie, "Reflections on Advocacy Planning," *ibid.,* XXXIV (March 1968), pp. 80–88; Roland L. Warren, "Model Cities First Round: Politics, Planning, and Participation," *ibid.,* XXXV (July 1969), pp. 245–252. Re advocacy law, cf. Jerome E. Carlin *et al., Civil Justice and the Poor; Issues for Sociological Research* (New York: Russell Sage Foundation, 1967). Re advocacy administration in a program agency, cf. George Hoshino, "The Public Welfare Worker: Advocate or Adversary," *Public Welfare* XXIX (January 1971), pp. 35–41.

CITIZEN PARTICIPATION IN PUBLIC ADMINISTRATION

Re farmer administration, cf. Charles M. Hardin, *The Politics of Agriculture* (Glencoe, Ill.: The Free Press, 1952), especially chap. 8; Reed L. Frischknecht, "The Democratization of Administration: The Farmer Committee System," *American Political Science Review,* XLVII (September 1953), pp. 704–727, arguing that the committees lack the power Hardin ascribes to them, emphasizing instead their administrative impotence; Herman Walker, Jr., & W. Robert Parks, "Soil Conservation Districts: Local Democracy in a National Program," *Journal of Politics,* VIII (November 1946), pp. 538–549, describing the (1500) soil conservation districts and raising questions about the reality of local democratic control through the districts; Phillip O. Foss, *Politics and Grass; The Administration of Grazing on the Public Domain* (Seattle: University of Washington Press, 1960). For an elaborate analysis, skeptical of "grass roots" administration of agricultural programs, cf. Philip Selznick, *TVA and the Grass Roots; A Study in the Sociology of Formal Organization* (Berkeley: University of California Press, 1949). Gladys Baker, *The County Agent* (Chicago: University of Chicago Press, 1939) is dated on details, but provides useful and skeptical insights into "citizen" and "local" control of government officials.

Re advisory committees, a useful summary of information is David S. Brown, "The Public Advisory Board as an Instrument of Government," *Public Administration Review,* XV (Summer 1955), pp. 196–204. Cf. Avery Leiserson, *Administrative Regulation; A Study in Representation of Interests* (Chicago: University of Chicago Press, 1942), for a discussion of interest representation in administration. For a critical view of advisory committees as servants of business, cf. Robert W. Dietsch, "The Invisible Bureaucracy," *The New Republic,* February 20, 1971, pp. 19–21.

Re draft boards, cf. Robert A. Shanley, "Selective Service: The Politics of Revision," *Public Administration Review,* XXX (September/October 1970), pp. 567–570, which reviews the recent literature, including: James W. Davis, Jr., & Kenneth M. Dolbeare, *Little Groups of Neighbors: The Selective Service System* (Chicago: Markham Publishing Co., 1968) and Gary L. Wamsley, *Selective Service and a Changing America* (Columbus, O.: Charles E. Merrill Publishing Co., 1969).

Re community action programs, cf. Altshuler, *Community Control;* Paul E. Peterson, "Forms of Representation: Participation of the Poor in the Community Action Program," *American Political Science Review,* LXIV (June 1970), pp. 491–507, for a comparison of the formal structure and the influence of citizen action committees in three cities. Cf. Daniel P. Moynihan, *Maximum Feasible Misunderstanding; Community Action in the War on Poverty* (New York: The Free Press, 1969), which is highly critical; Peter Marris and Martin Rein, *Dilemmas of Social Reform; Poverty and Community Action in the United States* (New York: Atherton Press, Inc., 1967), re efforts at citizen participation in the 1960's; "Planning and Citizen Participation," symposium, *Journal of the American Institute of Planners,* XXXV (July 1969), including useful articles by Arnstein, Mogulof, and Warren; "Alienation, Decentralization, and Participation," symposium, *Public Administration Review,* XXIX (January/February 1969), especially articles by Miller and Rein and by Kaufman; "Participation of the Poor: Section 202 (a) (3) Organizations Under the Economic Opportunity Act of 1964," *Yale Law Journal,* LXXV (March 1966), pp. 599–629. Re community control of schools, a sympathetic view, with special reference to New York City, is given in Mario Fantini, Marilyn Gittell, & Richard Magat, *Community Control and the Urban School* (New York: Praeger Publishers, Inc., 1970).

Re neighborhood government, for the argument in favor of its value and feasibility, cf. Milton Kotler, *Neighborhood Government: The Local Foundation of Political Life* (Indianapolis: The Bobbs-Merrill Co., Inc., 1969); Altshuler, *Com-*

munity Control, especially chap. 4; Suzanne Keller, *The Urban Neighborhood: A Sociological Perspective* (New York: Random House, Inc., 1968), analysis of the literature, leading to forcefully argued skepticism about revival or creation of urban neighborhoods. Cf. Alfred J. Kahn *et al., Neighborhood Information Centers; A Study and Some Proposals* (New York: Columbia University School of Social Work, 1966), a study of British and American experience and a proposal for Neighborhood Information Centers.

THE DEMOCRATIZATION OF PUBLIC ADMINISTRATION

Re the hopes for a new democratic administration, cf. Warren G. Bennis, *Organization Development: Its Nature, Origins, and Prospects* (Reading, Mass.: Addison-Wesley Publishing Co., Inc., 1969); Frank Marini, ed., *Toward a New Public Administration; The Minnowbrook Perspective* (Scranton: Chandler Publishing Co., 1971); S. M. Miller & Martin Rein, "Participation, Poverty, and Administration," *Public Administration Review,* XXIX (January/February 1969), pp. 15–25, for a good discussion of likely trends; Herbert G. Wilcox, "Hierarchy, Human Nature, and the Participative Panacea," *ibid.,* pp. 53–63, for a sophisticated critique of certain theories of nonhierarchical large-scale organizations. For a classic statement, but one subject to serious objections, against the possibility of democratic control of large-scale organizations, cf. Robert Michels, *Political Parties; A Sociological Study of the Oligarchical Tendencies of Modern Democracy,* trans. Eden & Cedar Paul (New York: Hearst's International Library Co., 1915).